The Character of a Nation

The Character of a Nation

John Witherspoon and the Moral Foundation of the United States

James Calvin Davis

BLOOMSBURY ACADEMIC
NEW YORK • LONDON • OXFORD • NEW DELHI • SYDNEY

BLOOMSBURY ACADEMIC
Bloomsbury Publishing Inc
1359 Broadway, New York, NY 10018, USA
50 Bedford Square, London, WC1B 3DP, UK
29 Earlsfort Terrace, Dublin 2, Ireland

BLOOMSBURY, BLOOMSBURY ACADEMIC and the Diana logo are trademarks of
Bloomsbury Publishing Plc

First published in the United States of America 2026

Copyright © Bloomsbury Publishing Inc, 2026

For legal purposes the Acknowledgments on p. viii constitute an extension
of this copyright page.

Cover design: Diana Nuhn
Cover image of chains © iStock.com/Cristina, Gaidau.
Bottom image © iStock.com/zimmytws

All rights reserved. No part of this publication may be reproduced or transmitted in any form or by any means, electronic or mechanical, including photocopying, recording, or any information storage or retrieval system, without prior permission in writing from the publishers.

Bloomsbury Publishing Inc does not have any control over, or responsibility for, any third-party websites referred to or in this book. All internet addresses given in this book were correct at the time of going to press. The author and publisher regret any inconvenience caused if addresses have changed or sites have ceased to exist, but can accept no responsibility for any such changes.

Library of Congress Cataloging-in-Publication Data Available

ISBN: HB: 978-0-567-72657-5
PB: 978-0-567-72656-8
ePDF: 978-0-567-72659-9
eBook: 978-0-567-72658-2

Typeset by Deanta Global Publishing Services, Chennai, India
Printed and bound in the United States of America

To find out more about our authors and books visit www.bloomsbury.com
and sign up for our newsletters.

With Gratitude for My Teachers
James F. Childress
David Little
Douglas F. Ottati

Contents

Acknowledgments	viii
A Note on Sources	x
Introduction	1
1 Calvinism and Common Sense	13
2 A "Public Spirit"	49
3 "The Obligation of Virtue"	87
4 Schools of Character	125
5 The Character of Dissent	157
6 The Failure of Character	187
7 Witherspoon and American Political Character	213
Bibliography	241
Index	247
About the Author	252

Acknowledgments

I have taught at Middlebury College for twenty-five years, and throughout that time my institution has supported my scholarly ambitions in important ways. Specifically, I have the honor of holding the George Adams Ellis Chair in the Liberal Arts at Middlebury, which has provided me with essential resources to do the research this project required. In addition, I am grateful for two sabbaticals granted during the preparation of this manuscript, one in 2019–20 that provided me extended time to immerse myself in Witherspoon's writings and map out the path of my argument, and another in the fall of 2023, without which I would not have finished writing in time for this book to contribute to anniversary celebrations of the Declaration of Independence.

Colleagues at Middlebury count among the conversation partners I have enjoyed through the evolution of this project, including Religion Department mates Elizabeth Morrison, Bill Waldron, Justin Doran, Jennifer Ortegren, Maria Hatjigeorgiou, Eunyung Lim, Robert Schine, and Ata Anzali. Other Middlebury colleagues who have engaged with me on this and related projects over recent years include Patricia Saldarriaga, Jacob Tropp, Elsa Mendoza, Luis Casteneda, and James Shinkyu Lee. Jim Ralph is not only a top-notch historian of the Civil Rights Movement, with whom I have enjoyed many scholarly conversations, but he also served as Middlebury's dean of faculty for a number of years, and in that role he enthusiastically supported faculty and their scholarly investments, including mine. Thank you, Jim, for your conviction that good liberal arts teachers are active scholars, and vice versa.

Friends beyond Middlebury who have been valuable interlocutors include Mark Douglas, Ward Holder, Elizabeth Hinson-Hasty, Roger Gench, and Mark Valeri. Richard Brown of Bloomsbury has been a persistent advocate for this project, and I am grateful for the work that he and Victoria Shi have done to make the book a reality. My spouse Elizabeth lent her professional copyediting skills to this text *pro bono*, as always. This manuscript (like my previous books) is crisper for her expertise, and my life is inestimably richer for her companionship. My sons Jae and Kisung had nothing at all to do with this book, but they would be disappointed if I did not mention them here, and indeed, watching them grow into remarkable young men has kept me grounded and humbled in the pursuits of the mind.

Finally, this book is dedicated to three teachers who made me a scholar. Jim Childress was my PhD advisor at the University of Virginia, and he is quite simply the source of any competence I have as a moral thinker. Besides training me in ethics, Jim taught me intellectual virtues worthy of infusion into one's scholarship, among them precision, clarity, grace, humility, and independence, and he gave me reason to think I could be an academic when I had no other basis for confidence. David Little taught me over a couple of semesters while I was at Virginia. From David I learned that thinkers from the classical Reformed tradition remain worthy source material for current consideration of topics like human rights, political order, religious freedom, and natural morality. David read over this entire manuscript, and his enthusiasm for it was the ultimate imprimatur. Of all my teachers, Doug Ottati has been my longest and most intimate instructor, mentor, and friend. Doug stoked my interest in Anglo-American Reformed theology while I was his seminary student thirty years ago, and he gently helped me navigate my years-long transition from first-generation college student to graduate student to college teacher. Throughout my academic career, Doug has provided consistent encouragement and the ultimate teacher-scholar role model. Everything I have written or taught has been an effort to live into the legacy of these revered teachers. For the providence that allowed me to be their student, I am forever grateful.

A Note on Sources

Unless otherwise indicated, all references to Witherspoon's writings in this book are drawn from *The Works of the Rev. John Witherspoon*, 2nd edition, four volumes. Philadelphia: William W. Woodward, 1802 (abbreviated *Works* in the notes). References to specific texts will include volume and page number (e.g., III:47) from this edition. Sermons found in Witherspoon's *Works* normally will be identified in the notes by the number they are given in the Woodward edition (e.g., Sermon 4), rather than by title. Other frequently referenced documents will be identified by the following abbreviations:

CM:	*Christian Magnanimity* (Graduation Address)
DPPM:	*Dominion of Providence over the Passions of Men* (Sermon)
EC:	*Ecclesiastical Characteristics or, the Arcana of Church Policy*
JHL:	*Essay on the Connection between the Doctrine of Justification by the Imputed Righteousness of Christ, and Holiness of Life*
LD:	*Lectures on Divinity*
LE:	*Lectures on Eloquence*
LMP:	*Lectures on Moral Philosophy*
PTR:	*A Practical Treatise on Regeneration*

Finally, my references to John Calvin's *Institutes of the Christian Religion* follow the common convention of including the book and chapter numbers, followed by the page number of the Battles/McNeil edition (e.g., *Institutes* IV.20, 1513).

Introduction

May 17, 1776. Despite it being a Friday, a preacher in an austere black robe punctuated by Genevan clerical tabs rose to his pulpit in Princeton, New Jersey. In leading his congregation in worship this day, he was doing what pastors all across the American colonies were encouraged to do. The Continental Congress had ordered May 17 to be observed as a day of "fasting, humiliation, and prayer, humbly to supplicate the mercy of Almighty God, that it would please him to pardon all our manifold sins and transgressions, and to prosper the Arms of the United Colonies, and finally, establish the peace and freedom of America, upon a solid and lasting foundation."[1] For nearly a year, the colonies had skirmished with British forces in Lexington and Concord, in Boston and Philadelphia. For longer, they had chafed under Parliament's taxation policies and the crown's condescension and disrespect. Now they were mobilizing for war, and the Continental Congress wanted the people to entreat God for the cause.

The precise cause was still being debated: some colonial leaders wanted the king to respect their right to self-governance but had little stomach for outright rebellion, while others insisted it was time for the United Colonies to become the United *States*, independent of the British Empire altogether. In less than two months' time, consensus would congeal around independence, with Congress declaring "That these United Colonies are, and of Right ought to be Free and Independent States" and "Absolved from all Allegiance to the British Crown." In that Declaration of Independence, they would "mutually pledge to each other our Lives, our Fortunes and our sacred Honor" and exhibit their "firm reliance on the protection of divine Providence."[2] On this day, assembled in their houses of worship, Americans were reassuring themselves that God was, in fact, on their side.

The Princeton preacher ascended his pulpit to convey just that assurance, and the sermon the Reverend John Witherspoon (1723–94) delivered would become one of the most consequential in American history. But in looking to assure his congregation that God was on their side, Witherspoon did not launch immediately into a defense of the revolutionary cause. Instead, he began with a dissertation on the "wrath of man." He began with the Bible—Ps. 76:10, to be specific—and its reminder that the destructive powers of human beings are no match for the providential designs of God: "Surely the Wrath of Man shall praise thee; the remainder of Wrath shalt thou restrain." This Psalm celebrates God's Providence and presence, assuring us that God is at work in the miraculous and the mundane events of history and in the threatening and beneficial moments of our lives. God is present in both beauty and ugliness, Witherspoon insisted—even the ugliness of human conflict.

In fact, Witherspoon argued, the "wrath of man" serves as a particularly potent conduit of the Providence of God, by reminding us of the "corruption of our nature" and our dependence on God's redemption.[3] All we need recall, he declared, is "the past history, or the present state of the world, but above all, to the ravages of lawless power" to "lead us to acknowledge the just view given us in scripture of our lost state."[4] Trials and tribulations lay bare our insufficiencies and our dependence upon God: "Both nations in general, and private persons, are apt to grow remiss and lax in a time of prosperity and seeming security; but when their earthly comforts are endangered or withdrawn, it lays them under a kind of necessity to seek for something better in their place."[5] Misfortune can serve as a reminder of our need for God and the reformation of our lives, and no misfortune brings our need for divine help into greater focus than the brutality of war: "Where can we have a more affecting view of the corruption of our nature, than in the wrath of man, when exerting itself in oppression, cruelty and blood?"[6]

War epitomizes humanity's insatiable greed and lust for power, warned Witherspoon, "that men should so rarely be satisfied with their own possessions and acquisitions . . . but should look upon the happiness and tranquility of others, as an obstruction to their own."[7] War decimates families, and long after the occasion of conflict is over "many days shall not put an end to the mourning of a parent for a beloved son . . . or of the widow and helpless offspring, for a father taken away in the fullness of health and vigor."[8] Worst of all, said Witherspoon, civil war marks an "abhorred scene" of national kin when they "butcher one another with unrelenting rage, and glory in the deed." War is hell, preached Witherspoon, or at least a reflection of the hellish potential of the depraved human species. Yet even this depravity speaks to God's providential glory, insofar as it reminds us of our need for redemption. Even in these moments of human wrath, the grace of God restrains the human capacity for evil and sometimes uses that capacity to accomplish God's good.

After this extended theological preamble, Witherspoon turned to the real subject of the day, the coming war with Britain, which he had foreshadowed in the sermon's first movement:

> To apply it more particularly to the present state of the American colonies, and the plague of war, The ambition of mistaken princes, the cunning and cruelty of oppressive and corrupt ministers, and even the inhumanity of brutal soldiers, however dreadful, shall finally promote the glory of God, and in the mean time, while the storm continues, his mercy and kindness shall appear in prescribing bounds to their rage and fury.[9]

Despite the conflagration to come, Witherspoon reassured his assembly that they should remain optimistic, for God was "the great object of our hope and trust, in our present situation." In the providential unfolding of history, even the wrath of man praises God; even the wrath of man can be turned into a vehicle for justice and good. This is our hope, Witherspoon declared, that God is at work even in the trials and tragedies that will befall us in the battles to come. "Put your trust in God," he preached, "and hope for his assistance in the present important conflict."[10]

None of this was to say that the coming war was morally justified, though Witherspoon believed it was. He would not get to making that point until he was over halfway into his sermon, and when he finally made his position clear, he did so hesitantly, reminding his congregation that this was the first time he had ever preached politics from the pulpit. Even now, as he broached the subject in the context of Christian worship, he did not dwell on the moral defense of revolution, and he certainly refused to paint American resistance as a crusade, the righteous execution of a divine cause. God would use this conflict for his purposes, despite the failing of men on both sides. Absent from Witherspoon's sermon was any of the demonizing rhetoric used by medieval church leaders to whip up fervor for assaults on Muslims in the Middle East (and Jews and Orthodox Christians they encountered along the way). Nor did his sermon resemble the jingoism often heard from American pulpits in the wars to follow this one. Witherspoon instead offered careful arguments in defense of war against Britain, judging it "not only lawful but necessary" that he "embrace the opportunity of declaring my opinion without any hesitation, that the cause in which America is now in arms, is the cause of justice, of liberty, and of human nature."[11] But his justification of revolution was couched in humility and reluctance, not enthusiasm for war. In fact, justification of the rebellion was not even his main point that day.

Instead, Witherspoon expounded on the importance of moral character to the struggle for independence and to the nation they were trying to create. After assuring his congregation that Divine Providence is powerful enough to convert even the wrath of man to the service of God, he focused most of the second half of his sermon on their collective moral duty in this time of war. He described those duties primarily in the language of virtue, insisting that when public virtue is cultivated, it strengthens a people against their enemies. He commended to them a litany of public virtues on which they should focus—patience with one another and fortitude for times when the war does not go well, unity in spirit so that their efforts may be coordinated and effective, industry (which he called "a moral duty of the greatest moment") so that they might be "prepared for the fatigues of a campaign," frugality and temperance that they might be prepared for the scarcities of war and committed to the material needs of the struggle. Most of all, Witherspoon commended the virtue of piety, for "it is in the man of piety and inward principle, that we may expect to find the uncorrupted patriot, the useful citizen, and the invincible soldier."[12] According to Witherspoon, independence would be won not primarily by superior arms or strategy, but by the steadfastness of moral character.

John Witherspoon was a Scottish Presbyterian clergyman, an early leader in American higher education, a political leader in the Revolution, and a signer of the Declaration of Independence. He was not born in the colonies, but his arrival in 1768 to assume the presidency of the College of New Jersey (later Princeton) gave the American cause one of its most eloquent and popular spokespersons and one of its most dedicated civilian servants. Besides his tireless service in state and national government during the war, and his oratorical success in making the case for the Revolution to patriots, allies, and loyalists on both sides of the Atlantic, Witherspoon is important to the history of the American Founding because of his efforts to provide a moral foundation for the independence movement and the new republic it would create. Throughout his career in America, he insisted on the importance of character to the health of the nation. This book explores his understanding of political character—what values and virtues it required, how they are cultivated in civic society, how they should shape American conduct in the war and expectations of government afterward, and how optimistic the United States should be in its efforts to create a benevolent society.

Witherspoon was well positioned to spread his moral vision for the United States. His address on May 17, 1776, would prove to be the most influential sermon preached from an American pulpit of that era. Beyond the congregants assembled in Princeton that day, *The Dominion of Providence over the Passions of Men* soon counted an audience of readers throughout the colonies and even back in Great Britain. It was published soon after the signing of the Declaration of Independence, along with a separate treatise in which Witherspoon gave his reasons for supporting the independence movement. In the following two years, it would be reprinted (in whole or in part) at least six times, in Scotland, London, and the colonies.[13] Depending on who was reading it, the sermon succinctly represented the righteousness of American independence, or it symbolized everything regrettable about those backward colonies and their unjustified rebellion.

Witherspoon had good reason to anticipate that people would pay attention to his sermon, for he was well known on both sides of the Atlantic even before the independence movement got hot. He was the most famous clergyman in America, but he was also president of an up-and-coming colonial college, and in that role educated a generation of religious and political leaders in America. As one biographer notes, "He drew so many of his students from leading families of the country, such as the Lees, Madisons, Randolphs, and Washingtons of Virginia, the Clymers and Hodges of Pennsylvania, the Morrises, Bruyns and Van Renssalears of New York, the Macons and Hawkins of North Carolina, the Reads of Delaware, and the Stocktons, Patersons and Livingstons of New Jersey."[14] His most famous student, James Madison, became president of the United States, but his classes also included a future vice president (Aaron Burr), ten members of presidential cabinets, six members of the Continental Congress, sixty members of the US Congress, twelve state governors, three justices of the US Supreme Court, and more than a hundred clergymen.[15] Beyond his ecclesial and educational work, he was a public figure of preeminence for his role in the colonial resistance. He was known in elite circles, said to have enjoyed George Washington's respect and been admired by John Adams (usually no friend of clergy) for his intellect and counsel. He was a political player, serving on numerous local, state, and national committees and helping to execute the nuts-and-bolts operations of the independence movement. He served two terms in the Continental Congress, including during the summer of 1776, when he signed his name to the Declaration of Independence.

Witherspoon was important enough to the independence movement that he even occupied the attention of British loyalists on both sides of the Atlantic. A critic in Glasgow reprinted his *Dominion* sermon in an attempt to show

Witherspoon's mother country just how destructive his emigration to America had been. The critic accused Witherspoon of dressing up "the most rebellious sentiments with the most sacred and important truths," giving religious cover to the insidiousness of the rebellion and deluding countless colonists in the process.[16] Another opponent dismissively referred to him as "Dr. Silverspoon Preacher of Sedition in America."[17] And an Anglican loyalist in New Jersey, a Reverend Dr. Jonathan Odell, wrote a satiric poem called "The American Times," in which, over the span of five stanzas, he implicated "Witherspoon the great" (as he sarcastically referred to him) as a chief instigator of the rebellion:

> Scotland confess'd him sensible and shrewd,
> Austere and rigid; many thought him good.
> But turbulence of temper spoil'd the whole,
> And show'd the movements of his inmost soul.
> Disclo'd machinery loses of its force;
> He felt the fact, and westward bent his course.
>
> Princeton received him, bright amidst his flaws,
> And saw him labour in the good old cause;
> Saw him promote the meritorious work,
> The hate of kings, and glory of the kirk.[18]

Odell labeled Witherspoon a warmonger and an anarchist bent on overturning law and order, declaring that "I'd rather be a dog than Witherspoon" and ending his poetic skewering with a promise to his reader: "Be patient reader—for the issue trust, \ His day will come—remember Heav'n is just." With a reputation like this, it is no wonder that British troops once burned Witherspoon in effigy, alongside General Washington and other treasonous military leaders.[19]

Witherspoon the preacher, teacher, and political servant was a figure of considerable importance and impact to the American Revolution. Yet today he ranks among the lesser-known heroes of the moment, eclipsed by Thomas Jefferson, John Adams, George Washington, and his student James Madison, and even less familiar than secondary actors like Thomas Paine and Samuel Adams. Those who have heard of him often know him only as the answer to a trivia question: Who was the only practicing clergyman among the signers of the Declaration of Independence? Or perhaps some identify him as the father of an American denomination, the Presbyterian Church. He certainly is not often regarded as one of the principal founders of the United States.

Why this is true has several possible explanations. As important as he was as an orator and leader of the time, much of his tangible service to the Revolution was in political grunt work, so to speak. He served on committees, often charged with relatively mundane responsibilities like procuring wagons for the war effort and clothing for its soldiers.[20] Furthermore, after the war, Witherspoon did not ascend to national leadership in the new nation, like Washington, Adams, Jefferson, and Madison. Instead, he returned to his day job as the president and primary faculty of a fledgling college. The legacy his writing might have left was blunted by the destruction of Princeton by British arsonists, as well as by his own frustrating decision to discard much of his corpus late in life. Thanks to the dedication of his students and friends, we still have some evidence of his intellectual and moral impact, though much of what remains of his writing consists of rather conventionally Calvinist sermons on primarily theological topics—not the kind of paper trail that lends itself to lionization in the annals of American political history. His moral philosophy has been preserved largely in the form of lecture notes his students published. While unpolished, they disclose the moral worldview that underwrites his more occasional writings on the Revolution itself, as well as his service to that effort. But even here, many historians have judged him too derivative a thinker to be worthy of attention, especially when compared to contemporaries in the Scottish Enlightenment, such as Francis Hutcheson, Thomas Reid, Adam Smith, or David Hume.

Yet it remains that he was an essential player in the American independence movement, and underwriting his leadership was a compelling political theology and philosophy. Beyond his practical work for the cause, Witherspoon was important because he emphasized the role that character would play in the health of the new nation he was helping to birth. He commended the cultivation of public virtue to citizens and leaders alike. He implored his fellow Americans to be a people dedicated to the common good and faithful to the protection of human rights. He reminded them that the right thing to do, in and after the war, would not always be what is politically or militarily expedient, but what accords with moral law. To Witherspoon, a commitment to human rights and the common good was fundamental not only to the justification of the American Revolution but also to the health of the nation they would forge together. His vision resonated with his fellow Americans in part because it synthesized the two dominant moral worldviews of his time, Calvinist political theology and Scottish Enlightenment moral philosophy. By virtue of this bilingualism, his intimacy with other movers and shakers, and his comfort in very different circles in the colonies—political, ecclesial, and educational—he served as a moral compass for the revolutionary effort.

He was also a slaveholder. Testimony from his estate indicates that at the time of his death, he owned two Black people. How long his household included enslaved people is difficult to know, nor do we know anything about his relationship with them or how he treated them. The answers to these questions ultimately do not matter because John Witherspoon owned other human beings, a moral crime that directly contradicts most of what he otherwise had to say on matters of political character, moral duties to other human beings, and the fundamental sacredness of human rights. We know now that participation in the institution of slavery was wrong, but many people in Witherspoon's time also recognized it as a moral abomination, so we cannot excuse Witherspoon with a simple appeal to historical context. Prominent voices within the theological tradition and the philosophical school to which he appealed for his public ethics wrote about the immorality of slavery. As dependent as he was on Calvinism and Scottish Enlightenment philosophy for his moral outlook, on the matter of slavery he was resistant to countervailing voices in both intellectual traditions. Not only did he participate in enslavement himself, but he ignored several obvious opportunities to contest the institution in his public work, despite at least once acknowledging at a conceptual level that involuntary enslavement violated the dignity and respect owed to other human beings.

In this way, John Witherspoon embodied the best and the worst of foundational American political thought. At a moment in which the United States celebrates an anniversary of its origins while also questioning the very sinews that bind the nation together as the *United* States, a return to Witherspoon may be useful. Witherspoon believed that collective political character was essential to the health of a nation, especially this new nation. He offered a vision of a moral politics, insisting that citizens and leaders must share an investment in the common good and respect for basic rights. He believed that an important function of government was to encourage (and reflect) these moral priorities and ensure a sense of collective moral duty among citizens. The cultivation of political character could be aided by the friendly support of religion, though Witherspoon recognized the dangers to both church and state in the official establishment of religion. Political character required deliberate civic education, he believed, and his own service to the College of New Jersey over thirty years testifies to the importance he placed on higher education as a vital source of moral formation.

The first four chapters of this book explore Witherspoon's understanding of political character, rooted in moral duty to the common good and the protection of human rights, and his conviction that a citizenry committed to this kind of character (including leaders who modeled and encouraged it) was essential to a flourishing nation, especially in moments of conflict, crisis, and political dissent. Chapter 1 argues that Witherspoon came to his commitment to political character not only through his Calvinist theological tradition but also by critically incorporating ideas from leading moral philosophers of the Scottish Enlightenment. His synthesis of theology and philosophy not only made for a compelling moral vision, but it also positioned him to speak to very different constituencies in his moment, adherents to traditional Christianity and less-than-orthodox intellectuals. Chapter 2, easily the most conceptual part of the book, takes a deep dive into Witherspoon's understanding of human moral capabilities, including our capacity for virtue. Witherspoon borrowed from both his Calvinist tradition and the philosophy current in his day to offer a cautiously optimistic expectation that Americans could create a nation based on the virtuous practice of benevolence, which he understood as genuine concern for others. Chapter 3 examines how Witherspoon defined the obligation of virtue by reference to God's moral law, a move that distinguished him from many of the philosophers from whom he otherwise borrowed ideas about virtue. His insistence that the duties of benevolence are defined by the obligation of divine law was perfectly at home in his Calvinism, however. For Witherspoon, the duty to others set upon us by God's law was best represented by the idea of rights, so much so that Witherspoon ultimately equated a virtuous nation with one that lives up to its moral duty through a commitment to the protection of natural rights.

After exploring the contours of Witherspoon's public ethics of political character, I consider how he thought this character could be cultivated. Chapter 4 shows how family, religion, and what we now call higher education each served as schools of character building in Witherspoon's vision of civic society. Chapter 5 then examines the ways in which Witherspoon thought political character should shape Americans' approach to the Revolution. Witherspoon believed that the cultivation of benevolent character and a respect for rights were the charge of good government, and when government abdicated that responsibility, dissent and reform were in order—and revolution could be justified. At the same time, Witherspoon maintained that the virtues of political character that justified revolution should also govern the conduct of that struggle. The means of dissent must match its objective: the reformation of character in political society.

Witherspoon persistently voiced this concern for benevolent virtue and respect for rights throughout the struggle for independence. He also reflected the sinister side of American character at the Founding in his participation in (and unwillingness to publicly critique) the institution of slavery. His complicity in the enslavement of other human beings represents an egregious departure from his own moral philosophy, a failure to extend his priority on virtue, rights, freedom, and moral responsibility to the plight of enslaved Black Americans. The important task of Chapter 6, then, is to make sense of this obvious hypocrisy, not to excuse it but to understand how someone like Witherspoon could exist within this moral disconnect. How does a compelling defense of basic rights, liberties, and virtues come from the minds and pens of slaveholders like Witherspoon? In his own hypocrisy, Witherspoon invites us to wrestle with the moral contradiction personified by our national heroes and baked into our foundational political documents.

Witherspoon's decidedly mixed moral record raises important questions about our invocation and celebration of men from the founding era, and these questions are among the issues I take up in the final chapter. Critics rightly raise sharp objections to the continued veneration of figures like Jefferson, Washington, and Witherspoon, when they dirtied their hands with complicity in slavery. By extension, some critics argue that the foundational documents of the United States, the Declaration of Independence and the Constitution, are also unworthy of continued appeal because they are the products and reflections of slaveholders. What do we do with Jefferson, Washington, Witherspoon, and other thinkers who reflected both the best aspirations of the United States and its most horrific failures? Do their sins fatally undermine the civic authority of the documents they penned and the political vision they bequeathed?

In Chapter 7, I argue that the study of a figure like Witherspoon is useful precisely because he simultaneously personified the foundational ideals of the United States and its "original sin," contradictory impulses that have shaped America's DNA from its beginning. To take seriously the good and the very bad in our national story, and to interrogate how we tell that narrative, as well as who gets to tell it, is to engage in what I call "chastened history." Chastened history considers carefully the choices we have made and are still making in how we understand our history. It invites what Emilie Townes calls "countermemories" to complement and question the dominant powers that control our collective narrative.[21] Chastened history also inquires how a more complicated understanding of our past provides insight into the political and cultural struggles of our own moment.

Because of his moral insights and his failures, the chastened history of Witherspoon I am offering here provides an instructive glimpse into the good and the bad of the "original intent" of the founding visionaries of the United States. At a time when questions of public character and the health of democracy are again acute, and as we still struggle to collectively admit to how deep racial bigotry and injustice run in our national core, perhaps the recovery of Witherspoon, his ethical vision and its myopia, can help us appreciate both our national sins and our better angels more poignantly. Perhaps the study of Witherspoon allows us to take seriously how deeply toxic racism is rooted in the American character, while also reminding us of the ideals that, however muddied their historical origins, provide the promise of an antidote. Wrestling with Witherspoon's vision of political character may provide wisdom regarding what to do with the moral murkiness of our history, perhaps suggesting alternatives to either whitewashing that history in antiseptic hagiography or dispensing with all of it—the good and the bad—in an expression of moral outrage over the worst of that legacy.

This study of Witherspoon is offered with the conviction that it is possible to utilize the resources from our political history constructively without ignoring the reality of their racist dimensions. In fact, without a proper reckoning with the failures in our history, we sentence ourselves to perpetuating the horrors and injustices that have persisted throughout the American narrative. But without the constructive ideals embedded in that same history, we undermine the bedrock on which a rehabilitation of the public good might be built. A chastened study of national origins can offer an occasion for collective repentance while also serving as a source of wisdom for a rejuvenated sense of public virtue and mutual obligation. The rediscovery of Witherspoon invites us to embrace this hard work as an expression of our own political character.

Notes

1 "General Orders 15 May 1776," Founders Online, National Archives, https://founders.archives.gov/documents/Washington/03-04-02-0243.
2 "Declaration of Independence: A Transcription," America's Founding Documents, National Archives, https://www.archives.gov/founding-docs/declaration-transcript.

3 John Witherspoon, *The Dominion of Providence over the Passions of Men* (hereafter DPPM) in *The Works of the Rev. John Witherspoon*, 2nd ed. 4 vols. (Philadelphia, PA: William W. Woodward, 1802), III:20.
4 Witherspoon, DPPM, III:22.
5 Witherspoon, DPPM, III:25.
6 Witherspoon, DPPM, III:20.
7 Witherspoon, DPPM, III:20.
8 Witherspoon, DPPM, III:21.
9 Witherspoon, DPPM, III:19.
10 Witherspoon, DPPM, III:35.
11 Witherspoon, DPPM, III:35.
12 Witherspoon, DPPM, III:39–45.
13 Varnum Lansing Collins, *President Witherspoon*, 2 vols. (Arno Press & The New York Times, 1969), I:223–30.
14 Collins, *President Witherspoon*, II:216–17.
15 Collins, *President Witherspoon*, II: 222, 229.
16 Collins, *President Witherspoon*, I:227.
17 Martha Lou Lemmon Stohlman, *John Witherspoon: Parson, Politician, Patriot* (Westminster Press, 1976), 115.
18 As quoted in Collins, *President Witherspoon*, I:184.
19 Collins, *President Witherspoon*, I:222.
20 Stohlman, *John Witherspoon*, 121.
21 Emilie M. Townes, *Womanist Ethics and the Cultural Production of Evil* (Palgrave Macmillan, 2006), 8.

1

Calvinism and Common Sense

John Witherspoon was born and raised in Scotland, the son of a Presbyterian pastor, in a hotbed of that particular brand of Calvinist Christianity. To the popular mind, Calvinism connotes little more than the doctrine of predestination, the belief that God elects some people for salvation and others for damnation before they are even born, independent of their desert. This common understanding of predestination hardly does justice to the subtlety and intent of that doctrine, and predestination scarcely captures what Calvinism meant to its adherents as a worldview. To be a devotee of John Calvin's theology meant to cast your hope on an all-powerful God whose sovereign will governs creation and history and whose irresistible grace ensures the salvation of God's elect. Early modern Calvinists believed that God's power had no equal, not even in the persistence of evil and sin. Christ's resurrection was proof of that, and his willingness to die to make the point was the promise that God is on the side of those whom God loves. For classical Calvinists, that meant that the Christian life was not about doing good things to earn God's approval and secure everlasting life in heaven. Instead, the Christian life was a life lived in gratitude for the good news that God had secured the believer's eternal salvation already. Predestination was an important part of the Calvinist worldview, but Calvin meant it as a doctrine of assurance, that salvation depends not on our capability to earn it but on the guarantee of God's grace in Christ. Classical Calvinism therefore was far from the theological fatalism it is sometimes portrayed to be. Rather, it was at its heart a hopeful interpretation of Christian religion, a celebration of the glorious futility in a sinful world's resistance to divine grace.

Presbyterians were not the only Calvinist Protestants in early modern Europe (and America); some Baptists and Anglicans adhered to Calvin's theology, as did the Independents who dominated the English and American Puritan movements a century before Witherspoon's time. What distinguished Presbyterians from these other flavors of Protestant Calvinism was ecclesiology, or their understanding of the proper structure of the church. Baptists and Independents believed that each congregation was an autonomous community that should govern its own commitment to faith and morals. By contrast, the Church of England emphasized the connectedness of the larger church and insisted that all local parishes were directly accountable to the hierarchy of Anglican authority. Anglican bishops defined and maintained discipline and orthodoxy, and each specific parish and its ministers reported directly to a local bishop, who himself was accountable to archbishops and ultimately the English monarch, the head of the Church of England.

On the matter of ecclesiology, Presbyterians were located somewhere between the high-church Anglicans and the low-church Baptists and Independents. Like the Baptists and Independents, Presbyterians invested a lot of governing authority in the leaders of local congregations, but Presbyterians also believed that those congregations were responsible to one another and to the larger church. In this broader vision of accountability, the Presbyterians resembled their Anglican kin, but they did not invest the authority of the larger church in a hierarchy of bishops—and certainly not in the crown, on whom they bestowed no ecclesial power. Instead, Presbyterians believed that each congregation was in direct relationship with other Presbyterian congregations through a regional network of ministers and lay leaders. This regional association was called a presbytery, and presbyteries, in turn, were responsible to one another through an even larger association made up of various presbyteries, called a synod. Presbyterian congregations enjoyed some self-governance, then, but they were accountable to the presbytery for the maintenance of orthodoxy, the mutual financial support of the churches in the region, and most notably the ordination and assignment of ministers. No congregation could hire or dismiss a minister without the approval of the presbytery, a restriction that caused a number of conflicts in which Witherspoon was embroiled while in Scotland. Presbyteries were often called on to resolve such disputes among ministers and congregations, and conflicts between presbyteries were adjudicated by their synod.

Witherspoon grew up in the home of a Presbyterian pastor, and from a young age seemed destined to become one as well. A committed student, when he was thirteen, Witherspoon was already prepared to matriculate to the University of Edinburgh, where he completed in three years the normally four-year curriculum for the Master of Arts degree. By the time he was twenty, he had advanced to become a Doctor of Theology, and his home presbytery declared him ready for a ministerial appointment. Perhaps because he was unusually young for the vocational moment, Witherspoon had to wait two more years for a local church to consider him for their pastorate. Finally, in 1745, he was called and ordained as the pastor of the congregation in Beith, a small village in Ayrshire.[1]

Witherspoon faithfully served the Beith congregation for twelve years, during which time he met and married his wife, Elizabeth. He began his public writing career there, publishing (among other things) a theological treatise called *Essay on the Connection between the Doctrine of Justification by the Imputed Righteousness of Christ, and Holiness of Life*, a satirical contribution to Presbyterian Church debates called *Ecclesiastical Characteristics*, and a diatribe against Christians going to the theater titled *Enquiry into the Nature and Effects of the Stage*. The ecclesial satire and the theater polemic each ruffled the feathers of their targets, causing some controversy, but the *Essay on Justification and Holiness* impressed many readers with its sound representation of Calvinist doctrine, so much so that it enjoyed several reprintings. His reputation as a formidably orthodox thinker grew among Scottish Presbyterians, and in 1757 Witherspoon was called to leave Beith to serve a larger congregation in Paisley. At least one other congregation would try (unsuccessfully) to poach him from the Paisley church, but he would stay there for a decade until his emigration to America, his reputation as a churchman and writer growing throughout his tenure.

During Witherspoon's service as a minister in Scotland, the Presbyterians there were enmeshed in conflict about both church governance and theology. The Popular Party in the Scottish kirk was devoted to traditional Calvinism, and members of the party regularly policed adherence to orthodox theology at the ordination examinations of new ministers in their presbyteries. Members of the Popular Party were equally committed to congregational self-governance, especially around the election and retention of their ministers. As Presbyterians, they recognized the importance of the broader church's endorsement of pastoral appointments, so they did not object to subjecting congregational calls to presbytery approval. They did bristle, however, at the outsized influence on ministerial calls that certain benefactors enjoyed in many Scottish congregations. Wealth and social standing seemed to give some individuals too much power over the leadership of local churches, sometimes in direct defiance of a congregation's majority will.

The Moderate Party was more theologically liberal than their Popular counterparts, invested in revising or disposing of traditional Calvinist theology in ways that made Christianity more palatable to the Enlightenment mindset dominating eighteenth-century intellectual culture. Many thinkers associated with the Enlightenment were less interested in traditional Christian doctrines than they were in the "reasonable" aspects of religion, primarily its moral teachings. Moderate Presbyterian clergy were enthusiastic mouthpieces for this revisionism, in part because it made the religion more culturally compelling than backward orthodoxy did. The Popular Party charged the Moderates with elitism, and the charge had grounds, intellectually but also in how the parties thought of ecclesiastical appointments. Moderate Presbyterians often distrusted popular will in their congregations, at least with important decisions like the selection of leaders, preferring the nomination of ministers from intellectual and cultural movers and shakers with whom they were aligned.

Theologically, Witherspoon was solidly at home in the Popular Party, and he quickly became one of its chief spokespersons. His theology was orthodox Calvinism, as his sermons and treatises like the *Essay on Justification and Holiness* made clear. He defended historic Calvinist doctrines like the sufficiency of grace and the reliability of God's Providence. He was "evangelical" in the traditional sense that he believed the Christian life required the experience of repenting of one's sins and being "born again" to God's grace in the death and resurrection of Christ. He also agreed with the Popular Party that ministerial appointments ought to substantially reflect the will of the congregation, and Witherspoon fought vigorously to protect congregational voice in the presbytery process of approving ministers. He strenuously objected to attempts to appoint ministers against the will of their congregations and out of deference to local patrons.

One such case hit particularly close for Witherspoon. His fame rising while he was at Paisley, the town fathers of Dundee orchestrated a call to Witherspoon to assume their pastorate. The Paisley congregation made clear that they wanted him to stay with them, and content to do so, Witherspoon refused the call. But after some back-room maneuvers by Dundee patrons, the presbytery approved the new call anyway and ordered him to move. Witherspoon and the Paisley elders contested the presbytery's decision, and the synod eventually overruled the presbytery and allowed Witherspoon to stay where he was. But at least one biographer has suggested that Witherspoon's close call with the powers of patronage may have contributed to his theological preference for democratic decision-making and representative governance, a disposition in church matters that he eventually would extend to his political priorities.[2]

While Witherspoon identified as a member of the Popular Party and defended their priorities on orthodoxy and congregational representation, he was by no means anti-intellectual. To be sure, he thought the Moderates abandoned traditional theology too readily in favor of rationalistic revisions. The most important work of his career in Scotland, *Ecclesiastical Characteristics*, is an extended satirical takedown of Moderate Presbyterians, and a major object of his ridicule is his belief that Moderates were too concerned with sounding smart and culturally refined to bother themselves with traditional doctrine, or even the Bible itself. Accusing them of an inordinate reliance on Francis Hutcheson's moral philosophy, Witherspoon sarcastically claimed that "it is therefore plain that the moderate man, who desires to enclose all intelligent beings in one benevolent embrace, must have an utter abhorrence at that vile hedge of distinction, the [Westminster] Confession of Faith."[3] Shortly after, in a hilariously dismissive discussion of Moderate preaching, he identified as a chief maxim of the average Moderate minister that "his authorities must be drawn from heathen writers, none, or as few as possible, from Scripture." For as Witherspoon observed, "it is plain a moderate preacher must confine his subjects to social duties chiefly and not insist on such passages of Scripture as will be the very repetition of them contaminate his style, and may perhaps diffuse a rank smell of orthodoxy through the whole of his discourse."[4]

Witherspoon's contempt for Moderate rationalism, however, should not be confused with a reactive opposition to new learning. For one thing, part of Witherspoon's indictment of Moderate preachers was that they were not learned *enough*, that they enjoyed the pretense of learning but were not nearly as educated as their more orthodox counterparts. Orthodox ministers trained in "the critical study of the Scriptures" and intensive education in church history and classical theology, but "we find that moderate men have mostly, by constitution, too much spirit to submit to the drudgery of [those] kinds of learning . . . and despise all who do so."[5] Instead, he claimed, the Moderates worked hard to create the impression of learning without committing to disciplined study. They dabbled in works of moral philosophy fashionable in the day, the writings of Hutcheson or Lord Shaftesbury, but not much else, for "much study is a great enemy to politeness in men, just as a great care of household affairs spoils the free careless air of a fine lady."[6] A good part of Witherspoon's disdain for the Moderates, then, was precisely because of the value he placed on a deeply learned clergy, a standard he embodied.

This is an important point to emphasize, given the modern stereotype of religious traditionalism as inherently anti-intellectual. John Witherspoon complicates the stereotype, as does the Calvinist tradition with which he identified, for Calvinism historically has been the most intellectually rigorous of all Protestant theological traditions. Shaped by a wide curriculum at Edinburgh, Witherspoon was a sharp thinker, and as he was contesting Moderates' overreliance on Enlightenment ideas and thinkers, he was learning from some of those same Enlightenment sources, without abandoning his orthodox Calvinist convictions. As a college president in America, he would assign and teach many of the Enlightenment thinkers he accused Moderates of relying on excessively, and his writings from his time in the colonies frequently reflected philosophical influence, even as he maintained his commitment to traditional Calvinism. In fact, his ability to synthesize two intellectual strands to formulate and disseminate a view on public character made him a popular moral leader of the American Revolution and a fascinating representative of this moment in history.

"Cousin America Has Eloped with a Presbyterian Parson!"[7]

Witherspoon served the Paisley church and his local presbytery until solicitors from the American colonies approached him with an offer he (eventually) could not refuse. Early in 1767, ambassadors from the College of New Jersey called upon Witherspoon and shared the trustees' invitation to be their next president. Convincing Witherspoon to emigrate to New Jersey, however, was a difficult task. By all reliable accounts, he was comfortable in his ministry in Paisley, and his congregants were not exactly eager for him to leave.[8] More problematic was the fact that Elizabeth Witherspoon was in no mood to make such a drastic move. When ambassadors of the College of New Jersey began calling on her husband, she made it quite clear that she would not approve a relocation to the colony, and each time she made her feelings known, John deferred to her wishes. It is likely that he remained attracted to the idea, though. Varnum Collins suggests that America always held special attraction for Witherspoon because he saw it as part of the solution to Scotland's entrenched poverty; perhaps his emigration would encourage others to follow, and the population reduction would help Scotland's economy and give impoverished Scots another avenue for avoiding pauperism.[9] Witherspoon himself suggested in the first sermon he preached in Princeton that his willingness to serve there was due to a straightforward sense of divine calling to serve the church in that part of the world. His interest in Princeton certainly was not motivated by a scarcity of opportunities to minister or teach in Scotland, for his relative celebrity there was regularly yielding invitations to upwardly mobile appointments.

Elizabeth would not budge, however. She may have had a problem with the salary offer, but her resistance was more deeply rooted in the fact that she simply did not like to move.[10] She had put up a fight over the transition from Beith to Paisley, and this was a much more drastic change. With his spouse's urging, then, Witherspoon declined the Princeton invitation several times, and finally the college's board moved on to their next candidate. In the meantime, though, one more college suitor came calling on the Witherspoons: Dr. Benjamin Rush, who himself would be an important player in the American Revolution and the maturation of at least two colonial colleges.[11] Rush visited John and Elizabeth, and after extended conversation, persuaded Elizabeth to relent. In August 1767, she agreed to allow the family to move, freeing John to accept the position. There was one hiccup, however: by the time word of Witherspoon's change of heart reached the Princeton trustees, they had made their offer to the backup candidate. Samuel Blair was a young tutor at the school, terribly young in fact, having only graduated seven years before being tapped for the presidency. Blair's youth was an issue in the board's consideration, but their options were limited, so when Witherspoon turned them down repeatedly, they elected Blair to the position. Apparently, though, Blair harbored similar reservations about his readiness for the responsibility, and when word finally reached the board that Witherspoon was willing to assume the presidency after all, Blair quickly and graciously stepped aside.[12]

In the spring of 1768, John and Elizabeth Witherspoon said goodbye to friends in and around Paisley, and after an arduous three-month journey across the Atlantic, they arrived in Princeton in August and were immediately embraced with enthusiasm. Witherspoon's reputation as a churchman preceded him, and he was especially welcomed because he was seen as a leader who could mend a conflict that had dominated the Presbyterian Church in the colonies for decades. In the early 1700s, the colonies had experienced waves of religious revivalism that revitalized Christianity in some ways and threatened it with discord and disunion in others. Revivalist preachers like James Davenport, the Tennent family, and most famously George Whitefield traveled throughout the colonies preaching against what they perceived to be a decided lack of religious fervor in the churches. Christians had come to approach their religion as a rote habit, these preachers argued, and they had lost the exhilarating and animating effect that the experience of God's Holy Spirit should have on someone called by Christ. Revivalist preachers argued that true Christian religion required the believer to be born again, to have an affective experience of the Spirit, and be forever changed by their conversion to Christ. Unwelcomed in many established pulpits, revivalists gathered crowds in town squares and open fields and oversaw the mass conversion of thousands of people to their enthusiastic understanding of Christian faith. Together, these waves of revivals and religious fervor have been deemed the Great Awakening, and it changed the face of American Christianity forever.[13]

The Great Awakening was an ecumenical event. It divided established denominations like the Anglicans, Congregationalists, and Presbyterians, and it birthed entirely new denominations like the Methodists. Largely a populist movement, it often produced conflict within congregations and with the formal pastors of those congregations. Presbyterians were not immune to this conflict. The revivalists in that denomination were called New Side Presbyterians, while those who resisted revivalism eventually came to be known as Old Side Presbyterians. New Side ministers argued that their Old Side counterparts were sapping the energy and integrity from faith in their effort to make Christianity intellectually respectable in an increasingly unorthodox age. Old Side Presbyterians thought the enthusiasm of New Side revivalism threatened the intellectual integrity of Calvinist Christianity. They tended to be more invested in the reinterpretation of classical Calvinism in terms that suited the modern rationalism emerging in Enlightenment-infused Euro-American culture, and they worried that the New Side emphasis on affective religion undermined their efforts by reverting to a less intellectual, too emotional premodern spirituality. They also charged the New Side leaders with disrupting their congregations and communities by calling into question their leadership and the authenticity of their religious experience. Truth be told, some of the revivalists were guilty as charged, claiming that Old Side preachers were not truly Christian at all because they had not been born again in the Spirit.

With the passage of time, some distance from the heat of the initial Great Awakening revivals, and the distraction of a common enemy in the threat of an established Anglicanism, the rift between these two Presbyterian factions cooled somewhat by the 1760s. Old Sides and New Sides were still vying for control over the Presbyterian college in New Jersey, however, when Witherspoon became a candidate for its presidency. Princeton began as an institution for New Side Presbyterians, but relying on revivalist sympathizers did not yield enough funding for the institution's budget. As reflections of the colonial establishment, Old Side Presbyterians had money on their side, and they desperately needed the school to educate their clergy too. After Old Side machinations to buy control of the college's board and promote their own presidential candidate fizzled, they fell in with their support of Witherspoon.

Witherspoon, it turns out, would appeal to both constituencies. His credentials as an orthodox interpreter of Calvinist tradition and his subscription to an affective version of Christian spirituality were solidly reflected in his verbal battles with the Moderate Party in Scotland. At the same time, his command of Enlightenment thinking—and his willingness to incorporate it into the college's curriculum—invited the Old Side Presbyterians' respect for his learning and intellectual orientation.[14] Witherspoon could preach a Christianity centered on the born-again experience of Christ's grace, and then utilize Enlightenment conceptions of the affections and virtue to explain what he meant. He was, in many ways, the perfect churchman to lead this institution into a synthesis of Old Sides and New Sides.

He also was well positioned to engage with a public beyond his church. When Witherspoon arrived in New Jersey in 1768, the colony was already actively engaged in conflict with the mother country. By the summer of 1774, twelve counties formed "committees of correspondence," local bodies that together would brainstorm appeals for redress to Britain, as preparation for a congress of colonial grievances that was in the works. Witherspoon was asked to join Somerset County's committee, and he played a major role in the resolutions his committee proposed for the new congress, as evidenced by the similarities in substance and prosaic style between those resolutions and his essay *Thoughts on American Liberty*, written soon thereafter.[15] Witherspoon continued to serve his country in this political role for more than a year, using the platform to urge the colonies to develop their economic independence from Britain at the same time they were contemplating political independence. He also served as a religious and political apologist for colonial demands for redress of grievances, and eventually for independence. By June 1776 he was a member of the provincial congress that deposed Governor William Franklin and set up a government in New Jersey independent of British oversight. That same month, Witherspoon was selected to represent New Jersey in the Continental Congress, and as a delegate to that body he would sign the Declaration of Independence, barely two weeks later. While in Congress, Witherspoon showed particular interest in the material well-being of the troops and the fiscal health of the revolutionary cause, serving on several procurement and financial committees.

Witherspoon continued his service to the Continental Congress until 1782, interrupted by a brief and largely unsuccessful attempt in 1780 to leave Congress and return to his primary responsibility of safeguarding his college. Indeed, Witherspoon was invited to Princeton to run a college, not forge a revolution, so throughout his service to the independence movement he was discharging the duties of college president, to varying degrees of distraction. The college itself suffered mightily during the war. Enrollment was compromised by a reduction in eligible students as well as teachers, and adequate funding was a chronic issue. Most disruptive of all was the arrival of British troops to Princeton in December 1776. The British army drove out the students and minuscule faculty, including its president, and for three weeks occupied Nassau Hall, the admirable main building of the college, until they were pushed out by General Washington's troops. While there, the British army housed its horses in the Princeton church and burned much of the furniture in Nassau as fuel for their fires. As an indicator of the prominence Witherspoon had achieved as a leader in the Revolution, they also hung him in effigy out of a window of the schoolhouse. When General Washington's forces drove out the British, however, colonial soldiers simply took their place, occupying the building as housing and a hospital and, by all accounts, doing more property damage than the British had.

Nonetheless, Witherspoon and Princeton persevered, and by July 1777, they resumed classes in a drastically scaled-back manner. The college persisted in its mission throughout the war, with Witherspoon periodically leaving his political duties to give the school more attention, only to return when the people of New Jersey asked him to serve their interests in the Revolution. When the war finally drew to a close, and other leaders transitioned into roles in the new nation's independent government, Witherspoon left politics and returned to Princeton, where he worked to reestablish momentum at his decimated college until his death in 1794.

Revolutionary Religion

A transplanted patriot, John Witherspoon served the American Revolution as a public apologist, moral leader, educator, and political servant. Throughout his service to the independence movement, Witherspoon consistently advocated for a public commitment to good character as not just a reflection of good religion, but also the goodness of the new nation. He insisted that the United States would only be as strong as its commitment to public virtue, mutual obligation, and the preservation of rights, and he believed that national survival required citizens to consistently put the needs of the whole above their own selfish motives, as a matter of moral habit. The moral development of the United States, insisted Witherspoon, was as important to its future as its political emancipation and economic maturation.

What made Witherspoon such an effective leader in the independence movement was his position at the confluence of two important moral traditions of his time: Calvinist Christianity and Enlightenment moral philosophy. Witherspoon was formed as a moral thinker and actor by the synthesis of these two intellectual veins, and his ability to speak both moral languages made him especially valuable to the project of inspiring widespread buy-in for the revolution in the colonies. Calvinism and the Enlightenment happened to represent (at least in general terms) the dominant moral traditions of influence in the American colonies. In particular, Christianity and Enlightenment philosophy were the worldviews of appeal as leaders and citizens alike sought to make sense of—and justify—the revolution in which Witherspoon was caught up. His bilingualism in these two moral vocabularies goes a long way in explaining his success as a public spokesperson for the revolutionary cause.

Oddly, though, biographers and historians have often failed to see both of these currents in Witherspoon's writings, instead debating whether it is more accurate to identify him with one over the other. Some historians maintain that Witherspoon was an evangelical Calvinist who largely opposed the intellectual innovations of his day. The Calvinist Witherspoon of the Scottish Popular Party, they say, who cut his teeth critiquing the Moderate fascination with modern philosophy, is the real Witherspoon, and he remained this staunch opponent of philosophy throughout his life. Whenever Witherspoon seems to be channeling Scottish Enlightenment thinkers in his later work, he was doing so only to mock or refute them.[16] By contrast, other historians acknowledge the evidence, obvious in his writings during his time in America, of a certain absorption of Scottish Enlightenment ideas. Some of these scholars conclude that this means Witherspoon eventually put off his outdated Calvinism when he became primarily an academic, serving at Princeton as a straightforward conduit of Enlightenment ideas.[17]

It is somewhat bewildering how modern students of Witherspoon fail to see the *simultaneous* commitment to theology and philosophy in Witherspoon's work, particularly after he arrives in New Jersey. Perhaps that is because many scholars assume that a commitment to orthodox religiosity and an openness to modern philosophy are somehow mutually exclusive. The assumption that Calvinism and Enlightenment philosophy must be polar opposite worldviews, however, betrays a lack of appreciation for their historical connection; many Enlightenment thinkers were influenced by, and evolved philosophically from, conceptual antecedents in Calvinist Christianity.[18] The assumption that Witherspoon was orthodox or philosophically astute—but could not be both—may also reflect modern assumptions about religion, fueled by binaries sometimes reinforced by religious spokespersons themselves. In modern debates over religion and science, for instance, it often seems that an evangelical commitment to Christianity requires a rejection of "secular" learning (and vice versa), but eighteenth-century thinkers did not necessarily subscribe to that intellectual either-or. It is also possible that readers of Witherspoon are guilty of assuming that his thought remained static throughout his career, even though the most straightforward read of his corpus is that, from his time in Scotland to his career in America, his enthusiasm for Enlightenment thought warmed considerably, especially as he learned to correlate the teachings of Hutcheson, Thomas Reid, and others with his orthodox Calvinist convictions. Our surprise that a person's thinking would change over time, and that he might be able to build bridges between seemingly different intellectual and ideological worldviews, is more a reflection of our time than Witherspoon's.

In any event, it is clear that Witherspoon did subscribe to both classical Calvinism and elements of Enlightenment philosophy, that he did manage to synthesize these two worldviews into a coherent understanding of human morality and politics, and that by the time he began his presidency at the College of New Jersey, he was an active student of both. His utilization of Enlightenment thought was always bound by his Calvinist convictions because he was, in his heart, an orthodox Presbyterian minister. But his interpretation of Calvinist Presbyterianism also occasionally changed as a result of the influence of the moral philosophy of his day, particularly (as we will see in the next chapter) around his moral expectations of human beings. The result was a fascinating synthesis, and a bilingualism that would give him equal gravitas in ecclesial settings as well as political circles dominated by the less-than-orthodox Washington, Adams, and Jefferson.

That he could converse deeply in the language of Calvinist Christianity was key to Witherspoon's popularity among the rank and file of the colonies, for the Christian religion was the worldview of many, if not most, of the colonies' residents. A surprisingly small percentage of colonists were members of a church, perhaps fewer than twenty percent, mostly Protestants of one flavor or another.[19] Membership is an inadequate measure of influence, however, and even among colonists who may not have darkened a church doorstep, Protestant Christianity had become the dominant moral tradition of Western Europe and, thus, the colonies. Calvinism (in its various evolutionary forms) prevailed in the North and maintained a strong minority presence in the South. The Anglican Church shaped the milieu of the southern colonies, while Quakers, Catholics, and others had political and cultural influence throughout British America, particularly in the Middle Colonies. European churches had transplanted their cultural influence in America, so much so that support from Protestant clergy from some of the established churches helped make the popular case for the Revolution.[20]

Besides the traditions with deep roots in European Christianity, America had birthed its own distinct brand of Protestantism in the Great Awakening of the 1720s and 1730s, a period of unusually intense piety stoked by traveling preachers who held religious revivals and called people to be born again in faith.[21] Revivalist Protestants would be especially important players in the Revolution as well, especially in defining the rights and freedoms for which it was fought. Normally a minority in their churches and towns, revivalist preachers and communities found themselves on the losing end of local restrictions on religious assemblies and activities, government sponsorship of particular traditions, and mandated taxpayer support of religious institutions. Preachers like Samuel Davies and Isaac Backus and evangelical communities like the Baptist Association in Danbury (Connecticut) were important public advocates for religious freedom in the early days of the new republic.

Given the cultural and political impact of Christianity, then, Witherspoon's fluency in orthodox Christianity was a major political asset, and because he was specifically a Calvinist, he was part of a sub-tradition that thought about politics in explicitly theological terms. Indeed, the Reformation that John Calvin helped lead was as political as it was religious, given the alignment between Europe's political powers and the various religious groups—Catholic and Protestant— vying for supremacy. Catholics and Lutherans jockeyed over the German states, while Calvinists entreated and resisted political leaders aligned with the Roman church in France, Geneva, and eventually Britain. Even the Anabaptists, that Protestant minority movement that gave us today's Mennonite and Amish communities, were political in their rejection of conventional political power and their withdrawal from the dominant cultures of the world. Reformation Christianity always had a political dimension.

As a result, Calvin had a lot to say theologically about politics, and his leadership in Geneva—which included the revision of civic structures of accountability as much as it did the reformation of religion—was an outworking of his theological understanding of the importance of political authority and responsibility. Calvin envisioned a cooperative relationship between church and civil life in Geneva, distinct from but not completely unlike the medieval understanding of church and state. Medieval popes had pushed an idea known as the "two swords theory" of church and state, based on a creative interpretation of an exchange Jesus had with his disciples in the Gospel of Luke.[22] According to this teaching, God entrusted all power on earth (ecclesial and political) to the pope, the vicar of Christ on earth. Popes then delegated the wielding of the political sword to kings and emperors, but the implication of this theory of delegation was that the church retained ultimate jurisdiction over occupants of political offices. Since a king's power derived from the church, the church could disregard political authorities, and in cases when political rulers deviated from the church's teaching or authority, the pope could declare a king or emperor excommunicated and deprive him of his power. The "two swords" theory not only emphasized the theological importance of politics and political power, but it also underwrote the ultimate supremacy of church over state.

Like other Protestant reformers, Calvin rejected the claim that political authority was derived from the pope, but he did not let go of the idea that politics has theological significance. Against Catholic doctrine, Calvin insisted that church and civil power should be distinguished: "whoever knows how to distinguish between body and soul, between this present fleeting life and that future eternal life, will without difficulty know that Christ's spiritual Kingdom and the civil jurisdiction are things completely distinct."[23] At the same time, he also opposed the rejection of political authority he saw at work in Anabaptist movements of his day. The Anabaptists argued that the call to faith in Christ was a call to purity requiring Christians to separate themselves from the profanities of this world to maintain lives of righteous piety. Because politics is a coercive arena in which political authority is exercised violently, and violence is antithetical to the peace-loving imperative that Christ gave his followers, politics was one of those worldly profanities from which Anabaptists often retreated. Many Anabaptists argued that Christians could never serve in political office without a threat to their lives of faith, so they advocated withdrawal into alternative communities living outside the conventional political world.

In response to the Anabaptist rejection of politics as corrosively violent, Calvin claimed that government is a gift of God, and he assured Christians that service in government could be undertaken as a religious duty. Calvin insisted that the distinction between the authority of church and civil government need not "lead us to consider the whole nature of government a thing polluted, which has nothing to do with Christian men."[24] Instead, government is a profound good; "its function among men is no less than that of bread water, sun, and air; indeed, its place of honor is far more excellent," he said, because "it provides that a public manifestation of religion may exist among Christians, and that humanity be maintained among men."[25] Government ensures a stable society and the conditions necessary for human beings to flourish. It creates conditions of peace and social cooperation, and, to Calvin's mind, it cooperates with the church to assure the vitality of religion and the cultivation of morals. Those who serve in government rightly understand that service as a religious calling, for "they have a mandate from God, have been invested with divine authority, and are wholly God's representatives, in a manner, acting as his vicegerents."[26]

Civic life had religious significance for Calvin because, like the life of the church, the life of the *polis* exists underneath the umbrella of the gracious Providence of God. Confidence in divine Providence is one of the main axes of classical Calvinism, the conviction that God alone is creator, redeemer, and sustainer of the universe, and nothing happens that God does not determine to occur. Providence is a major theme of the first book of Calvin's magnum opus, the *Institutes of the Christian Religion*, where he argued strenuously against the idea of chance or fortune, insisting that "anyone who has been taught by Christ's lips that all the hairs of his head are numbered [Matt. 10:30] will look farther afield for a cause, and will consider that all events are governed by God's secret plan."[27] God's providential care extends to our public lives, said Calvin, and he understood political structures, laws, and offices as provisions that God makes for human flourishing in society.[28]

The centrality of God's Providence in Calvin's thought had several implications for his political theology. The first is that it encouraged Calvinists to see the hand of God in human events, including politics. If nothing escapes the prerogative of God's gracious sovereignty, then everything that happens can be seen as an extension of God's providential will. This includes not only natural occurrences but also developments in human society:

> For in administering human society he so tempers his providence that, although kindly and beneficent toward all in numberless ways, he still by open and daily indications declares his clemency to the godly and his severity to the wicked and criminal. For there are no doubts about what sort of vengeance he takes on wicked deeds. Thus he clearly shows himself the protector and vindicator of innocence, while he prospers the life of good men with his blessing, relieves their need, soothes and mitigates their pain, and alleviates their calamities; and in all these things he provides for their salvation.[29]

Calvin believed that righteous contemplation sometimes could reveal the hand of God working in human events to achieve God's ends, the protection of the righteous and the punishment of the wicked. But he admitted that the correlation between gracious Providence and the events of human history was not always easy to discern:

> Indeed the unfailing rule of his righteousness ought not to be obscured by the fact that he frequently allows the wicked and malefactors to exult unpunished for some time, while he permits the upright and deserving to be tossed about by many adversities, and even to be oppressed by the malice and iniquity of the impious.[30]

Calvin admits that the righteous are often surrounded by, and subject to, "many adversities," but he assures his readers that even trials and tribulations are the machinations of a gracious God.

Calvin argued that hardship is often God's mechanism for testing the pious or reminding them of their reliance on God: "It [suffering] teaches us, thus humbled, to rest upon God alone, with the result that we do not faint or yield. Hope, moreover, follows victory in so far as the Lord, by performing what he has promised, establishes his truth for the time to come."[31] This sentiment was likely the inspiration for Witherspoon's assurance that Providence works even through "the wrath of man." At the same time, Calvin also warned that the apparently unjust blessing of sinners could be a means of bringing them to faith: "what great occasion he gives us to contemplate his mercy when he often pursues miserable sinners with unwearied kindness, until he shatters their wickedness by imparting benefits and by recalling them to him with more than fatherly kindness!"[32] Sometimes unfortunate events are the tools of a providential effort to bring us to good, and like Witherspoon after him, Calvin believed that "knowledge of this sort, then, ought not only to arouse us to the worship of God but also to awaken and encourage us to the hope of the future life."[33]

Another implication of Calvin's linkage between God's Providence and the realities of politics is that it encouraged Calvin to see political participation as participation in the work and world of God. Because politics carried theological importance and meaning, political participation could be seen, in a real sense, as a religious vocation. In another departure from medieval Catholic thought, Calvin (like Luther) expanded the notion of religious vocation well beyond the calling to be a church minister. "The Lord bids each one of us in all life's actions to look to his calling," wrote Calvin. Those who are among God's elect are justified in the grace of Christ and empowered to live improved lives of piety. Their responsibility, then, is to live that piety out in whatever social office or role they find themselves. God "has appointed duties for every man in his particular way of life," said Calvin, "and that no one may thoughtlessly transgress his limits, he has named these various kinds of living, 'callings.'"[34]

By describing social roles and functions this way, Calvin gave religious significance to the work done in them, and in his discussion of vocation, he specifically lifted up political leadership ("magistrates") as an example of worldly work with righteous importance. The identification of political duty with religious vocation is, of course, compatible with his description of rulers as the "vicegerents" of God, individuals who, by virtue of their office, are doing the work of God, ensuring the stability and order of society, defending good religion, and creating the conditions for people to live flourishing lives. Calvin's discussion of vocation was meant to augment the religious significance of mundane work, including but not limited to political service—"no task will be so sordid and base, provided you obey your calling in it, that it will not shine and be reckoned very precious in God's sight."[35] But the doctrine of vocation was also meant to warn readers against striving for a lot in life that is not their calling. The Puritans would call this the virtue of "contentment," being happy with the work God has called you to do in your station, and avoiding aspirations to power or responsibilities that God has not given you. In his discussion of vocation, Calvin again used political power as a specific example of the kind of role satisfaction he is commending.

Calvin's understanding of providential design, the religious importance he invested in the vocation of political leadership, and his static understanding of social roles all contributed to his conservative stance on political resistance and rebellion. Calvin counted oppressive political rule among the "adversities" that could obscure God's benevolence, but which ultimately served the ends of God's providential design. "There is no erratic power, or action, or motion in creatures, but that they are governed by God's secret plan in such a way that nothing happens except what is knowingly and willingly decreed by him."[36] Confident in God's Providence, Calvin cautioned against resisting bad rulers, declaring directly that "the magistrate cannot be resisted without God being resisted at the same time."[37] He warned that God normally regards political disobedience as "contempt toward himself" because resistance to political structures, laws, and offices is resistance to God's providential design for human community. The world is simply an array of "secondary causes" through which God actualizes his own objectives, so Christians ought to ponder the ultimate meaning of the seemingly mundane things happening around them, including in their political lives.[38]

His theology of Providence, then, made obedience to political authority a religious duty. His stance on political resistance was inspired by Romans 13: "Let every person be subject to the governing authorities; for there is no authority except from God, and those authorities that exist have been instituted by God." Calvin recognized that "it is the example of nearly all ages that some princes are careless about all those things to which they ought to have given heed," but he warned that neither incompetence nor self-serving tyranny justifies resisting a properly ordained ruler. For one thing, said Calvin, bad rulers can be instruments of God's chastisement on us. Even when a ruler's abuses seem unjustified, however, Calvin's concern for the importance of civil order led him to commend obedience: "In a very wicked man utterly unworthy of all honor, provided he has the public power in his hands, that noble and divine power resides which the Lord has by his Word given to the ministers of his justice and judgment. Accordingly, he should be held in the same reverence and esteem by his subjects, in so far as public obedience is concerned, in which they would hold the best of kings if he were given to them."[39]

Calvin's understanding of government as a divine tool for maintaining civil order and of political authority as a divine vocation made it hard for him to justify political resistance, but not impossible. Rebellion against ordained political rulers was rebellion against God's order, and thus was a transgression against God himself—except when it was not. Calvin could create theological room for justified political revolution, but when he did so, he based that justification in the same doctrine of God's Providence through which he understood the authority of magistrates. God expects ultimate loyalty from those whom God sets in positions of leadership, so when political leaders abandon their divine responsibility, God may arrange for the removal of those leaders. But in these cases, Calvin did not have popular rebellion in mind: "if the correction of unbridled despotism is the Lord's to avenge, let us not at once think that it is entrusted to us, to whom no command has been given except to obey and suffer."[40] Calvin did allow for individual civil disobedience when a ruler demands something that transgresses the obligations of Christian faith: "If they [kings] command anything against him [God], let it go unesteemed."[41] But tyranny does not excuse popular uprising.

Instead, Calvin directed the victims of oppression to look to other legally ordained political entities to execute God's justice. Near the end of his *Institutes*, Calvin offered this remarkable call to representative political bodies to protect the people against tyrant kings:

> For if there are now any magistrates of the people, appointed to restrain the willfulness of kings (as in ancient times the ephors were set against the Spartan kings, or the tribunes of the people against the Roman consuls, or the demarchs against the senate of the Athenians; and perhaps, as things now are, such power as the three estates exercise in every realm when they hold their chief assemblies), I am so far from forbidding them to withstand, in accordance with their duty, the fierce licentiousness of kings, that, if they wink at kings who violently fall upon and assault the lowly common folk, I declare that the dissimulation involves nefarious perfidy, because they dishonestly betray the freedom of the people, of which they know that they have been appointed protectors by God's ordinance.[42]

Calvin's assumption was that God normally works to remove tyrants through other established means of his providential order. The other political entities of that established order have a responsibility to chastise, challenge, or even remove leaders who deviate from God's expectations. In this way, they serve as "the arm of the Lord" when an ungodly king abandons God's law.

As we will see later, Calvin's theological descendants in Britain would take Calvin's restrained justification of political resistance further, deepening the rationale for civil disobedience and expanding the responsibility to resist unjust leaders to articulate a theological right of the people to serve as the means of God's judgment on bad rulers. They agreed with Calvin that in a contest between God's expectations and the behavior or demands of human rulers, when rulers deviated from their duties as the guarantors of God's providential ordering, God could work through other means to establish that order. But more explicitly than Calvin, they were willing to entertain the possibility that the people themselves could serve as "the arm of the Lord." A variation on a theme that Calvin offers sparingly and reluctantly would become, in England and Scotland, a theological rationale for popular rebellion as godly judgment on ungodly rulers. Appeal to God's Providence could justify rebelling against—and sometimes beheading—occupants of the throne, a theological development that would help underwrite the American colonies' Declaration of Independence from the English crown.

For Calvin, then, the political realm was theologically significant, political order was a divine good, political participation and leadership were vocational duty, and political resistance could sometimes be seen as a product of providential design. Witherspoon's inheritance of this theological understanding of politics is on full display in his *Dominion* sermon. Indeed, the entire theological setup for his commentary on the Revolution is the doctrine of Providence. He reminded his hearers that God's Providence "extends not only to things which we may think of great moment, and therefore worthy of notice, but to things the most indifferent and inconsiderable."[43] He insisted that God's sovereign will not only provides the obvious blessings in life but also works behind the tragedies and corruptions, including "the wrath of man" and the realities of war. And he assured his audience that the providential design of all human events, good and bad, is ultimately directed toward the glory of God.

God's sovereign reign includes politics, argued Witherspoon, and it included the present war. Having established the doctrine of God's Providence, he encouraged his hearers to look for signs of God's investment in their break from Britain. "It would be a criminal inattention not to observe the singular interposition of Providence hitherto, in behalf of the American colonies."[44] He gave them examples, including moments of uncharacteristic confusion among normally hyper-disciplined British troops, victories in skirmishes that resulted in remarkably low American casualties, and the British retreat from Boston. "How many discoveries have been made of the designs of enemies in Britain and among ourselves, in a manner as unexpected to us as to them, and in such season as to prevent their effect? What surprising success has attended our encounters in almost every instance?" God's providential oversight of the American resistance confirmed God's presence in the political moment for Witherspoon, and it served to confirm that the resistance was justified.

In the sermon, Witherspoon emphasized a point that he repeated elsewhere, that the mistakes of the British were a particularly obvious sign that God was directing the war effort. "The management of the war itself on their part, would furnish new proof of [God's machinations], if any were needful."[45] Witherspoon took the unusual strategic blunders of the British as a signal that something miraculous was at work. He would make this point again in another public commentary on the war two years later:

> As to the public cause, I look upon the separation of America from Britain to be the visible intention of Providence; and believe that in the issue it will be to the benefit of this country, without any injury to the other—perhaps to the advantage of both. It seems to me the intention of Providence for many reasons, which I cannot now enumerate, but in a particular manner for the following—that I cannot recollect any instance in history, in which a person or people have so totally and uniformly mistaken the means for attaining their own ends, as the king and parliament of Britain have in this contest.[46]

Witherspoon was clear in his conviction that God governed all human affairs, including the political realm, and that signs everywhere indicated God was at work in the colonies' resistance. This assured him that the resistance was justified and that participation in the struggle was a religious calling as well as a political duty. In his theological understanding of politics, Witherspoon was quintessentially Calvinist.

We see Witherspoon's religious interpretation of politics and political duty at work throughout his public and private remarks about the war. For example, during the war, he wrote a letter of support to General Washington on behalf of the faculty of the College of New Jersey, hitting many of the high points of Calvinist political theology:

> We contemplate and adore the wisdom and goodness of divine Providence, as displayed in favor of the United States, in many instances during the course of the war; but in none more than in the unanimous appointment of your Excellency to the command of the army. When we consider the continuance of your life and health—the discernment, prudence, fortitude and patience of your conduct, by which you have not only sacrificed, as others have done, personal ease and property, but frequently even reputation itself, in the public cause, chusing rather to risque your own name than expose the nakedness of your country—when we consider the great and growing attachment of the army, and the cordial esteem of all ranks of man, and of every state in the Union, which you have so long enjoyed—we cannot help being of opinion, that God himself

has raised you up as a fit and proper instrument for establishing and securing the liberty and happiness of these States.[47]

According to Witherspoon, Providence was responsible for Washington's leadership in the war, for the personal attributes that made him the perfect man for the job, and for the success he enjoyed in the role. And because Washington served as a matter of providential design, Witherspoon again implied that such public service is not just a political obligation but a religious calling God had issued to the general.

In invoking Providence on behalf of the American cause, Witherspoon certainly was not unique among revolutionary leaders; a similar reference shows up in the Declaration of Independence. In case we are tempted to read Witherspoon's invocations of Providence in the vein of Deists like Thomas Jefferson, though, it is worth recalling Witherspoon's Princeton *Lectures on Divinity*, in which his broader theology is on systematic display. In these lectures, Witherspoon dedicated several sessions to the defense of orthodox trinitarianism, demonstrating his deep understanding of the Constantinian-era debates over the essence of God. He rehearsed the ancient objections to orthodox trinitarianism, including Sabellianism and Arianism. He appealed to the authority of the Council of Nicaea and the reflections of God the Father, Son, and Holy Ghost in biblical texts. In contrast to Deist depictions of God, Witherspoon clearly subscribed to an orthodox trinitarianism, and he defended the apparent incoherence in God's three-in-one nature as a mystery, above the capability of human reason to understand but not unreasonable or irrational:

> Therefore though we say that the trinity in unity is incomprehensible, or above reason, we say nothing that is absurd or contrary to reason; so far from it, I may say rather it is consonant to reason and the analogy of nature that there should be many things in the divine nature that we cannot fully comprehend. There are many such things in his providence, and surely much more in his essence.[48]

Witherspoon's divinity lectures demonstrate that he was a conventional Calvinist in his understanding of the nature and activity of God. For instance, after representing the controversies around a strong belief in providential design and decrees, particularly around the implications of a strong emphasis on God's sovereignty on the concept of free will, Witherspoon aligned himself with the Westminster Confession and declared himself willing to live in the traditional paradox: "It does not appear difficult to me to believe precisely in the form of our confession of faith—to believe both the certainty of God's purpose and the free agency of the creature. Nor does my being able to explain these doctrines form an objection against one or the other."[49] God's Providence is the point of revelation, said Witherspoon: "one of the chief reasons why any thing is revealed to us concerning the decrees of God, is to give us an awful impression of his infinite majesty, his supreme dominion, and the absolute dependance of every creature upon him."[50] The Calvinist God of predestination and election, not Jefferson's deity, was the referent of Witherspoon's insistence that the dominion of Providence was working through the passions of men in his political moment.

One additional aspect of Witherspoon's religious orientation likely played a powerful role in shaping his political commitments. Witherspoon was a Calvinist *Presbyterian*, and as such was committed to a particular understanding of proper ecclesiastical structure. As we have seen, Presbyterians believed that congregations should enjoy substantial autonomy in governing their affairs, but that they should also be accountable to the larger church in relationships of mutual accountability through presbyteries and synods. Presbyteries and synods served as mechanisms of shared governance, helping to ensure orthodoxy among congregations and protect against the proliferation of significant theological and ethical deviance. Presbyteries also served as courts of appeal in conflicts between congregations, as synods did for conflicts involving more than one presbytery.

Witherspoon was deeply involved in the governance structure of both the Presbyterian Church of Scotland and the Presbyterian Church in the American colonies. In Scotland, he engaged in moments of tension between the Popular and Moderate parties, many of which played out in presbytery meetings (including the fight over whether he would involuntarily relocate to the church in Dundee). In America, he was instrumental in revising the Westminster Confession for local use, beginning the process of constructing a constitution for the American church, and bringing to fruition the first General Assembly—a collective meeting of synods—in the new United States. Witherspoon's investment in Presbyterian polity likely deepened his political convictions as well—the importance of shared governance, the definition of roles as functionary rather than honorary, the need for a balance of power, the importance of national solidarity and accountability, and a commitment to representation from local to national levels. Each of these commitments was baked into the Presbyterian system, and Witherspoon's immersion in them may have inspired his pursuit of parallel ideals in the politics of his new nation.

Enlightened Character

The political thought of John Witherspoon was profoundly shaped by his theological tradition. As central as theology was to his moral and political worldview, however, it was not the only intellectual influence on him, especially by the time he became active in the American revolutionary cause. The man who critiqued Moderate clergy in Scotland for their infatuation with philosophers like Shaftesbury and Hutcheson would increasingly utilize some of those same Enlightenment philosophers in his own teaching, at least to the degree that he could reconcile their views with his basic Calvinist convictions.

The "Enlightenment" is a slippery term, historically and conceptually. Part of its slipperiness is because, as an intellectual movement, it developed in different areas of Europe at different times and featured different thinkers and priorities. Even within these regional variations, there was a range of perspectives on philosophical, moral, social, and economic ideas, and thinkers who now share a common association with the Enlightenment often disagreed vehemently with one another. But perhaps the German philosopher Immanuel Kant gives us a starting point for considering what it meant to be part of this movement. Kant defined Enlightenment as "man's emergence from his self-incurred immaturity."[51] By "immaturity," Kant meant deference to authority or convention rather than a commitment to understanding through the independent use of one's reason. By "self-incurred," Kant meant a failure to employ one's reason not as a result of lack of talent or intelligence but as a result of a "lack of resolution and courage." For Kant, Enlightenment was the commitment to use the freedom that comes from reliance on one's own reason, and to offer one's reasoning in public discourse and debate as a member of society. An enlightened society is one in which its citizens are free to consider important social and moral questions through the employment of their reason, with no restriction or fear of reprisal. We accept explanations for things not because they have been taught to us as true, but because we have reasoned them to be true on our own account. The commitment to thinking reasonably and freely, then, was the central mark of the Enlightenment for Kant, and he contrasted this commitment primarily with deference to religious authorities because he believed that "religious immaturity is the most pernicious and dishonourable variety of all."[52]

As we have noted, Kant's dichotomy between religion and reason (a binary that gets a lot of traction in our day) is complicated by figures like Witherspoon, who managed to hold together respect for his Christian tradition and a commitment to critical thought and investigation. Nor is the dichotomy an entirely useful description of the broader Scottish Enlightenment, given the overlap between Christian ideas and philosophical thought in that country. But the priority placed on unfettered reason, and the implication that no line of critical inquiry can be preemptively declared off limits, was as much a mark of the Enlightenment in Scotland as it was in Kant's Germany.

The number of Scottish intellectuals who contributed to Enlightenment thought on moral, social, political, economic, and religious matters is too many to name here, but it will be helpful to identify a few thinkers who show up time and again in Witherspoon's corpus as his conversation partners. Francis Hutcheson (1694–1746), a professor of moral philosophy at the University of Glasgow, propagated the idea (borrowed from Anthony Ashley Cooper, Lord Shaftesbury) of a "moral sense," a natural capacity that allows us to recognize virtue and vice and directs our actions toward the maximization of benevolence toward others. His commitment to the reality of a moral sense was embedded in a broader understanding of the human condition that prioritized the importance of affections and an aesthetic appreciation for beauty, as a rejoinder against overly dogmatic or rationalistic accounts of human nature. Thomas Reid (1710–96), also of the University of Glasgow, was the chief representative of "common sense" philosophy, an approach that prioritized philosophical consistency with fundamental principles that all human beings know through immediate perception. He argued for his commonsense approach in response to the idealism of David Hume and others, but also as a broader protest against philosophical speculation that was increasingly disconnected from the reality of actual human experiences. Hugh Blair (1718–1800) was a Presbyterian pastor and later Professor of Rhetoric and Belles Lettres at the University of Edinburgh. His multi-volume set of *Sermons* emphasized the importance of Christian morality, and his lectures on rhetoric were likely a source for Witherspoon's own *Lectures on Eloquence*. Adam Smith (1723–90) is famous for his contribution to modern economic thought (specifically, free-market economics) in *The Wealth of Nations*, but he also contributed to the Scottish school of "sentimentalism" with his equally important *Theory of Moral Sentiments*. Smith, who studied with Hutcheson, understood human moral performance to be based not in Hutcheson's "moral sense," but in a natural capacity for empathy, an ability to recognize the feelings and experiences of others that we develop through observation and interaction, which he called "moral sympathy."

David Hume (1711–76), arguably the most famous representative of the Scottish Enlightenment, was also its most controversial in his day. He was widely vilified (including by Witherspoon) for his apparent atheism, having written dismissively about miracles and arguments for the existence of God. Hume was also criticized for his philosophical skepticism, which called into question the popular belief in the existence of innate ideas. Hume argued that ideas do not exist independent of our mental associations and assumptions. True knowledge is limited to what we can experience, and he suggested that much of what we think we are perceiving in the world is a product of connections we make in our own minds. For instance, what we perceive as causal connections between events and experiences are simply assumptions we make mentally about their relationship, by habit or cultural custom. Actual causality cannot be empirically verified, nor can the assumption that allegedly causal correlations in the future will follow the patterns of the past. Hume extended a version of his philosophical skepticism to the arena of ethics, where he argued that human morality was fundamentally an experience of the passions, not reason, and that ethical principles like justice are not eternal ideas embedded in a natural law or the innate workings of conscience as much as social conventions designed to ensure the mutual benefit of members of society.

Many of these Scottish thinkers were debating fundamental questions about human nature, including the origins of morality itself. Is moral concern for others an instinct, feeling, or sentiment, or is it a judgment and exercise of reason? Is moral evaluation rooted in an objective standard, meaning that things are in their essence right or wrong, according to an unchangeable moral law discoverable to human beings in scripture, nature, or the conscience? Or is moral judgment subjective, meaning that we perceive things to be right and wrong when they affect us in certain ways? Is there a reliable source for moral truth, a kind of natural law that we internalize and apply to moral decision-making, or are moral standards just social constructs, developed and externalized in order to ensure social stability and order?

Witherspoon was educated and ministered in a context deeply affected by the intellectual evolution around these basic questions. To be sure, while in Scotland he opposed the Moderate Party's wholesale adoption of the new philosophy at the expense of traditional Calvinist doctrines. But these ways of thinking were everywhere, and as an educated man, Witherspoon could not help but be shaped by them. This does not mean he was uncritically influenced; Witherspoon offered rebuttals to philosophical ideas he judged incompatible with the Calvinist theology he refused to abandon, or when he just thought they were wrong on other grounds. He was particularly dissatisfied with dissertations on virtue that described moral capacities as social constructs or a kind of universal human nature, with no connection to God. Throughout his career, Witherspoon insisted that true virtue was more than a social contract or a species of aesthetic beauty; it was the formation of character around the obligations of divine moral law, a stance that put him at odds with most Scottish sentimentalists. Witherspoon's willingness to criticize excessive philosophical innovation is on potent display in his vilification of Hume, whom he called "beyond the reach of conviction by reasoning" and considered "worthy of the highest contempt," because of Hume's depiction of virtue, which Witherspoon found to be "an insult upon reason itself, and human nature."[53] But Hutcheson, Shaftesbury, and others are also subject to critique, particularly in his moral philosophy lectures, albeit with more nuance than Witherspoon's disdain for Hume reflects.

Sometimes critic and sometimes enthusiast, then, Witherspoon was influenced by the Scottish Enlightenment, and he melded it with his Calvinist theology. It should not surprise us that this synthesis is possible, for Calvinism is one of the intellectual raw ingredients for the Enlightenment movement. Contrary to the way historians sometimes tell the story, the Enlightenment did not emerge *de novo* in Europe. It was itself an evolution made possible in part by a liberal vein in European Calvinism in the seventeenth and eighteenth centuries. John Locke's depiction of political rights and toleration, for instance, was clearly influenced by the struggle of Puritan Calvinists against monarchical power during the English Civil War.[54] Many of Locke's arguments for religious toleration echo the same defense of religious liberty that Roger Williams made (in England and Massachusetts) a generation before him, though Locke entertained more limits on religious toleration than Williams did.[55] Principles of popular political consent and conceptions of natural rights emerging in this same period were rooted in Calvinist antecedents, and the Enlightenment education at Scottish universities was happening at institutions that retained considerable investment in Christian identity and intellectual heritage. In fact, Scottish thinkers like Reid and Blair were ministers of the established Kirk.

We might say that the synthesis happening in Witherspoon's mind simply modeled an evolution in Calvinism itself. His understanding of political character certainly reflected the influence of these philosophical sources. Of obvious impact was his commitment to something akin to Reid's "common sense" philosophy, the conviction that our philosophical understanding of the world and of human nature ought to resonate with our actual experience of it. Witherspoon's practical piety synthesized naturally with Reid's grounded approach to morality. In the sixth installment of his *Lectures on Moral Philosophy*, Witherspoon interrupted his discussion of modes of reasoning for the existence of God to invoke Reid and others, specifically as a rebuttal of Hume. He noted the impact of Hume's radical philosophical skepticism on religious belief and, more broadly, on confidence in the reality that we can perceive through human reasoning. In response, Witherspoon invoked "some late writers" who have asserted "that there are certain first principles or dictates of common sense, which are either simple perceptions, or seen with intuitive evidence." Witherspoon seemed to have Reid principally in mind here, and he endorsed Reid's argument that commonsense principles "are the foundation of all reasoning," because without this foundation, "to reason is a word without meaning."[56] He returned to this commonsense approach in the "Recapitulation" to his philosophy lectures, where he advised his students that "it is always safer in our reasonings to trace facts upwards, than to reason downwards upon metaphysical principles." Here he credits James Beattie for this commonsense approach, but similarities to Reid are evident as well.

Besides this insistence on a correlation between intellectual work and the commonsense realities of the world we live in, Witherspoon adopted a modified version of Hutcheson's idea of the moral sense. As we will explore in the next chapter, Witherspoon found Hutcheson's language of a moral sense compatible with his theological understanding of the conscience, and his adoption of Hutcheson's language (in his philosophy lectures and elsewhere) gave him the philosophical vocabulary to explain the thoroughly Calvinist idea that all normally functioning human beings have some natural capacity for basic moral performance. Again, Witherspoon deviated from Hutcheson's description of the moral sense in that he thought Hutcheson made it sound too much like a natural appetite for moral beauty. For the Calvinist Witherspoon, there had to be a way to talk about the connection between the intuitions of the moral sense and the objective requirements of God's law. Witherspoon was more than happy, however, to co-opt Hutcheson's concept to at least approximate his Calvinist understanding of conscience.

Witherspoon's adoption of the idea of a moral sense reflected another element of Enlightenment influence, a guarded optimism about human moral potential. Classical Calvinists were not exactly known for emphasizing human beings' capacities for goodness. Calvinists certainly affirmed that human beings were created good, but their moral theologies tended to stress the liabilities of our sinful state. For Calvinists, sin manifested particularly as inordinate self-love or the pursuit of self-interest at the expense of others, and this focus on sin as self-interest influenced their political theology and ethics. They tended to view law and social order as necessary mechanisms for curbing people's selfishness and protecting a commitment to the common good. They justified the coercive nature of political authority as a divinely ordained tool for protecting people from one another. And they tended to be circumspect about how optimistic we should be about the moral performance of individuals and societies.

Calvinists were not without theological resources for articulating some moral ambition on the part of individuals and societies, but their political theologies tended to be realist in their expectation that people normally pursue their own self-interest, even at others' expense. Witherspoon inherited this realism from his theological tradition, but at times he appeared more optimistic about human moral accomplishment than the conventional classical Calvinist, possibly because of the influence of Enlightenment moral thinkers. As reflected in the idea of a moral sense, most Scottish philosophers were convinced that human beings are naturally equipped for considerable moral accomplishment and cooperation. Goodness is our natural state, they argued, and vicious habits are a correctable signal of an unhealthy moral system. Scottish thinkers also tended to assume that the "state of nature" of human beings is not one of isolation and the pursuit of self-interest but sociableness; in other words, human beings constitutionally need fellowship and cooperation. Unlike Thomas Hobbes and some versions of Calvinism, then, the Scots saw social order and government primarily as assets to the fulfillment of human potential, not necessary restrictions on selfish human nature. To stress the ends of civic kinship and social cooperation led to a more positive regard for government and society than social theories that defined political government as the protection of citizens from the brutalizing power of others.

Ideas like Hutcheson's moral sense and the Scots' priority on sociableness conspired with elements of Calvinist anthropology (like the conscience) to give Witherspoon grounds on which to expect a moderate degree of social cooperation from society, especially when compared with more pessimistic spokespersons from his tradition (including at times Calvin himself). And to the degree that Witherspoon adopted the interpretation of the human condition as including a natural capacity for moral performance, he could be relatively ambitious in his hopes for social morality regardless of how many members of society were active

Christians. We see this relative moral optimism on display in a column he wrote on "the philosophy of human nature and of human life" under the pseudonym The Druid. In the first installment, he appealed to a picture of human nature that, "with all its defects, is certainly the noblest and most valuable in this lower world, and therefore the most worthy of cultivation."[57] He observed that commentaries on the human condition tend to fall into two categories, subscribing to either an unjustifiably optimistic portrait of human moral capabilities or an unhelpfully pessimistic one. In response, Witherspoon argued for a kind of positive realism that takes seriously human failings but also acknowledges and appeals to our constructive moral capabilities. Even cautious appeals to a common morality like this one reflect more optimism than is normally associated with Calvinist moral theology, and it may be because in making this appeal, Witherspoon was putting his particular synthesis of Calvinism and Scottish sentimentalism on display.

From his moral philosophy lectures and other writings, a selective incorporation of Scottish Enlightenment ideas becomes apparent, refracted as always through his primary Calvinist worldview. That refraction governed which philosophical ideas were persuasive to him, and it affected his interpretation of those ideas. From time to time, however, we also see ways in which Enlightenment thought reshaped Witherspoon's understanding of his theological tradition, no more obviously than in his greater optimism (relative to other Calvinists) regarding social cooperation, an optimism vital to his rhetorical leadership during the Revolutionary War. Without the belief that a society of mixed religious pedigree could come together to accomplish something in the name of goodness, justice, and right, his broad appeals to the moral imperative of war—and his commendation of public character during and after it—would seem pointless.

A Bilingual Appeal for Political Character

Calvinist political theology and Scottish Enlightenment moral philosophy shaped Witherspoon's public ethics, including his priority on healthy political character. He emphasized the theme of character in his lectures at Princeton and his wartime public essays. The *Dominion* sermon exemplified his ethical preoccupations, for Witherspoon spent little of that sermon justifying his support of the war itself. Instead, after discharging his Calvinist duty to provide adequate biblical exegesis, he launched into an extended discussion of the obligation the colonists had to one another and the collective moral traits the struggle would require from its leaders and citizens. Courage, fortitude, patience, unity in spirit, a commitment to piety, industry, frugality, and temperance were all reconstituted as moral contributions to the war effort. But Witherspoon was careful to emphasize that these public virtues would be important long after the war had concluded. Collective character was as vital to the maturation of the new nation as it was to its birth. Without good character, a sense of mutual obligation to one another (and to God), and a commitment to the protection of basic liberties, the American project would be doomed from the start.

We see this priority on character running through a number of his public works on the war itself. For instance, in the letter to General Washington referenced earlier, we see Witherspoon commend Washington's "discernment, prudence, fortitude and patience" as gifts of God and assets to his leadership. In an op-ed he wrote *On Conducting the American Controversy*, Witherspoon went to great pains to distinguish between a virtuous pursuit of independence and a vicious one, even as he was adamant that the American cause against the British was justified. Of utmost importance to him was maintaining respect for the British monarch, and he modeled that virtue of respect in his own pledge of "love and honor" to the person of George III.[58] And in a congressional speech on the colonies' financial obligations to their creditors, Witherspoon warned Congress about not only the practical consequences of default but the resultant impact on the moral reputation of the new nation: "We are just beginning to appear among the powers of the earth, and it may be said of national, as of private characters, they soon begin to form, and when disadvantageous ideas are formed, they are not easily altered or destroyed."[59]

While Witherspoon emphasized a commitment to character in his private correspondence and public remarks during the war, he also was instilling it in the future citizens and leaders who were his college students. The best example of his pedagogical priority on public virtue is his benedictory address to graduating Princeton students, *Christian Magnanimity*. Witherspoon first delivered *Christian Magnanimity* at Princeton in 1775, then modified it at least once for a subsequent graduating class. In his address, Witherspoon defined magnanimity as "spirit, dignity, or greatness of mind."[60] He described it as the ambition to "attempt great and difficult things," to have "great and valuable possessions," and to do so with "resolution," fortitude, and perseverance in the face of danger or struggle.[61] He admitted that, at first glance, aspiring to greatness may seem antithetical to the teachings of Christianity, which emphasize humility and self-denial over ambition. Witherspoon argued, though, that magnanimity may be understood as a supreme Christian virtue as long as the "great and difficult things" Christians strive for are to "live and act for the glory of God and the good of others."[62] Christians can strive for "great and valuable possessions," as long as the possession they crave is piety and the satisfaction of God's wishes. In other words, Witherspoon argued that magnanimity becomes a Christian virtue when the ends to which the magnanimous person strives are the ends of God and the good of other people.

Witherspoon's focus on magnanimity in his benedictory address is a fitting example of his synthesis of Calvinist moral theology and Enlightenment thought. Scottish philosophers of the eighteenth century were preoccupied with magnanimity as a public virtue, most notably Hume and Smith, who each developed the trait as a socially useful virtue. For Hume and Smith, though, magnanimity was an example of how natural egoism can be constructively directed toward the public good, as the pursuit of personal greatness and renowned reputation leads men to contribute constructively to society in pursuit of those self-centered goals.[63] In his benedictory address, Witherspoon was recalling their well-known arguments, but for him, magnanimity had to be based in something other than publicly directed self-centeredness to be compatible with Christian morality. He translated magnanimity theologically by redirecting it toward a Calvinist end. The pursuit of public greatness is virtuous from a Christian perspective when it is motivated by a desire "to glorify God and enjoy him forever," as the Westminster Catechism puts it. In Witherspoon's vision of political character, pious striving to fulfill God's will replaces self-interest as virtue's intention, object, and motivation. Given that God's will includes the imperative to serve the needs of others, according to Witherspoon, this theological end gave his understanding of magnanimity a decidedly outward, other-regarding vector. Magnanimity consists of striving for greatness by serving the common good.

Witherspoon understood magnanimity as a virtue consistent with Christian ideals, then, but he did not restrict his expectation of magnanimity only to professed Christians. Magnanimity could be a "worldly virtue" as well as a Christian one. Even without the effects of piety, individuals can strive for admirable magnanimity if their pursuit of greatness is more than egoistic, if it has a genuine concern for justice as its object and its ambitions are discharged with wisdom and prudence. Magnanimity as a worldly virtue takes as its "principle of action"—by which Witherspoon seems to mean intention and motivation—not "merely to make [one's] name famous" but "doing signal service to mankind."[64] Without a noble public cause, ambition and fortitude cease to be virtuous and instead "degenerate into vice and assume the names of pride, ambition, ambition, temerity, ferocity, and obstinacy."[65] Motivated by a concern for justice and the common good, however, ambition becomes virtuous, even if its focus and motivation fall short of the pursuit of the glory of God. Witherspoon's "worldly" magnanimity bears a bit of resemblance to Hume's and Smith's, but even in its non-theological form, his virtue is defined by a principal commitment to other-regard, not the self. In this way, it reflects the distinct moral orientation of Calvinism while providing for recognition of admirable moral potential in people beyond the community of redeemed Christians.

Describing magnanimity as both an admirable component of Christian character and a more widely applicable "worldly virtue," Witherspoon demonstrated his indebtedness to Calvinist theology and Scottish moral philosophy, as well as his efforts to synthesize the two moral traditions to speak to a mixed constituency of committed Christians and a wider American public. More broadly, his graduation address demonstrated his investment in the cultivation of character as essential to the health of the American political endeavor. In the chapters to follow, we consider more closely what good political character looked like for Witherspoon, the specific virtues he thought important, and their roots in a commitment to the common good and the protection of human rights.

Notes

1 Stohlman, *John Witherspoon*, 20–1.
2 Stohlman, *John Witherspoon*, 99.
3 John Witherspoon, *Ecclesiastical Characteristics*, in *The Selected Writings of John Witherspoon*, ed. Thomas P. Miller (Southern Illinois University Press, 1990), 70.
4 Witherspoon, EC, in Miller, *Selected Writings*, 71.
5 Witherspoon, EC, in Miller, *Selected Writings*, 79.
6 Witherspoon, EC, in Miller, *Selected Writings*, 78–9.
7 This exclamation is attributed to the Whig Horace Walpole and is generally understood to have been a reference to Witherspoon. See Kevin DeYoung, "John

Witherspoon and Slavery," *Theology Today* 80:4 (2024), 358. By contrast, Jeffry Morrison doubts that Witherspoon is the reference; see Jeffry H. Morrison, *John Witherspoon and the Founding of the American Republic* (University of Notre Dame, 2005), 13.

8 Collins, *President Witherspoon*, I:94.
9 Collins, *President Witherspoon*, I:96.
10 Collins, *President Witherspoon*, I:80–1.
11 For more on Rush's contributions to early American higher education, see Harlow Giles Unger, *Dr. Benjamin Rush: The Founding Father Who Healed a Wounded Nation* (Da Cap Press, 2018), especially 83–4.
12 Collins, *President Witherspoon*, I:88.
13 For more on the importance of the Great Awakening to the evolution of Christianity in the United States, see Mark A. Noll, *America's God: From Jonathan Edwards to Abraham Lincoln* (Oxford University Press, 2002).
14 Stohlman, *John Witherspoon*, 48–55.
15 Stohlman, *John Witherspoon*, 98–9.
16 See, for instance, Gideon Mailer, *John Witherspoon's American Revolution* (The University of North Carolina Press, 2017). The strength of Mailer's study is his insistence that we honor the theological orientation at the heart of Witherspoon's work and writings, but Mailer overstates his case, arguing for a forced reading of all references to Scottish Enlightenment philosophy as ironic or oppositional. For a more nuanced argument on Witherspoon's Calvinist orthodoxy, see Kevin DeYoung, *The Religious Formation of John Witherspoon: Calvinism, Evangelicalism, and the Scottish Enlightenment* (Routledge, 2020). DeYoung's focus on Witherspoon's career in Scotland prevents him from offering extensive interpretations of his time in America, but generally DeYoung allows that over time Witherspoon could have embraced ideas from Scottish philosophy without completely abandoning his religious beliefs.
17 The most influential of these interpretations of Witherspoon is Mark A. Noll's in *America's God*, chapter 6.
18 See, for instance, David Little's assertion that Locke's political philosophy developed in large part from the ethical ethos of the Puritan parliamentary debates, and thus reflected the influences of Roger Williams, the Levellers, and other theological perspectives. See David Little, *Essays on Religion and Human Rights: Ground to Stand On* (Cambridge University Press, 2015), 188–91.
19 Roger Finke and Rodney Stark, *The Churching of America 1776-2005: Winners and Losers in Our Religious Economy* (Rutgers University Press, 2005), 24–8.
20 For a compelling argument for the importance of clergy justifications of the American Revolution, and for the ways those justifications were derivations (and

not deviations) from dominant theological traditions in the colonies, see Gary L. Steward, *Justifying Revolution: The American Clergy's Argument for Political Resistance, 1750–1776* (Oxford University Press, 2021).

21 The Great Awakening in America was distinct but not unique. Europe experienced its own evangelical revival in the eighteenth century, and in fact, participants in the European revivals influenced the British colonial experience. See Mark A. Noll, *The Rise of Evangelicalism: The Age of Edwards, Whitefield, and the Wesleys* (InterVarsity Press, 2003).
22 Lk. 22:38.
23 John Calvin, *Institutes of the Christian Religion*, ed. John T. McNeill. (Westminster Press, 1960), Book IV, chapter 20, 1486. Subsequent references to Calvin's *Institutes* will follow this book/chapter/page format.
24 Calvin, *Institutes*, IV.20, 1487.
25 Calvin, *Institutes*, IV.20, 1488.
26 Calvin, *Institutes*, IV.20, 1489.
27 Calvin, *Institutes*, I.16, 199.
28 Calvin, *Institutes*, III.19, 847.
29 Calvin, *Institutes*, I.5, 60.
30 Calvin, *Institutes*, I.5, 60.
31 Calvin, *Institutes*, III.8, 704.
32 Calvin, *Institutes*, I.5, 60.
33 Calvin, *Institutes*, I.5, 62.
34 Calvin, *Institutes*, III.11, 724–5.
35 Calvin, *Institutes*, III.10, 725.
36 Calvin, *Institutes*, I.16, 201.
37 Calvin, *Institutes*, IV.20, 1511.
38 Calvin, *Institutes*, I.17, 221.
39 Calvin, *Institutes*, IV.20, 1513.
40 Calvin, *Institutes*, IV.20, 1518.
41 Calvin, *Institutes*, IV.20, 1520.
42 Calvin, *Institutes*, IV.20, 1519.
43 Witherspoon, DPPM, III:17.
44 Witherspoon, DPPM, III:33.
45 Witherspoon, DPPM, III:37.
46 "On the Contest between Great Britain and America," in *Works*, IV:375.
47 Witherspoon, "Address to General Washington," in *Works*, IV:363.
48 John Witherspoon, *Lectures on Divinity* (hereafter LD), Lecture IX, *The Works of the Rev. John Witherspoon*, IV:66.
49 Witherspoon, LD, Lecture XIII, *Works*, IV:90.

50 Witherspoon, LD, Lecture XIII, *Works*, IV:83.
51 Immanuel Kant, "An Answer to the Question: 'What Is Enlightenment?,'" in *Kant: Political Writings*, ed. Hans Reiss (Cambridge University Press, 1991), 54.
52 Kant, *What Is Enlightenment?*, 59.
53 See Witherspoon's *Essay on Justification*, 58nb. Witherspoon's primary objection here seems to be Hume's inclusion of "natural advantages," like good health and physical attractiveness, among the virtues, and disease among the vices. To Witherspoon's mind, Hume's understanding of virtue as physical traits is the extreme consequence of what he is critiquing in this moment of the *Essay*, the philosophical description of virtue entirely as a feature of universal human nature, rather than as a manifestation of the commitment to God's law.
54 See Little, *Religion and Human Rights*, 189–91.
55 See my introductory essay in *On Religious Liberty: Selections from the Works of Roger Williams* (Harvard University Press, 2008), 40–4.
56 John Witherspoon, *Lectures on Moral Philosophy* (hereafter LMP), Lecture VI, in *The Works*, III:394.
57 *The Druid*, I, in *Works*, IV:427. Witherspoon's positive realism about human nature is also reflected in his arguments in "Part of a Speech in Congress, Upon the Confederation" (*Works*, IV:347–50). In this speech, he pushes back on the attitude that a confederation between the states will never work because the selfish nature of people will inevitably undermine it. In response, Witherspoon articulates a chastened optimism and a progressive view of history, arguing that the "liberal sentiments that now prevail" make an imperfect union possible, even while acknowledging that the "depravity of human nature" will always require proper governmental checks to be established to keep the union together.
58 Witherspoon, "On Conducting the American Controversy," in *Works*, IV:305.
59 Witherspoon, "Part of a Speech in Congress, on the Finances," in *Works*, IV:343.
60 Witherspoon, *Christian Magnanimity*, in Miller, *Selected Writings*, 117.
61 Witherspoon, CM, in Miller, *Selected Writings*, 118–19.
62 Witherspoon, CM, in Miller, *Selected Writings*, 121.
63 See Ryan Patrick Hanley, "Magnanimity and Modernity: Greatness of Soul and Greatness of Mind in the Enlightenment," in *The Measure of Greatness: Philosophers on Magnanimity*, ed. Sophia Vasalou (Oxford University Press, 2019), 176–96.
64 Witherspoon, CM, in Miller, *Selected Writings*, 120.
65 Witherspoon, CM, in Miller, *Selected Writings*, 121.

2

A "Public Spirit"

When he rose to his pulpit that day in May 1776 to preach *Dominion of Providence over the Passions of Men*, John Witherspoon offered far more than moral justification for the Revolution. He called on his parishioners to imagine the nation they were fighting to establish, warning them that their new republic would need to aspire beyond political independence to ensure a healthy future. They would need to build a society that could count on the good character of citizens and leaders: "Nothing is more certain," he preached, "than that a general profligacy and corruption of manners make a people ripe for destruction. A good form of government may hold the rotten materials together for some time, but beyond a certain pitch, even the best constitution will be ineffectual, and slavery must ensue."[1] Of course, there was tragic irony in his invocation of slavery as the consequence of an absence of public character, and we must attend later to the hypocrisy that this irony lays bare. But we can see that, for Witherspoon, the kind of people the colonists would strive to become was important to the Revolution's justification and its prospects for success. The struggle for independence had to be for the right reasons, but it also had to be undertaken with the right *attitudes*, including a commitment to industry and sacrifice, a sense of humility, concern for the common good, and respect for the humanity of the enemy. These traits and others represented the virtues of a "public spirit" that Witherspoon invoked several times in his fast day sermon, a spirit he believed was a necessity if their new nation was to succeed. Beyond the fight for independence, the cultivation of public character among citizens and leaders of the new republic would be essential to the longevity of this American experiment in representative democracy.

Moral philosophers and theologians use the language of *virtue* and *character* to describe the dispositions, traits, and habits that make someone a good person. (By contrast, of course, *vices* are those character traits or dispositions that we say make someone a bad person, or at least not a morally admirable person.) Moralists disagree about which virtues are most important to good character. Among the virtues Aristotle identified as important to the ethical life were fortitude, temperance, justice, and prudence. The Stoics were fond of wisdom, justice, courage, and moderation as classes of character traits reflecting good virtue. In the Christian tradition, the apostle Paul listed love, peace, joy, forbearance, kindness, goodness, faithfulness, gentleness, and self-control as the "fruit of the spirit," suggesting that these dispositions reflected a Spirit-filled character.[2] Regardless of any disagreement over which specific virtues are most important, virtue theorists generally argue that right behavior comes from good character, but good character is also reinforced and deepened by habitually doing the right thing. What different virtue ethics have in common is that they do not define moral performance first and foremost as *doing* the right thing. Instead, they suggest that *being* a certain type of person is fundamentally what makes one morally admirable.

Witherspoon talked a lot about moral character or virtue, including the virtues necessary to the "public spirit" he thought essential to national health. But what exactly does good public character look like? How is it cultivated, and what does it require? Witherspoon answered those questions by drawing upon the resources of his Calvinist theological tradition, refracted often through the moral language of the Scottish Enlightenment. The result was a vision of public character that spoke to eighteenth-century evangelicals as well as devotees of Enlightenment thinking.

Although Witherspoon's theological and moral convictions are evident throughout his writings, the philosophical foundations of his public ethics can be found in his *Lectures on Moral Philosophy*, which he delivered each year to his students at the College of New Jersey. What we have in these lectures are actually notes, not a fully developed dissertation on the moral life. As a result, the lectures are somewhat sparse, neither exhaustive as a source of moral philosophy nor deep in their elaboration of many of the ideas captured in them. In fact, during his lifetime, Witherspoon never intended these notes to be published. Only after his death did some of his loyal students and friends see fit to print them, in honor of their beloved teacher and with the conviction that Witherspoon's wisdom should have a wider impact.

Nonetheless, with the help of the *Lectures*, and drawing on other sermons and treatises, we can piece together Witherspoon's understanding of the political character necessary for citizens and leaders to contribute to a healthy society. Assessing Witherspoon's understanding of character requires us to start with what moralists sometimes call *moral anthropology*, or the assumptions we make about human beings' moral capacities. Is moral performance primarily a matter of the head or the heart? Is moral choice a function of our reason, our will, or our affections? Are human beings basically good creatures who occasionally make mistakes, or fundamentally flawed beings whose capacity for goodness is significantly limited? These questions and others get at foundational convictions we hold about human beings as moral actors, which in turn shape our moral expectations of individuals and societies, including how optimistic we can be regarding the prospects for a society of justice, peace, and flourishing.

An Affection for Virtue

When Witherspoon described the inner workings of the moral life, he talked in terms of human "faculties," consistent with the long-standing rhetoric of classical Western moral theology and philosophy. "The faculties of the mind are commonly divided into these three kinds," he lectured to his students, "the understanding, the will, and the affections."[3] Also consistent with his religious and philosophical traditions, Witherspoon did not regard the understanding, will, and affections as separate moral organs so much as mental functions of moral activity—or as he put it, "different ways of exerting the same simple principle."[4] The understanding stands for our intellectual capacities, our ability to ascertain truth, to absorb and comprehend facts, and to engage in logical reasoning. The will represents the inclination to love, desire, and choose; we desire and choose what we consider good, and we experience aversion to what we regard as bad. The affections were arguably the murkiest of the moral faculties, and it often seems that no two thinkers of this era understood them quite the same way. Generally, though, the affections were understood as nonrational or semi-rational sensory responses. Some affections were captured in the commonly recognized external senses— sights, sounds, tastes, smells, and tactile feelings. But other affections were aesthetic (a response to beauty), emotional (e.g., anger), or ethical (a sense of sympathy or fairness, for instance). Rather than being the product of intentional deliberation, the affections are something we experience almost instinctively.

Whether imagined as operations, modes, or something else, the placement of priority among the intellectual, volitional, or affective faculties indicated what a thinker considered the ultimate compass of the moral life. Those who emphasized reason or judgment considered moral decision-making to be primarily an intellectual exercise. Doing what is right requires that we first understand what is right, and only a proper moral understanding can direct the will (and the affections) to desire and choose the right thing. People do bad things because they do not understand their moral duties; bad moral choices indicate faulty reasoning. For moral philosophers who prioritized understanding, better ethical reasoning was the way to admirable moral performance.

By contrast, moralists who considered the will or the affections to be the heart of moral performance argued that our loves and our dispositions dictate our choices and our evaluation of truth. Before we can understand what is good, we must desire the good. A priority on the will and affections was particularly compatible with how most British Calvinists thought about sin and piety. Most Calvinist thinkers adopted Calvin's views on the pervasive nature of sin's corruption of our entire moral faculty. For his part, Calvin followed Augustine's understanding of sin as principally a matter of willful disregard of God's commands rather than ignorance of them. According to Augustine, the act of choosing represented in the will is determined by our ultimate love; we choose and pursue that which we love. God created human beings to love the good, to love God, and the fact that we were created this way testifies to the goodness of God's creation, including the human species. But, observed Augustine, "the love which is the root of good things is quite different from the cupidity which is the root of evil things."[5] Sin corrupts us, and a human will that is designed to love God no longer recognizes true goodness. Instead, "cupidity" drives the will's desire, and we chase after our own constricted interests.

The distortion of the will is how Augustine interpreted his own life of sin, prior to his Christian conversion. As he tells the story in his *Confessions*, he was often surrounded by admirably pious role models, but he could not overcome the inclination to pursue his own pleasures and priorities, particularly around sex, simply by learning from their examples. "I was . . . thus bound, not with the irons of another, but my own iron will," he wrote. "My will was the enemy master of, and thence had made a chain for me and bound me. Because of a perverse will was lust made; and lust indulged in became custom; and custom not resisted became necessity."[6]

Here Augustine illustrates the connection between a moral anthropology based in the will and an ethics focused on character. To describe the moral life as one of virtues and character is to claim that who we *are* as people is more fundamental to our moral standing than what we *do*. To be sure, our actions help shape our moral lives, but to be a virtuous person requires more than a net sum of good deeds. To be good requires that we love and desire the right things. Good or bad, our loves direct our choices and actions, and those actions habituate and deepen our loves. A person who inordinately loves herself will desire things that feed that self-love. Left unchecked, this self-indulgence will habituate in practice over time, and the inclination to serve the self will only deepen. By contrast, a person who loves God and the good of others will desire things that contribute to the happiness of God and others. The practice of that kind of other regard also will habituate over time, deepening virtuous love in the character of the person who aims for it and practices it. Augustine believed that his inability to break free from his love of "the world" to love God above all else was not a matter of insufficient wisdom or understanding: "The unlearned start up and 'take' heaven, and we, with our learning but wanting heart, see where we wallow in flesh and blood!"[7] For Augustine, true virtue was a practice of the heart, of desiring and loving the good—that is, God. A heart corrupted by sin cannot love properly; only a will reset by the intervention of divine grace possesses the capacity to love and choose the good.[8]

Calvin and his theological followers were, for the most part, good Augustinians, so they adopted much of Augustine's anthropology as their own. Calvin viewed the corruption of sin in holistic terms: "we are so vitiated and perverted in every part of our nature that by this great corruption we stand justly condemned and convicted before God." Calvin was clear that "whatever is in man, from the understanding to the will, from the soul even to the flesh, has been defiled and crammed with this concupiscence."[9] But that term, "concupiscence," betrays that Calvin, like Augustine, thought of sin fundamentally as a matter of wrong desires more than corrupted understanding. His interpretations of the first sin of Adam and Eve were all about destructive attitudes and myopic aspirations: pride, disobedience, apostasy, reproach, ambition—all ill-directed desires, not misunderstandings. For Calvin, sin corrupts the whole person, but we feel the impact of sin most acutely in the narrowing of our desires. Rather than desiring the glory of God and obedience to God, we denigrate into constricted self-love.

Like Calvin, the Puritan William Ames (1576–1633) was clear that moral performance, or "observance" of God's commands, was fundamentally a matter of desire, a "conformity between the will of God and ours."[10] In his discussion of morality, Ames was of course careful not to imply that works have any salvific effect. Instead, most of his discussion assumes that he was talking about the moral actions of redeemed Christians, whose goodness is not a result of their actions but whose actions are empowered to be good by God's grace. "For since sin came, man cannot of himself do anything acceptable to God . . . except it be done in Christ through faith and sanctifying grace."[11] At the same time, Ames insisted that the necessity of grace for true virtue does not make moral striving unimportant to the unregenerate: "Yet these duties are not to be omitted by a man who does not yet believe, for they are good in themselves—they impede the increase both of sin and the punishment of sinners and they are often recompensed with various benefits from God . . . through his abundant and secret kindness."[12]

Whether regenerate or unregenerate, Ames described human moral striving as a matter of reason and will, of knowing and desiring the good, but like Calvin (and Augustine), he gave priority of place to the will. "As the zeal of the will consists chiefly in love and hatred, observance acceptable to God is found in a love of good and a hatred of evil."[13] Ames believed that moral performance is driven by a "love of good," and that a motivating "zeal" for the good contributed significantly to whether a specific act was good. He distinguished the "inward act" of desiring some particular action from the manifestation of that desire externally in "performing power," and it is that inward inclination that establishes the goodness of the outward performance.[14] In fact, Ames insisted that presumably good actions without a genuine desire to do good are hypocritical and morally worthless, while the opposite is not necessarily true; a desire to do good with no means to perform that goodness can still be good, just "incomplete."[15] For Ames, then, "the goodness of an act depends first and chiefly upon the will." Reason is implicated in the practice of virtue because the intellect is needed to understand the law of God, adherence to which is the obedience that makes one virtuous. But Ames argued that virtue is not primarily a matter of thinking rightly. Virtue resides in the shaping of our wants and desires toward love of God and increase in the common good.[16]

In fact, Ames thought the fundamental desires of our will, from which our character derives, were so powerful that they can move us to act contrary to what we know in our minds is right. Ames believed that the conscience is a "storehouse" of moral principles placed in our intellect by God. Essentially the voice of God in the mind of human beings, that reservoir of moral principles could not err, but a corrupted will could direct a person to act in violation of what his conscience was telling him was God's command. "The Will can move itself, towards an object that is apprehended and judged good for profit or pleasure in some respect, though reason judge that it is not lawful but sinful." In other words, sometimes our conscience tells us something is wrong, but we do it anyway. Ames thought it obvious that people do things they know are wrong all the time. These sins of "malice" are evidence that our misdirected desires are sometimes powerful enough to overrule our knowledge of God's commands: "If the Will do necessarily follow the judgment of the understanding, then there should (in proper speaking) be no sin of malice, distinct from those sins which are committed through ignorance or passion."[17] In describing the operations of conscience this way, Ames not only assumed the independence of the will from reason, but he also suggested that our desires enjoy a certain amount of power over reason and intellect. In fact, Ames argued that the will can turn the understanding, including conscience, away "from the consideration of any object," by which he meant that our misdirected loves distort our understanding of obligations or circumstances.[18] As a result, he says, "by reason of this commanding power, the Will is the first cause of unadvisedness, and blameworthy error in the Understanding."[19]

The Calvinist description of sin tells us a lot about their understanding of moral striving and failure. While Calvinists were at great pains not to collapse salvation into moral performance (salvation comes by grace, after all), a priority on the will served many Calvinist explanations of the moral life, saved or otherwise. Being good requires more than knowing what is right, and moral failings result from more than just ignorance. The moral life is fundamentally a matter of the *heart*. It is about loving and seeking what is right and good, and seeking the right and the good requires more than just information; it requires the right inclination. Moral performance depends on the desire to be good; it is a matter of character.

Calvinists in the sixteenth and seventeenth centuries primarily used the concept of the will to represent fundamental desires or "loves" that shape and direct our moral character, for good or bad. By the eighteenth century, though, moral thinkers were increasingly utilizing the language of the affections to capture a moral attraction to the good. For centuries of Western moral philosophy and theology, the affections had been referred to as "passions" and were normally considered expressions of our baser, more animalistic impulses. Passions like anger or sexual attraction were nonrational reactions to stimuli that often impeded a person's moral performance, requiring reason to regulate the passions for a person to achieve an admirable level of human moral accomplishment. The quintessential example of this suspicion of passions in Christian theology appears in Augustine's diatribes against lust, greed, and "cupidity," a theological concern for the passions rooted in his own spiritual pilgrimage.[20] The Puritan divine William Perkins (1558–1602) was still operating with the pejorative connotation of affections when he described the affections as a "fountain" of sins that derive from "hatred, grief, anger, sorrow," and arrogance.[21]

In the eighteenth century, however, moral philosophers were beginning to regard the affections as a positive moral force, and in fact, some philosophers considered them the seat of morality. Much of the rehabilitation of the affections among British thinkers can be traced to the work of Anthony Ashley Cooper, better known as the Third Earl of Shaftesbury (1671–1713). Shaftesbury argued that human morality is rooted in a broader natural appreciation for order and harmony. Human beings possess a "moral sense" that causes us to experience moral goodness as a kind of aesthetic beauty. Specifically, we naturally invest in the happiness of others as conducive to moral harmony, he argued, so when we encounter actions and attitudes that concern themselves with the happiness of others, we experience those actions and attitudes as morally good. Importantly, Shaftesbury emphasized that it is the motive of the actor, rather than the consequences of any particular action, that invokes our experience of goodness. In that way, the moral sense is an affective response to another's affect, a second-order experience of concern for others as morally pleasant (or the experience of disregard for another as morally repugnant). This moral sense of right and wrong, argued Shaftesbury, is a natural impulse, not a product of deliberative reason but an affective experience that prompts virtuous action.[22]

Later thinkers like Francis Hutcheson followed Shaftesbury's lead in regarding the affections as an important constructive contributor to human morality, rather than an impediment to moral performance. Hutcheson's first major work, *An Inquiry into the Original of Our Ideas of Beauty and Virtue*, was meant as a defense of Shaftesbury's understanding of the affections, and by extension, his depiction of human morality as a matter of the affections. Hutcheson agreed with Shaftesbury that all normally functioning human beings are born with a moral sense that is more instinctual than rational. Based in the affections, the moral sense renders a "perception" of moral beauty and harmony, and "the Pleasure [that this perception invokes] does not arise from any Knowledge of Principles, Proportions, Causes, or of the Usefulness of the Object; but strikes us at first with the Idea of Beauty."[23] We recognize "an immediate moral goodness" as beautiful, and we respond to that beauty with a sense of approval, independent of any sense of advantage that we might gain from the attitude or action in question.[24] This last point was as important to Hutcheson as it was to Shaftesbury, both of whom were responding to the likes of Thomas Hobbes, Bernard Mandeville, and others who (in different ways) interpreted moral standards as constructions that fundamentally appeal to people's natural self-interest.[25] Rather than innately selfish creatures, Hutcheson believed we are hardwired to revel in other people's happiness. He called this a natural inclination toward benevolence. When we see an attitude or action that aims toward the happiness of others, especially a great number of other people, we instinctually approve of such attitudes and actions with our moral sense. We perceive virtue with our affections, and we experience it as the love of benevolence.[26]

Hutcheson's assumption that virtue derives from our love of benevolence is roughly compatible with Augustine's description of the redeemed moral life as the restoration of our ability to will—to love and desire—God and the good of others. The difference, of course, was that Hutcheson thought this love of the good was our natural default, whereas Augustine believed that our loves are significantly misshaped by the pervasiveness of sin. Hutcheson's failure to account for sin was the main problem New England Calvinist Jonathan Edwards (1703–58) had with Hutcheson's moral philosophy, despite his willingness to incorporate other aspects of it. In an essay he contributed to the controversy surrounding the Great Awakening, titled *A Treatise Concerning Religious Affections*, Edwards described the affections as "sensible exercises of the inclination and will of the soul," where the soul includes both the will and understanding.[27] He believed that "true religion, in great part, consists in holy affections," by which he meant that genuine Christian faith exhibits a desire for and pursuit of the moral excellence of God, made possible by the gift of an "inward sensation, or kind of spiritual sense, or feeling" given by the Spirit of God.[28] In other words, like Augustine, Calvin, and Ames before him, Edwards understood true religion, and thus true virtue, to be fundamentally a matter of the heart, a conversion in our loves.[29] Edwards utilized the popular philosophical language of his century to make this Augustinian point, describing the conversion of the will to love the good as divine manipulation of the affections. He even mirrored Hutcheson's description of virtue as benevolence, though he specified that for him, genuine "benevolence to being in general" had God as its ultimate object.[30] As we will see, Edwards maintained an Augustinian insistence that only the redeemed exhibit such an affective conversion to true love for the good, by the grace of God.

Like Edwards, Witherspoon was faced with the task of reconciling the moral philosophy of his day with his Calvinist theological principles. The older President Witherspoon was more enthusiastic about the project of synthesizing

Calvinism with the ideas of Hutcheson, Reid, and others, even if in his younger days he had regarded Christian theology and modern moral philosophy in somewhat oppositional terms. Even Witherspoon's earlier writings, though, give us glimpses of the Calvinist moral anthropology that would prove amenable to combination with Enlightenment thought later in his career. Witherspoon's *Essay on the Connection between the Doctrine of Justification by the Imputed Righteousness of Christ, and Holiness of Life* (1756), for instance, was written in response to Moderate objections to the traditional doctrine of justification by faith alone, on the grounds that it undermined motives for moral striving. Witherspoon rejected the idea that a priority on grace dissuades people from lives of piety; in fact, he argued, justification sets people on the only true path to right living. The main objective of his treatise was the defense of this doctrinal pillar, but in the process of describing the relationship between justification by faith and the sanctified life of piety, Witherspoon gives us a look at his moral anthropology, which locates him solidly in the lineage of Augustine, Calvin, and the Puritans.

Like Augustinians before him, Witherspoon described sin not primarily as ignorance but as constricted loves, misdirected desires, and (invoking the traditional Augustinian metaphor for the will) a bad heart. He referred to sin as "alienation in heart from God," a "corruption of heart" and "an inward opposition to the law of God."[31] Invoking quintessentially Augustinian language, he identified sin as "the love and pursuit of inferior objects on their own account, and giving them that place in our affections which is due only to God."[32] Sin is misdirected or myopic love, and "there is then a diametrical opposition between the love of God, and the service of sin."[33] Furthermore, the things we do necessarily travel in the same direction as "the heart and affections," so Witherspoon was certain that constricted loves would manifest in actions that were insufficiently other-regarding or God-affirming.

Witherspoon insisted that intellectual knowledge of right and wrong was no match for a constricted will:

> No human reason, no argument whatever, drawn from worldly conveniency, is at all sufficient to contend with violent and sinful habits. We see many examples of persons of excellent understanding and knowledge in other matters, nay, who can reason strongly and justly upon the bad consequences of vice in others, sometimes even in themselves, who will yet go on to ruin their name, family,

fortune and health, while they are slaves to evil habits: nothing will change them but the grace of God.[34]

Even the wisest person (according to human standards) does not have the heart to love and desire God if not redeemed:

> Though an unholy person may have a very penetrating genius and capacity, may think acutely, and perhaps reason justly upon many, or most of the natural attributes of God, he can neither perceive nor admire his moral excellence. Instead of perceiving the glory of God as infinitely holy, he hates, and sets himself to oppose this part of his character, or to substitute something quite different in its room. Or, if we can suppose him able, or from any particular reason inclined, to tell the truth, as to what God is, he can never discern or feel his glory or beauty in being such. For why, he himself is unholy: that is to say, in other words he supremely loves, and hath his affections habitually fixed, upon something that is not God, something that is contrary to God's nature, and a breach of his law.[35]

What is interesting here is the way in which Witherspoon wraps together a number of themes in a classical Calvinist moral anthropology: love of God equips a person to appreciate and revel in God's moral excellence, God's excellence invokes loathing and hatred in the heart of the unredeemed, and the focus of one's love, the end on which "his affections habitually fixed," determines the moral performance of one's actions. All of these themes locate the experience of spiritual and moral "unholiness" in a person's loves, that is, in the will.

Correspondingly, Witherspoon's account of redemption was also volitional and affective. He described conversion as "the renovation of their natures, to be inclined and enabled to keep the commandments of God."[36] Love of God is the disposition of the heart that empowers holiness and piety, for love of God begets desire for the moral excellence that is God, which propels a person in positive moral striving:

> A supreme love of God, therefore, where it really hath place in any heart, must mean the love of a character in some measure understood, though not fully comprehended. In short, according to the Scriptures, it is a supreme love of the source and pattern of moral excellence, of a being of infinite holiness and purity, with whom "evil cannot dwell." Is not this, in truth and reality, the love of holiness itself, the supreme love of it? Can we love holiness then, and not aspire after it? Can we love it and not endeavor to practice it?[37]

This is not the language of intellectual wisdom but volitional change; the redeemed have their inclinations transformed, so that they now desire affinity with God and conformity to the commands of God. Sometimes Witherspoon described this change of inclination as an infusion of gratitude. Sometimes he referred to religious conversion explicitly as an "inclination of the will." Frequently, he described this change as being "possessed of a supreme or superlative love to God, which is not only the source and principle, but the very sum and substance, nay, the perfection of holiness." Conversion to the redeemed life is a matter of correcting and expanding our loves, so that (as Augustine would say) we can love the good.

What we have in the *Essay on Justification and Holiness* is Witherspoon's Calvinist understanding of moral anthropology, even while he is contrasting that theological understanding of morality with some of the popular theories of the day. The essay is preoccupied with religious conversion and salvation, but *moral* conversion—holiness—is part of that religious experience, so that he is also describing (at least in part) how he thinks people work morally, how it is that our loves determine our ethical orientation. To be sure, at this early stage of his career, Witherspoon believed that Christian redemption was the only sure way to a life of true morality, which is why he found most contemporary philosophical accounts of virtue so wanting:

> There is one circumstance in which this "doctrine according to godliness" essentially differs from all other schemes or systems of morality. It is, that any of these systems a man may understand, embrace and defend, without having his heart made better, or his morals secured or improved by it at all; whereas it is impossible, that any man can really, and from the heart, embrace the doctrine of Christ's imputed righteousness, without being sanctified by it.[38]

Between his writing the *Essay on Justification and Holiness* and his arrival as president and lecturer on moral philosophy at the College of New Jersey, Witherspoon evidently changed his mind about some of those "modern accounts" of the nature of virtue. He found more that was translatable to his Calvinist point of view than he evidently recognized earlier in his thinking. Perhaps he discovered that there was more reference to God in the works of Hutcheson and Reid than he first acknowledged. He also seems to have moved to a broader affirmation of the natural moral capacities of human beings, independent of saving grace. The result was that the relationship between his scriptural understanding of the conversion of heart and popular moral philosophies went from oppositional to critically complementary.

By the time he began lecturing on moral philosophy in Princeton, his own moral theory clearly reflected considerable influence from the philosophical discourse of his time, while remaining classically Calvinist at its core. He acknowledged and incorporated the work of Hutcheson and Shaftesbury, even as he critiqued them and sought to reconcile them with some of their philosophical opponents he also found (partially) useful. He was particularly indebted to them for their work on the affections. Similar to Hutcheson and Shaftesbury, Witherspoon defined affections as sensations or "propensities, implanted in our nature," that are "excited by external objects." He distinguished between moral affections and passions that "have their seat in the body," emotions like "fear and rage" that Witherspoon implied are stoked by baser appetites rather than the impulses of a reasonable species.[39] He described moral affections as being of "the mind," like the perception of beauty, harmony, order, proportion, uniformity, variety, and other aesthetic sensations we instinctually find pleasing. Moral affections, said Witherspoon, are of this general mental order, though he pushed back on Shaftesbury's equation of moral sense with an aesthetic perception of ethical beauty.[40] Nonetheless, Witherspoon agreed with the two philosophers that human beings possess a "moral sense" by which these affections "contribute not a little to bias the judgment, or incline the will."[41]

Like Calvin and Edwards before him, Witherspoon subscribed to a holistic moral anthropology where the affections influenced both our moral judgments and our basic moral loves and desires. In contrast to his earlier work, however, in his *Lectures on Moral Philosophy*, Witherspoon had very little to say about the will. After a short description of the will in Lecture II, where he attributed to the will Hutcheson's two basic affective moves of desire and aversion, he described human morality almost exclusively in terms of reason and affection. The traditional Calvinist language of the will drops out, and the affections become the "faculty" representative of a felt love and desire for the good.

This set up Witherspoon to weigh in on a prominent debate in Scottish moral philosophy, the degree to which virtuous conduct is a matter of reason versus sentiment. Thomas Reid, Samuel Clarke, and others criticized sentimentalist philosophers like Hutcheson and Shaftesbury for transforming human morality into an instinct or sensory experience, rather than a reflection of that distinctive marker of the human creature, rational apprehension. For these rationalists, morality was primarily a product of our reason. We access, understand, interpret, and apply moral principles in our pursuit of right conduct. The "Business of Ethicks," wrote Reid, is "the Duty we owe to God and to one another."[42] This duty is made known to us by the apprehension of basic moral principles, which are discerned by reason. More than a sensory experience of the beauty of moral harmony, virtue is assent to fundamental self-evident principles.[43]

Witherspoon referenced this debate in his moral philosophy lectures at Princeton, acknowledging that "it has been disputed whether good be in any degree the object of the understanding." He observed that "persons of equal intellectual powers" often have "opposite moral characters," and judged that it is therefore a legitimate conclusion to draw that intellect itself does not determine moral performance. At the same time, he also observed that in moments of moral decision-making, "the choice made by the will seems to have the judgment or deliberation of the understanding as its very foundation." For this reason, Witherspoon ultimately judged that in the "considerable opposition" between sentimentalist philosophers and their rationalist critics, "perhaps neither the one nor the other is wholly right. Probably both are necessary." As he did with a lot of the theological and moral debates of his time, he saw some usefulness on both sides. From the intellectualists, Witherspoon wanted to hold on to the idea that rational ascertainment of fundamental principles is an important part of moral reasoning and performance. This point was especially significant given his commitment to a Calvinist reverence for moral law, which we will explore more deeply in the next chapter. From the sentimentalists, he embraced the notion that the core of human morality is not simply our knowledge of what is right but our love of what is good. Moral performance requires having a heart invested in furthering good.[44]

For Witherspoon, then, morality was not just an intellectual judgment but a matter of the heart, a desire to be good. While he retained an important role for the intellect and reason in the moral life, the foundation of Witherspoon's ethic remained a characteristically Augustinian-Calvinist concern for our loves. He began his moral philosophy lectures with the language of affection and virtue, and those concepts served as the framework within which he developed the importance of duty, law, and rights. Moral striving was for him fundamentally shaped by the orientation of our basic desires and aspirations. Virtuous character was the yield from a heart inclined toward love of others and a devotion to God.

Natural Virtue?

As we have seen, in his younger days Witherspoon equated the life of true virtue with the life of piety, similar to Edwards's thinking. Even the older President Witherspoon tied piety and public virtue together to a certain extent, as we see in his *Dominion* sermon, where he included an appeal for the public support of religion as part of his call for public virtue. Later we will look closely at Witherspoon's understanding of the relationship between the institutions of church and state, but for now, his close association of good religion with the cultivation of public virtue raises an obvious question: Did Witherspoon think that citizens needed to be Christian to be truly virtuous?

Early Witherspoon certainly sounds like he did, and if so, he hardly would have been unique in the Christian tradition. John Calvin assumed that true virtue is only possible from people justified and sanctified in Christ. On the one hand, Calvin acknowledged that efforts at virtue are confirmable among people who are not saved:

> In every age there have been persons who, guided by nature, have striven toward virtue throughout life. I have nothing to say against them even if many lapses can be noted in their moral conduct. For they have by the very zeal of their honesty given proof that there was some purity in their nature. . . . These examples, accordingly, seem to warn us against adjudging man's nature wholly corrupted, because some men have by its prompting not only excelled in remarkable deeds, but conducted themselves most honorably throughout life.[45]

On the other hand, Calvin was quick to say two things about these displays of virtue among unbelievers. First, he reminded his readers that even these natural moral capabilities are reflections of the benevolent grace of God, for it is God who bestows this moral capacity on people in order to restrain some of the violence and harm of sin. "All these virtues," he writes, "or rather images of virtues—are gifts of God, since nothing is in any way praiseworthy that does not come from him."[46] Second, as evidenced by Calvin's self-correction in the preceding quote, Calvin considered displays of virtue among the unredeemed to be *images* of virtues. Unredeemed moral performance is distinguished from the virtue of the truly saved in both substance and motivation. The virtues of the unsaved are counterfeit because they are not motivated by service to God. Only moral actions motivated by genuine self-denial and deference to the command of God, enabled by the spirit of Christ, reflect true virtue. By contrast, he wrote, "wherever denial of ourselves does not reign, there either the foulest vices rage without shame or if there is any semblance of virtue, it is vitiated by depraved lusting after glory."[47] Doubting that the unregenerate possess the capacity to pursue virtue for its own sake, Calvin assumed that theirs was usually motivated by a desire for public accolade: "Show me a man, if you can, who, unless he has according to the commandment of the Lord renounced himself, would freely exercise goodness among men. For all who have not been possessed with this feeling have at least followed virtue for the sake of praise." Unredeemed virtue, according to Calvin, is ultimately rooted in the same "self-love" that animates vice.[48]

Witherspoon's fellow American Calvinist, Jonathan Edwards, similarly distinguished between what he called "true virtue" and "natural virtue," the former being the character possible in a born-again Christian in whom the Spirit of God operates, and the latter being the moral performance possible from people who have not been redeemed by grace and therefore operate out of self-love.[49] Like Witherspoon, Edwards used the language of Scottish sentimentalism to describe the moral life, describing true virtue as "beautiful" and defining it as "a disposition to benevolence towards being in general."[50] But Edwards insisted that "true virtue must chiefly consist in love to God," by which he meant that the more particular exercises of benevolence in the truly virtuous derive from their appreciation of God's excellence.[51] This appreciation for the beauty of God's excellence is possible only in the redeemed, only in those in whom the Holy Spirit has planted that "new perception or sensation" to love God. Only those who have been changed by religious conversion can cultivate and exercise true virtue.

Edwards did not ignore the moral accomplishments of unredeemed people, but he refused to label them as true virtue. He granted that there may be such a thing as a moral sense or natural conscience that elicits in us feelings like gratitude, justice, guilt, or anger, but he seemed to argue that its function is just to stimulate appreciation for a kind of natural agreement between things. Other times he attributed "natural virtue" to the selfishness that motivates people who remain in a sinful state. Through our imagination, cultural conditioning, or even education, we come to associate with others what we ourselves would want, even in cases that have nothing to do with us, so that what the sentimentalists called a natural public spirit animating our moral sense was, for him, the projection of our own self-interest onto other persons and circumstances.[52] Edwards acknowledged that the character of unredeemed persons might "have something of the general nature of virtue" in them, but it is a resemblance to rather than a participation in true virtue.[53] Sinful individuals can love "by natural instinct" other persons or specific communities, but these are not expressions of benevolence to being in general. Even the most extensive practice of natural virtue, if not rooted in grace-enabled love of God's excellence, ultimately amounts to nothing more than extended self-love.[54] As Edwards puts it, "nothing is of the nature of true virtue, in which God is not the *first* and the *last*."[55]

In several of Witherspoon's works written while in Scotland, he employed a similar distinction between true virtue and an unregenerate counterfeit. In the *Essay on Justification and Holiness*, Witherspoon channeled the conventional Calvinist view that the "imputation" of Christ's righteousness is what makes Christians truly righteous, and that it is Christ's grace in them that empowers "the renovation of their natures, to be inclined and enabled to keep the commandments of God."[56] The presence of the Spirit awakens the believer to the depth of sin and the inner workings of grace, and only the Spirit can enable them to live righteously, in gratitude for that grace.

In this text, Witherspoon took a moment to compare his explanation of the sanctified life with the teachings of contemporary moral philosophers: "It may probably occur to some readers, that this reasoning will not accord with the accounts given by many moderns of the nature and foundation of virtue." Then he recited some of the popular theories of the day: morality is just the pursuit of one's own happiness (Mandeville), or the pursuit of the good of others (Hutcheson's theory of benevolence), or the reasonable assessment of the proper fit of things (the rationalism of Clarke and Reid). He noted the language for virtue common among many philosophers, that virtue is a sense of beauty, harmony, or order in moral relations. He granted a certain amount of usefulness to this language but ultimately judged it "figurative" rhetoric of limited substance. All of these options Witherspoon found wanting because they did not root virtue explicitly in the love of God. "This indeed seems to me the great defect of these accounts of the nature and foundation of virtue, that they keep our relation and obligations to God at a distance at least, and much out of view."[57] He did not categorically dismiss the usefulness of philosophical accounts of morality, but he considered them deficient because they did not emphasize allegiance to God as the axis on which true morality pivots: "Upon a fair and just examination, the supreme love of God will be found the most consistent and rational account of the nature of virtue, and the true source from which all other virtues, that are not spurious, must take their rise, and from which they derive their force and obligation."[58]

In *A Practical Treatise on Regeneration*, another work from his Scotland days, he argued that the understanding, will, and affections are given "a new direction" in conversion, reoriented toward renouncing sin and loving God.[59] Grace enables "the recovery of the moral image of God upon the heart" so that a believer may "love him supremely and serve him ultimately, as our highest end; and to delight in him superlatively, as our chief good."[60] Witherspoon admitted that this moral reorientation remains imperfect in this life, but it renders a qualitative difference in the character of a born-again person. A redeemed person is able to know and love God and goodness to a degree unattainable by "an unholy person," even if that unredeemed person has "a very penetrating genius and capacity, may think acutely, and perhaps reason justly upon man, or most of the natural attributes of God."[61] Young Witherspoon recognized that unredeemed persons can live good lives, but, like Edwards, he distinguished even a high level of good character from the true virtue of redeemed Christians. The difference was "between human virtue and religion, between a decent and blameless carriage upon motives of present conveniency, and a new nature, or a gracious state."[62] What he called "human virtue" he elsewhere referred to as "counterfeit graces," capturing (like Calvin) a resemblance to holy virtue in something less authentic.[63]

There is thus ample evidence to conclude that the Witherspoon of the Scotland days, like Edwards and other Calvinists, assumed that authentic moral character required a religious experience of the grace of Christ and the power of the Holy Spirit. But there is also clear evidence to suggest that Witherspoon's thinking on this front moved with time. By the time he was in Princeton, removed from the need to defend orthodoxy against Moderate Party revisionists, he seems to have incorporated more of Scottish sentimentalism into his own thinking, not abandoning his Calvinist theological principles but expanding and synthesizing them with these philosophical sources. The most obvious bit of evidence, of course, lies in his moral philosophy lectures, where Witherspoon described (and partially endorsed) a number of ethical theories that locate the seat of moral performance in human nature, in reason or the affections. He joined Shaftesbury and Hutcheson in their rejection of the theory, represented in different ways by Hobbes, Mandeville, and Hume, that all human moral motivation derives from the pursuit of self-interest, an interpretation that resembles a conventional Calvinist assumption that natural morality is based on self-love. Furthermore, his embrace of the concept of a moral sense was itself a claim that all normally functioning human beings possess some natural capacity for moral virtue and performance, not a conviction that the younger Witherspoon would emphasize.

To confirm this movement in Witherspoon's thought toward a more positive embrace of natural moral potential, we need only to look to a series of columns entitled *The Druid*, which Witherspoon wrote in 1776 for the *Pennsylvania Magazine*, the "general subject" of which he claimed would be "the philosophy of human nature and of human life."[64] In the first entry of *The Druid*, Witherspoon acknowledged "no small degree of error, ignorance, prejudice and corruption to be found among men," an apparent confirmation of his theological tradition's emphasis on the pervasiveness of sin in the human condition. Immediately after this admission, however, he insisted that "there are not only particular instances in which the human mind has discovered the most exalted virtue as well as amazing powers, but the human race in general, with all its defects, is certainly the noblest and most valuable in this lower world." Witherspoon acknowledged that "it is very common for authors to go to an extreme on the one hand or on the other, in speaking of human nature." He noted that some philosophers tend to exalt the moral capacities of human beings in a way that Witherspoon thought was unsubstantiated by "present experience and the history of past ages," that is, by past and present displays of our basest inclinations. At the same time, he thought it was easy to exaggerate human moral failings too. Despite the reality of our failures, Witherspoon wanted to affirm that our intellectual and moral potential had not been fatally compromised by sin. In fact, this intellectual and moral potential is what sets us apart from other creatures, he argued, and remarkably (for a Calvinist), he claimed the impact of sin on that potential is "but a narrow sphere."

Later, in the fourth installment of *The Druid*, Witherspoon pointed to the idea of "plain common sense," to which he attributed humanity's "good character," and he made clear that this sense is a "gift of nature."[65] Perhaps adapting both Reid's and Thomas Paine's use of the term, Witherspoon distinguished plain common sense from scientific knowledge or the benefits of formal education. Common sense, he said, manifested in prudence or sound judgment, and it could be improved by education but ultimately was a natural gift. He implied that some persons have more common sense than others, but his development of the idea and its location in our natural constitution is further evidence that in the latter half of his intellectual career, Witherspoon was working with a moral anthropology that had moved away from an earlier assertion that true moral performance is possible only among the regenerate. President

Witherspoon articulated expectations of human morality that were realistic in their acknowledgment of error and vice, but cautiously optimistic regarding the capacity for virtue that most members of society possessed.

If it is true that Witherspoon expanded his appreciation for the capacity for virtue among the unredeemed in a way that resonated with some of the moral philosophy of his day, he did not need to step out of his Calvinist tradition to do so. For Calvinism itself hosts theological explanations for the empirically obvious moral performance of people who are not Christians. Despite the way many interpreters have characterized him, Calvin did not believe that sin obliterates our intellectual, artistic, or moral capacities. Many Calvin interpreters have imposed on him a view of "total depravity" that suggests that people possess no capability for goodness whatsoever outside an explicit relationship with Christ. But that is not what Calvin argued. He insisted that no part of the human experience is immune from the effects of sin, and he emphasized that our ability to know, love, and live toward God is decimated by sin, so that no one can have a relationship with God until God reaches out to them in the grace of Christ.

But Calvin also reminded his readers that God created us as good creatures, and through God's "common grace" some of the residue of that original goodness remains in us. For instance, Calvin argued that the "natural gifts" of human reasoning, understanding, and judgment are only "partly weakened and partly corrupted."[66] As a result of this partial corruption, our intellectual, social, and moral activity is constantly undermined by the effects of sin, but we are still capable of imperfectly pursuing knowledge, wisdom, and constructive social ends. Calvin believed that most human beings retain a natural appreciation for art and beauty and that scientific accomplishment should be celebrated as a divine gift, whether those who produce scientific knowledge are pious or not.[67] Sin compromises our creative and intellectual capacities, but it does not eliminate them.

Calvin made a similar claim about human moral capacities. He taught that the natural law in our conscience represents a "natural light of righteousness" that still gives us an imperfect compass for "right and justice" that allows us to coexist with some semblance of social order.[68] He believed that we retain a "natural instinct to foster and preserve society," including "universal impressions of a certain civic fair dealing and order."[69] By this, Calvin acknowledged that within and beyond Christian faith, human beings are capable (imperfectly) of discerning right and wrong, of living in orderly societies, and of at least approximating a spirit of social justice, despite the pervasiveness of sin. His muted but genuine confidence in human beings' natural gifts for science, art, practical wisdom, and basic social morality was rooted in his conviction that sin does not obliterate the effect of God's "common grace" with which God created the human species.

None of this is to say that Calvin was incredibly optimistic about human beings' moral potential outside of Christ's grace, but he offered a theological way to explain what was easily observable to him, that non-Christians exhibit admirable moral virtue all the time. In fact, Calvin argued that it was strange to deny this reality:

> When we so condemn human understanding for its perpetual blindness as to leave it no perception of any object whatsoever, we not only go against God's Word, but also run counter to the experience of common sense. For we see implanted in human nature some sort of desire to search out the truth to which man would not at all aspire if he had not already savored it. Human understanding then possesses some power of perception, since it is by nature captivated by love of truth.[70]

His explanation for residual human intellectual and moral capacities was that we have retained, by God's design, some semblance of the grace with which God created us. Again, we are not capable of restoring ourselves to a right relationship with God, so we cannot be *truly* good on our own. But human beings—including non-Christians—generally retain an imperfect ability to live and cooperate morally. That ability comes from God, a product of God's common grace bestowed on all humanity in our creation.

Theological descendants of Calvin sometimes emphasized the insufficiency of our natural striving for salvation so vehemently that it squeezed out any acknowledgment of the constructive potential of human beings' residual moral capabilities. For instance, the Scots Confession affirmed "that no man on earth, with the sole exception of Christ Jesus, has given, gives, or shall give in action that obedience to the Law which the Law requires," but it said nothing about what human beings are capable of, short of perfectly living up to God's expectations.[71] Expressing a similar sentiment, the Westminster Larger Catechism discussed God's moral law in the Ten Commandments extensively, but when it got to the relationship between God's moral expectations and "unregenerate" persons, it left very little room for the moral accomplishment of nonbelievers:

> Q. 96. What particular use is there of the moral law to unregenerate men? A. The moral law is of use to unregenerate men, to awaken their consciences to flee

from the wrath to come, and to drive them to Christ; or, upon their continuance in the estate and way of sin, to leave them inexcusable, and under the curse thereof.[72]

According to the Catechism, the only relationship between "unregenerate men" and the moral law is a convicting one; the law testifies to how incapable nonbelievers are of living the intentions of God.

Younger Witherspoon's theology matched these confessional documents, which ought not to surprise us, given how important they were to the Scottish Kirk of his time. Some of Calvin's theological descendants, however, chose to emphasize Calvin's recognition of residual moral capacity in unregenerate sinners and developed it much more than the above confessions (and young Witherspoon) did. The English Puritan William Perkins, for instance, argued that God's goodness permeates the world in multiple ways. Besides the general goodness we can discern in the created order, Perkins acknowledged a "special or moral goodness" that is such because it is consistent with "the eternal and unchangeable wisdom of God, revealed in the Moral Law." He subdivided this moral goodness into two parts, things that "are either good in themselves alone, or good both in themselves and in the doer." With this distinction, he acknowledged that unregenerate people do morally worthwhile things, and those things deserve the label good, in a restricted sense. But they are "good work only in itself, but not good in the doer, because it is not done in faith, and from a good conscience." Perkins distinguished true virtue, which is good both because of the goodness of the deeds and also because of the godly character from which it derives, from "all the virtues of the Heathen." He still insisted on calling the virtue of the unredeemed a species of good, however. Believers' actions are truly virtuous, "both good in themselves and in the doer also," but persons without faith are also capable of character that yields imperfect good, what Perkins (less flatteringly) called "beautiful sins."[73]

The most explicit celebration of the moral capacity of non-Christians to be found among classical Reformed thinkers, and the one most willing to separate that celebration from any theological concerns about the sufficiency of saving grace, is that of seventeenth-century Puritan Roger Williams (1603–83), founder of Rhode Island. In his written debates over religious liberty with the New England Puritan establishment, Williams argued that uniform subscription to Christianity was not necessary to ensure a stable society, because non-Christians were capable of exercising socially useful virtues just as well as (and sometimes better than) Christians. He found evidence to back up that claim in numerous historical examples of non-Christian societies that enjoyed generations of peace, stability, and success. He also pointed to the indigenous American communities with whom he spent so much of his life, observing how capable they were of moral and social cooperation even while they subscribed to "pagan" religion:

> Hence it is that so many glorious and flourishing cities of the world maintain their civil peace, yea the very Americans and wildest pagans keep the peace of their towns or cities, though neither in one nor the other can any man prove a true church of God in those places. . . . The peace spiritual . . . is of a higher and far different nature from the peace of the place or people, being merely and essentially civil and humane.[74]

Williams agreed with Calvin's distinction between saving grace ("peace spiritual") and the common grace with which God equips human beings to engage in moral relationships and cooperate on moral projects, but he insisted that the latter had integrity, too. A natural moral capacity was real, was on regular display among non-Christians, and often was more evident among non-Christians than Christians, which he saw as an indictment on the church of his time.

That Williams was making this point in the context of a defense of religious liberty speaks to its importance to a discussion of public virtue. How ambitious we can be in our expectations of public virtue among citizens of a religiously pluralistic society conceptually depends on how optimistic we are about human beings' natural capacities, without religion. By the time he began his service in Princeton, Witherspoon's assumptions about human beings' moral potential lay closer to Williams than Westminster. Witherspoon was enough of a Calvinist to believe in the potency of sin and its effect on how we interact with one another. He still sometimes distinguished between the virtuous performances of Christians imbued with saving grace and the moral accomplishments of the unsaved. But Witherspoon was not pessimistic about the moral potential of admittedly sinful human beings. He rejected outright the assumption of Hobbes, Mandeville, and Hume that people are capable of nothing more than the pursuit of self-interest. Witherspoon thought it was important to acknowledge human beings' penchant for moral corruption while also affirming their potential for constructive moral performance. A realistic call for public virtue depended on this potential, and both his recognition of sin and his ambitions for human morality had roots in Calvinism.

Benevolent Character

In the American portion of his career, then, Witherspoon regularly called on his students and fellow citizens to lead lives of virtue, with little regard to their salvific status. In fact, he thought the health of their new nation absolutely depended on them doing so. The prominence of this theme in his teaching and his public advocacy of independence would be nonsensical if Witherspoon did not believe it was possible for his fellow citizens to take up the challenge, with the proper encouragement. There is no reason to think that Witherspoon the theologian retreated from his Calvinist assumption that there was a qualitative difference between the moral performance of those with saving grace and those without, and he certainly never gave any evidence that he thought natural virtue contributed in any way to a person's salvation. But it is clear that President Witherspoon believed there was considerable good to be gained in cultivating natural virtue among the citizens and leaders of a nation at large. Like others in his Calvinist tradition, Witherspoon took the reality of sin seriously, but this same Calvinism offered resources to theologically endorse moderately aspirational expectations for the moral accomplishments of individuals and societies of mixed religious status. Theologically, philosophically, and politically, Witherspoon insisted that a nation of benevolent virtue and "public spirit" was possible, and he was certain that no nation could survive long term without such a commitment to character.

What did this public spirit of benevolent virtue look like for Witherspoon? Like his moral anthropology, Witherspoon's assumptions about the specific requirements of public virtue represented a synthesis of his theological tradition and his philosophical context, wedding the characteristically Calvinist priority on self-denial with the sentimentalists' emphasis on benevolence.

Calvin believed the character of the sanctified Christian was one of self-denial out of obedience to God and for the good of others. The root of vice, wrote Calvin, was "self-love," so putting aside concern with the self was the necessary step toward a life of virtue.[75] In fact, Calvin argued that self-denial in the spirit of Christ was the heart of all virtue, and his entire discussion of the Christian life is structured around self-denying virtues like humility, compassion, and love.[76] Denying self-interest, the Christian is positioned to embrace a life of piety centered on reverence for God. That reverence is shown chiefly in respect for God's commands and concern for the good of others. Referencing Augustine,

Calvin identified "obedience that is paid to God" as "the mother and guardian of all virtues, sometimes their source."[77] Our obedience is measured by our adherence to God's law, and Calvin understood the law not as arbitrary negative commands but requirements that have as their end the formation of persons, oriented along the dual axes of reverence for God and the good of others.

Calvin's interpretation of the Decalogue, for instance, goes beyond a minimalist read of the prohibitions to connect each commandment with a broader set of dispositions that Calvin believed served the glory of God and the common good. The prohibition against working on the Sabbath cultivated a deep spirit of trust in the loving Providence of God, while the obligation to honor parents encouraged gratitude and respect for authority of all types. The commandments that outlawed adultery, theft, and bearing false witness were, in Calvin's hands, expanded to encourage modesty, justice, and truthfulness, while the prohibition against killing was taken to commend a character of mutual concern.[78] In interpreting the commandments this way, Calvin teased positive virtue out of the prohibitions of the law, so that the law served a pedagogical purpose, the formation of godly character.

Seventeenth-century English Puritans followed Calvin's lead in emphasizing God-fearing and other-regarding virtue in their descriptions of the Christian life. Typical of (and prominent among) Puritan writers, William Ames defined virtue as "a condition or habit [habitus] by which the will is inclined to do well." In other words, virtue is a disposition of character, developed over time, that "makes the subject behave in a certain manner."[79] Ames preferred to talk of virtue as a collective rather than as discrete virtues, reflecting his conception of virtue as a unity of traits that together contribute to the character of a pious individual. In his *Marrow of Theology*, he refused to cite any specific list of virtues as exhaustive, not even from Scripture, but he was clear that virtue was a matter of loving and desiring the right things, namely obedience to God and the good of others.

By the time we get to the eighteenth century, the language of virtue had become a dominant vocabulary for describing moral aspiration. Building on his theory of affections and the moral sense, Hutcheson was typical of this reliance, defining virtue as the "Instinct, antecedent to all Reason from Interest, which influences us to the Love of others; even as the moral sense . . . determines us to approve the Actions which flow from the Love in our selves or others."[80] Like Ames, Hutcheson talked more often about "virtue" than the "virtues," but for Hutcheson this was because he thought all virtue amounted to benevolence.

Actions and attitudes that encouraged the good of others reflected virtuous character; by contrast, the absence of any "Regard for the Publick" was a sign of vice, which he defined as "the absence of moral Good or Virtue" and declared "positively evil and hateful."[81] To be virtuous, however, it is not enough to execute only occasional benevolent acts. "What then properly constitutes a virtuous Character," wrote Hutcheson, "is not some few accidental Motions of Compassion, natural Affection, or Gratitude; but such a fix'd Humanity, as uniformly excites us to all Acts of Beneficence, according to our utmost Prudence and Knowledge of the Interests of others."[82] In other words, virtue is not simply the sum total of discrete actions but a consistent disposition to serve the good of others. Persons who "appear to have the most universal unlimited Tendency to the greatest and most extensive Happiness" of others, these our moral sense identifies as virtuous.

Like the theological and philosophical thinkers who influenced him, Witherspoon thought good character reflects love of God and the good of others. The importance of benevolent character shows up in some of Witherspoon's earliest preaching. In a pair of sermons on Gal. 6:14 that Witherspoon preached in his time in Scotland, he identified as his focus the "disposition" indicative of "the character of a servant of God." The title of the sermons, "The World Crucified by the Cross of Christ," borrows from the scriptural text to expose "worldliness" as the "inward principle" or inclination that manifests in excessive investment in our own pleasures. By contrast, he used the language of virtue to explicate what it means to be "crucified" to the world. Like Calvin, Witherspoon believed that the character of the Christian should be one of self-denial, a person dead to the world and focused on obedience to God. A pious Christian is one who lives with the "conviction of the unsatisfying nature of all earthly enjoyments" and with "an inward persuasion" that the excellence of God far outweighs the value of "earthly things." God is the "supreme delight" of the Christian, and this disposition leads the Christian to regard the world as a gift of God without making any aspect of life in this world a rival for allegiance to God.

Importantly, Witherspoon cautioned his hearers against interpreting crucifixion to the world as a call "to retire from the employment or business of the world altogether." While acknowledging that there is always risk that our work in this world will become too important to us, he insisted that he was not calling for otherworldly asceticism or "monkish austerity." To withdraw from our social and economic responsibilities in the world is not a reflection of positive character but of sloth and irresponsibility, for virtue's proper end is the glory of God through our contributions to the common good. Already in these early sermons, we see Witherspoon interpreting virtue as living out love of God through the pursuit of the good of others. He warned that a retreat from our public responsibilities "is not doing, but deserting our duty" to "the Publick." He even offered practical advice for discerning between godly indifference to the world and excessive avoidance of our duty to and for the world. He suggested that we ask "whether the mortification renders us more spiritual, and more active, or, by excess of scrupulosity, we are consuming our time, and neglecting our duty." The avoidance of "worldliness," suggested Witherspoon, should not come at the expense of our investment in the good of others.

By the time he became president of the College of New Jersey, Witherspoon had fused his Calvinist commitment to self-denial with the theories of virtue developed by Shaftesbury, Hutcheson, Reid, and others to deepen his ethic of benevolent character. In his *Lectures on Moral Philosophy*, after dispensing with some foundational material, Witherspoon launched immediately into a consideration of the meaning of virtue, reflecting prominent debates among moralists of his day. The positioning of virtue near the beginning of his ethics lectures signals the importance of the concept to his moral philosophy, for virtue comes before any discussion of law, duty, or rights, even as those ideas feature prominently in subsequent lectures and deepen his understanding of the life of character. Witherspoon argued that a sense of duty to God and God's law was the heart of our "obligation of virtue," and that same "sense of duty is the primary notion of law and rights."[83] We shall look closely at the relationship between law, rights, and virtue in the next chapter, but virtue comes first in Witherspoon's moral lexicon; it featured early in his students' course of study, and his lectures retained an occupation with virtue throughout.

Witherspoon disagreed with Hutcheson's complete equation of virtue with benevolence, and given how important obedience to God's law was to his moral outlook, it is no surprise. He thought Hutcheson's commitment to maximizing the good of others could lead to choosing actions incompatible with adherence to the law, with nothing more than a simple calculation of the greatest good for the greatest number. His main problem was not with the idea of benevolence itself but with Hutcheson's assumption that it would be easy to count up what was truly in service to the common good, independent of an objective standard. What seemed at face value to be a choice that maximized public good may not be what is in fact the greatest good, thought Witherspoon, especially if it leads us to choose things that violate explicit parameters of God's law. At the same time, Witherspoon believed that obedience to God always promotes the greater good because it is always in the best interest of the common good to live in accordance with divine law. A person of virtue could expect that the well-being of others and the common good usually travel in the same direction as the demands of God's law, and obedience to God's law thus will always serve the greater good. Ultimately, then, Witherspoon had little problem declaring that "true virtue certainly promotes the general good." A life lived in pursuit of general benevolence, at the expense of private gain when necessary, was for Witherspoon an apt description of godly character.[84]

Because he believed the heart of virtue was obedience to God through attention to the good of others, Witherspoon's discussion of specific virtues tended toward those ends as well. In his classroom, Witherspoon offered a range of examples of specific virtues he considered important for his students to cultivate, as future civic leaders and citizens. He commended humility, contentment (with one's circumstances in life), and patience as reflections of healthy character.[85] Commenting on the traditional cardinal virtues of Aristotelianism and medieval Thomism, Witherspoon also affirmed the importance of justice, temperance, and fortitude as beneficial to the public good.[86] He lifted up labor, ingenuity, bravery, sobriety, and patience as "active virtues" particularly important for contributing to a modern economy and a political society in turmoil.[87] And he made a compelling argument for how careful and chastened patriotism could be considered virtuous, insofar as it reflects an investment in the common good of one's fellow citizens.[88] These were just some of the virtues Witherspoon thought a healthy "public spirit" included because they positioned a person to contribute positively to the common good. Many of the public virtues he commended to his students he would repeat in his *Dominion* sermon. Humility, patience, "firmness" (or perseverance), industry, frugality, moderation, self-denial, and other regard were all traits of the virtuous citizen cited in that revolutionary address as essential to the American cause of new nation-building.

One of the most interesting reflections on virtue penned by Witherspoon comes in the form of *An Address to the Students of the Senior Class* graduating from the College of New Jersey in September 1775.[89] Standing before a cohort of students preparing to commence their public lives, Witherspoon offered them a range of advice, the theme of which was care for the cultivation of benevolent character. The address is peppered with insinuations that while they were students, they had not always conducted themselves with the maturity he would have preferred—confirming a certain timelessness to the mischievousness of the American college student. Now, preparing to release them to adulthood, he charged them to live lives of constructive virtue. Ever the preacher, he began his counsel with a concern for their religious lives, cautioning them to care for their souls, whether they had trained to be ministers (most had not) or were embarking on other vocations. Beyond their spiritual lives, Witherspoon commended a character befitting the society they would serve, one that exhibited traits like practical wisdom, industriousness, respect for others, and a managed temper. He asked them to respect public order, to work hard at whatever contribution to society they had trained to make, and to commit to a life of learning. Respectful intercourse, hard work, and the accumulation of wisdom were the marks of a virtuous citizen, he argued, as were a constitution of moderate passions and a well-governed tongue, especially in matters of public dispute. Finally, he warned them that they would need "a firmness of mind, and steady perseverance" to pursue their personal goals and discharge their duty to society.

Witherspoon urged his students to maintain good character as they embarked on their private and public lives after college, and he suggested a couple of helps for the way. For one thing, he advised them to develop friendships with other good people, relationships of moral support (literally) when the circumstances of life taxed their character. Perhaps with an ear toward the political upheaval already brewing in the colonies, Witherspoon warned his students that, with "so much opposition to encounter" in life, they will "need the assistance of others" for their own emotional good and for support in their maintenance of character. Virtuous friends "comfort each other in distress, they assist each other in doubts and difficulty, they embolden each other by their example, and assist each other by their prayers." In celebrating the importance of friendship to the life of virtue, Witherspoon channeled a prominent theme in Western virtue theory: virtue is habituated over time, and it is done so most successfully in community. Virtuous friends reinforce one another's positive character through both affirmation and constructive correction. Without the context of friendship, virtue is difficult if not impossible, and Witherspoon thought the reverse was true as well: "There is no true friendship, but what is founded upon virtuous principles, and directed to virtuous purposes."

Another way his students could measure their success in cultivating virtuous lives was to attend to their public reputation. To be clear, he cautioned them against obsessing about what others thought about them. If we pay too much attention to the public praise we receive, we risk becoming haughty about our own self-importance. If we take too seriously the critical things people say about us, we risk becoming discouraged. Nonetheless, Witherspoon recommended moderate attention to public reputation as a measure of our attempts to develop a "public spirit." Without being totally dependent on others' opinions, he thought public perception could be an effective sounding board. Are we having the positive public impact we should be having? Do we or our actions achieve more harm than good? Learn from the counsel of others, Witherspoon advised, ignore criticisms that seem to have no grounding, and exhibit enough "humility of heart" to avoid getting puffed up from others' praise. On this last front especially, he advised them to "do as much as you can to deserve praise, and yet avoid as much as possible the hearing of it."

The virtues of a benevolent public spirit were a prominent theme for Witherspoon, and his commencement advice emphasized the duty to live and work with consideration of the good of others. "Think of others as reason and religion require you, and treat them as it is your duty to do, and you will not be far from a well-polished behaviour," he advised. Witherspoon made clear that he was referring not simply to a responsibility to politeness, but a substantive commitment to the satisfaction of others' needs and the common good: "I mean to recommend to you a disposition to oblige, not merely by civil expressions, and an affable deportment, but by taking a real interest in the affairs of others." This commitment to public benevolence should govern the personal, professional, and economic affairs of the virtuous citizen. Treat others with respect and patience in your personal relationships, use your education and skills to improve the common good, and commit your financial resources to public causes, especially in this time of political upheaval, he preached. On this last front, he said, the practice of economic frugality is indeed virtuous, as long as it does not denigrate into miserliness. Personal scruples cease to be virtuous when their practice is no longer aimed at the good of others.

Equally important to Witherspoon's vision of public character was a commitment to the truth. Witherspoon ended his address to his students by emphasizing the importance of truth, the defense of truth, and the practice of truth-telling to the life of virtue and the common good of a society. It was a long-standing and familiar theme for him. Throughout his career in Scotland and America, Witherspoon had made clear that he considered lying and slander some of the most egregious transgressions we can commit against one another.[90] Even lies told for benign purposes, for the sake of humor or politeness, he considered erosions of truth-telling as a bedrock of a stable political and economic society. Citizens need to be able to trust each other's commitment to honest dealings and discourse, and they need to be able to trust their leaders as truthful, Witherspoon argued.

On his way out of his address to his graduating students, then, he pleaded with them to "preserve a sacred and inviolable regard to sincerity and truth." He reminded them of how often he had stressed this obligation of virtue during their time in Princeton, taking one last chance to reinforce the necessity of truthfulness to good personal character and the health of a nation:

> Let me therefore recommend to you a strict, universal and scrupulous regard to the truth—It will give dignity to your character—it will put order into your affairs; it will excite the most unbounded confidence, so that whether your view be your own interest, or the service of others, it promises you the most assured success. I am also persuaded, that there is no virtue that has a more powerful influence upon every other, and certainly, there is none by which you can draw nearer to God himself, whose distinguishing character is, that he will not, and he cannot lie.[91]

Truthfulness is "so very sacred a thing indeed," so essential to private and public virtue, "that the very shadow of departure from it is to be avoided." And when others direct falsehoods against them, Witherspoon recommended that his students respond not with public protests or vengeful counterattacks, but with an honest rebuttal that neutralizes the falsities, accompanied by behavior that stands in relief to the bad character of those who peddled in slander. To Witherspoon's mind, a commitment to truth was a bedrock expression of the public spirit required of citizens.

Witherspoon's commendation of benevolent public virtue was meant for all citizens, but he believed that leaders have a special responsibility to exhibit and encourage concern for the good of others. In his fast day sermon near the beginning of the war, he said, "To this let me add, that if all men are bound in some degree, certain classes of men are peculiar obligations, to the discharge of this duty." He reminded them that people in positions of power—parents and political and religious leaders in particular—have an obligation to demonstrate a commitment to "the glory of God and the good of others." Not only should they exhibit laudable character themselves, but they should hold strictly accountable those who are under their authority. Ignoring the bad habits of people under your care is not mercy or patience, he argued; it is a dereliction of the duty to lead others to lives of deeper virtue.[92]

If Witherspoon was at great pains to commend good character to the citizens and leaders of his fledgling new American republic, he correspondingly was quite concerned with the negative impact of bad character on the revolutionary cause and the prospects for the new nation. Witherspoon seemed particularly concerned with whether his fellow colonists had the industry and perseverance to see the war effort through to its conclusion. He also warned his audience against hubris and immodesty in a time of conflict and political dissent. Having a justified cause, he said, was no reason to boast, belittle, or taunt, and he extended this obligation to the colonists' treatment of the British with whom they were contending. Witherspoon tried to model his point by pledging not to engage in disparaging slander against British officers or the crown: "You shall not, my brethren, hear from me in the pulpit, what you have never heard from me in conversation, I mean railing at the king personally, or even his ministers and the parliament, and the people of Britain, as so may barbarous savages."[93] Witherspoon insisted that political difference, dissent, and even rebellion were compatible with the exercise of basic respect, and that the lack of such comportment was an ominous sign of deleterious character in a people: "I look upon ostentation and confidence to be an outrage upon Providence, and when it becomes general, and infuses itself into the spirit of a people, it is a forerunner of destruction."[94]

Ultimately, for Witherspoon, the cultivation of a virtuous public spirit was a collective responsibility that the nation's citizens had to God, but also to themselves and others: "We contribute constantly, though insensibly, to form each other's character and manners; and therefore, the usefulness of a strictly holy and conscientious deportment is not confined to the possessor but spreads its happy influence to all that are within its reach."[95] In making this point, Witherspoon showed a sophisticated understanding of the social nature of moral norms and behavior. As members of a society, we do not exist as atomistic individuals, but rather we influence one another, for good and for bad. For a society to be of sound moral character, its citizens have to commit to developing virtuous habits in themselves, to supporting (and keeping accountable) their fellow citizens, and to sharing in an investment in the common good. When citizens display less admirable dispositions, fail to keep one another accountable, and pursue their own private interests at the expense of the common good, the effect can be contagious and socially destructive.

Notes

1. Witherspoon, DPPM, III:41.
2. Gal. 5:22–3.
3. Witherspoon, LMP, Lecture II, *Works*, III:373.
4. Witherspoon, LMP, Lecture II, *Works*, III:373.
5. Augustine, *On the Grace of Christ and on Original Sin*, in *Basic Writings of Saint Augustine*, vol. 1., ed. Whitney J. Oates (Baker Books, 1992), 597.
6. Augustine, *The Confessions*, VIII.5, in *Basic Writings of Saint Augustine*, vol. 1, 116.
7. Augustine, *The Confessions*, VIII.8, in *Basic Writings of Saint Augustine*, vol. 1, 121.
8. "It is not by law and teaching uttering their lessons from without, but by a secret, wonderful, and ineffable power operating within, that God works in men's hearts not only revelations of the truth but also good dispositions of the will." *On the Grace of Christ*, 601).
9. Calvin, *Institutes*, II.1, 251.
10. William Ames, *The Marrow of Theology*, trans. John Dykstra Eusden (Baker Books, 1968), 219–20.
11. Ames, *Marrow of Theology*, 221.
12. Ames, *Marrow of Theology*, 221.
13. Ames, *Marrow of Theology*, 223.
14. Ames, *Marrow of Theology*, 234.
15. Ames, *Marrow of Theology*, 235.
16. Ames, *Marrow of Theology*, 225. Ames rejects the concept of an "intellectual virtue," a category that is common to Aristotelian and Thomistic ethics. The closest Ames comes to acknowledging something like an intellectual virtue is in his discussion of prudence, which he considers the practice of reason necessary for us to understand our obligation to God's law. See Ames, *Marrow of Theology*, 228.
17. William Ames, *The Marrow of Theology*, trans. John Dykstra Eusden (Baker Books, 1968), 25.
18. Ames, *Conscience*, 23.
19. Ames, *Conscience*, 24.
20. See, for instance, Augustine's views on sexual attraction in his *Confessions* (chapters 7 and 11) and *The Good of Marriage* (sections 3 and 6).
21. William Perkins, *The Whole Treatise of the Cases of Conscience* (Cambridge: John Legat, 1606), 21.
22. Anthony Ashley Cooper, Earl of Shaftsbury, *An Inquiry Concerning Virtue in Two Discourses* (London: Printed for A. Bell, E. Castle, and S. Buckley, 1699), 27–9.
23. Francis Hutcheson, *Inquiry into the Original of Our Ideas of Beauty and Virtue*, ed. Wolfgang Leidhold (Liberty Fund, 2004), 25.

24 Hutcheson, *Beauty and Virtue*, 88.
25 See Thomas Hobbes, *Leviathan*. 1651 (J.M. Dent and Sons, 1973).; Bernard Mandeville, *Fable of the Bees: Or Private Vices, Publick Benefits. 1714*, ed. by Phillip Harth. (Penguin Classics, 1959).
26 Hutcheson, *Beauty and Virtue*, 101.
27 Jonathan Edwards, *The Works of Jonathan Edwards*, vol. 2, *Religious Affections*, ed. John E. Smith (Yale University Press, 1959), 96. Edwards distinguished affections from mundane willing by attributing a special degree of vigor to the love, desire, hope, hatred, fear, and other manifestations of desire or aversion the affections invoke in us. He distinguished affections from passions by implying that there was something more rational about the affections, in contrast to the "animal spirits" that make up the passions. The latter often "are more violent, the mind being more overpowered, and less in its own command." Edwards, *Religious Affections*, 98.
28 Edwards, *Religious Affections*, 99, 114.
29 See Edwards, *Religious Affections*, 106–8, 116–17. Edwards also identifies the "heart," by which he means "the disposition and will," as the seat of morality at the beginning of *The Nature of True Virtue* in *The Works of Jonathan Edwards*, vol. 8, *Ethical Writings*, ed. Paul Ramsey (Yale University Press, 1989), 539.
30 Edwards, *Nature of True Virtue*, 540.
31 John Witherspoon, *Essay on the Connection between the Doctrine of Justification by the Imputed Righteousness of Christ, and Holiness of Life* (hereafter *JHL*), in *Works* I:50, 54.
32 Witherspoon, *JHL*, I:73.
33 Witherspoon, *JHL*, I:73.
34 Witherspoon, *JHL*, I:85.
35 Witherspoon, *JHL*, I:72.
36 Witherspoon, *JHL*, I:50.
37 Witherspoon, *JHL*, I:73.
38 Witherspoon, *JHL*, I:84.
39 Witherspoon, *LMP*, Lecture II, III:372.
40 Witherspoon, *LMP*, Lecture III, III:381.
41 Witherspoon, *LMP*, Lecture II, III:374.
42 Thomas Reid, *Practical Ethics: Being Lectures and Papers on Natural Religion, Self-Government, Natural Jurisprudence, and the Law of Nations*, ed. Knud Haakonssen (Princeton University Press, 1990), 109.
43 See Terence Cuneo, "Reid's Moral Philosophy," in *The Cambridge Companion to Thomas Reid*, ed. Terence Cuneo and Rene van Woudenberg (Cambridge University Press, 2004), 259.

44 Witherspoon's endorsement of both sides of this philosophical debate resulted in a typically Calvinist portrait of the moral life, incorporating reason, will, and sense. To focus on the will and affections at the expense of the importance of understanding and moral reasoning could lead to an unintellectual understanding of the moral life, but Witherspoon avoided that mistake by locating the content referent for "the obligation of virtue" in our compliance with divine and moral law. Nowhere is Witherspoon's synthesis of the rational and nonrational elements of morality more evident than in his appeal to the classic Christian idea of conscience. Witherspoon argued in his lecture that the conscience was essentially what philosophers like Hutcheson and Shaftesbury were calling the moral sense: "This moral sense is precisely the same thing with what, in scripture and common language, we call conscience." But Witherspoon also inherited a Calvinist understanding of conscience as the "storehouse" (to use Ames's term) of principles of divine law. He combined these rational and sensory dimensions in his equation of conscience with the moral sense: "It [the moral sense] is the law which our Maker has written upon our hearts, and both intimates and enforces duty, previous to all reasoning" (*Lectures on Moral Philosophy*, III). In equating moral sense with a Calvinist understanding of conscience, Witherspoon transformed the moral sense from a largely sensory moral faculty into one that has a clear intellectual component, even if that intellectual component (namely, an apprehension of moral law) exists in us "previous to all moral reasoning." This is Witherspoon's attempt at a "both-and"—the moral sense or conscience is both a reflection of the objective moral good and the locus of our subjective desire to be governed by it.

45 Calvin, *Institutes*, II.3, 292.
46 Calvin, *Institutes*, III.14, 770.
47 Calvin, *Institutes*, III.7, 691.
48 Calvin, *Institutes*, III.7, 693–4.
49 For Edwards's comparison of self-love and a grace-enabled appreciation for God's moral excellence, see *Religious Affections*, Part III.
50 Edwards, *Nature of True Virtue*, 541.
51 Edwards, *Nature of True Virtue*, 550.
52 Edwards, *Nature of True Virtue*, 561–88.
53 Edwards, *Nature of True Virtue*, 610.
54 Edwards, *Nature of True Virtue*, 554.
55 Edwards, *Nature of True Virtue*, 560.
56 Witherspoon, JHL, I:50.
57 Witherspoon, JHL, I:75.
58 Witherspoon, JHL, I:75.
59 John Witherspoon, *A Practical Treatise on Regeneration*, in *Works*, I:144.

60 Witherspoon, PTR, I:156.
61 Witherspoon, JHL, I:72.
62 Witherspoon, PTR, I:115.
63 Witherspoon, PTR, I:171.
64 Witherspoon, *The Druid* I, *Works*, IV: 425–30.
65 Witherspoon, *The Druid* IV, *Works*, IV: 445–57.
66 Calvin, *Institutes*, II.2, 270.
67 Calvin, *Institutes*, II.2, 273–5.
68 John Calvin, *Commentary on Romans*, trans. R. Mackenzie, in *Calvin's New Testament Commentaries*, ed. David W. Torrance and Thomas F. Torrance (Eerdmans, 1991), 48–9.
69 Calvin, *Institutes*, II.2, 272.
70 Calvin, *Institutes*, II.2, 271
71 Scots Confession (1560) in *Book of Confessions, The Constitution of the Presbyterian Church (USA)*, Part I (2016), 3.15.
72 Westminster Larger Catechism in *Book of Confessions, The Constitution of the Presbyterian Church (USA)*, 7.206.
73 Perkins, *Cases of Conscience*, 8.
74 Roger Williams, *The Bloody Tenent of Persecution*, in *On Religious Liberty: Selections from the Works of Roger Williams*, ed. James Calvin Davis (Harvard University Press, 2008), 98.
75 Calvin, *Institutes*, III.7, 693.
76 Calvin, *Institutes*, III.7, 690–701.
77 Calvin, *Institutes*, II.8, 372.
78 Calvin makes the point that "the commandments and prohibitions" of the Law "always contain more than is expressed in words" in *Institutes*, II.8, 374. Soon after this preface, he launches into a detailed exposition of the Ten Commandments, from which he teases both positive commendations as well as prohibitions.
79 Ames, *Marrow of Theology*, 224.
80 Hutcheson, *Beauty and Virtue*, 112.
81 Hutcheson, *Beauty and Virtue*, 120.
82 Hutcheson, *Beauty and Virtue*, 132.
83 Witherspoon, LMP, Lecture V, III:389.
84 Witherspoon, LMP, Lecture IV, III:387.
85 Witherspoon, LMP, Lecture IX, III:409–10.
86 Witherspoon, LMP, Lecture IX, III:410. Witherspoon raised questions about the status of prudence as a moral virtue, though. His concern with prudence rested on his suspicion that the ancient Greeks were more preoccupied with status as "great men" in the public eye than he thought befits a truly virtuous citizen.

87 Witherspoon, LMP, Lecture X, III:422.
88 See Witherspoon, LMP, Lectures VIII and XIV.
89 Witherspoon, *Works*, III:99–119.
90 Interestingly, his concern for truth-telling was part of his objections to the theater, which he found not only a frivolous display of questionable moral ideas but also specifically a means of deadening both the actors' and audience's appreciation for truthful representation, in that the stage encouraged the suspension of factual belief in telling a pretend story.
91 Witherspoon, *Works*, III:119.
92 Witherspoon, DPPM, III:43.
93 Witherspoon, DPPM, III:36.
94 Witherspoon, DPPM, III:34.
95 Witherspoon, DPPM, III:42.

3

"The Obligation of Virtue"

For John Witherspoon, political ethics was principally a matter of character, the virtues that give a citizen or leader the "public spirit" necessary to contribute positively to the common good. Classic Calvinist that he was, Witherspoon thought redeemed Christians were capable of a special (though imperfect) level of virtue, but, drawing on both his theological tradition and philosophical influences, he also expressed considerable confidence in the virtue possible from citizens regardless of their religious state. In fact, Witherspoon was certain that the success of the revolution and the new republic depended on widespread investment in this public spirit—in other words, a collective commitment to character.

In the eighteenth century, virtue-talk was all the rage among moral philosophers of the Scottish Enlightenment, and Witherspoon borrowed a lot of their vocabulary to make his own case for the importance of character to the common good in America. As important as the language of virtue was to his understanding of the moral life, though, Witherspoon did not just adopt wholescale the explanations of Shaftesbury or Hutcheson. For one thing, Witherspoon was unwilling to describe human virtue as exclusively an affective or aesthetic experience. He insisted that the cultivation of virtue depended on reasoned moral judgment. Reason and judgment were important because it was through reason that the virtuous person determined *how* to live virtuously in each particular moment, that is, what exactly to do to fulfill one's duty to God and neighbor. As Witherspoon put it, reason helps us determine the precise "obligation of virtue."[1]

In the history of Western ethics, duty and virtue often have been distinct, if not mutually exclusive, vocabularies for describing the moral life. To talk of virtue is to describe the kind of people we ought to *be*, but to describe the moral life primarily as the fulfillment of duty focuses our attention on the things we should *do*. Duty-based ethics are primarily concerned with actions and decision-making, specifically how we decide which actions we should choose and which we should avoid. To guide those choices, duty-based theories focus on moral laws, principles, or rules—norms that help us determine which actions we ought to take (or avoid) in particular moral circumstances. Different duty-based ethical theories emphasize different governing principles, but they have in common the assumption that to be an ethical citizen is primarily to do the right thing, to fulfill one's obligation as defined by some authoritative source of moral guidelines.

To give an example, a Christian duty-based ethic might regard the Ten Commandments as a set of principles that (with the required amount of interpretation) tell us what we should or should not do to fulfill our obligation to God. In this kind of Christian ethic, the prohibitions (e.g., murder, theft, and false witness) serve as action-guides, explicitly ruling out certain behaviors as immoral, and perhaps also implicitly encouraging the opposite actions as the fulfillment of moral duty. A Christian ethic that regards the Ten Commandments as its core moral principles would still need to interpret and apply those principles to specific circumstances (e.g., is killing in self-defense a violation of the sixth commandment?), and it might entertain exceptions to some of the principles (e.g., is the threat of starvation a justification for stealing?). The need to interpret the principles opens the door, of course, for disagreement among people who share a commitment to the commandments. Even with different interpretations, however, duty-based ethics that regard the Ten Commandments as binding principles would use the commandments to determine what a person should or should not do to fulfill their moral obligations.

For another example, consider a Christian duty-based ethic that prioritizes the Golden Rule: "In everything do to others as you would have them do to you, for this is the Law and the Prophets."[2] This ethic would judge actions that we would not want others taking against us as immoral for us to choose as well, and actions we would be willing to have done to us would be acceptable for us to choose. The Golden Rule would serve as a moral principle by which we would determine whether particular acts or decisions fulfill or violate our obligations to others. An ethic with this principle of reciprocity at its heart does not directly say anything about what kind of person we should be. It is primarily talking about not virtue but duty, the things we should feel morally obligated to do or not do. Like the Ten Commandments, the Golden Rule needs to be interpreted and applied to specific circumstances, and the need for interpretation creates room for disagreement among adherents to this shared principle. Whatever the interpretation, the mode of ethical reasoning is the same: compare this principle to my options and choose the action that satisfies the imperative in the principle.

A duty-based ethic, then, is focused on performing right actions, while a virtue-based ethic emphasizes the traits that make someone a good person. These types of ethical theories offer different answers to the fundamental ethical question, "What makes a person moral?" Duty-based ethics respond "right actions," while virtue ethics respond "good character." In the history of Western ethics, these two approaches to the moral life have often been regarded as quite distinct, with thinkers prioritizing one approach over the other. Witherspoon, however, treated virtue and duty as two sides of the same coin. For him, the performance of moral duty was "the obligation of virtue," and good character was the result of habituated commitment to moral duty. The encouragement of political character may have been his larger project, but the persons of character he valued most were those invested in the performance of their moral duty—to God, other people, themselves, and the common good. And for Witherspoon, the moral duty of a virtuous nation was best captured in two commitments: respect for God's moral law and protection of people's natural rights.

Virtue and the Moral Law

"When we speak of the foundation of virtue, we ask or answer the question, Why is it so? Why is this course of action preferable to the contrary? What is its excellence?"[3] The answer, said Witherspoon, is that the satisfaction of our moral duty makes a life morally beautiful. For Witherspoon, the commitment to moral duty was an essential part of virtue, including political virtue. But how do we know what our duty is? How do we know "by what law we are bound, or from what principles we ought to be obedient to the precepts which it contains or prescribes?"[4] On one level, the answer to this question was straightforward for Witherspoon. Our moral duty is defined by God's will; our fundamental moral obligation is to follow the intentions of God.[5] But how do we know what God's intentions for humanity are? Witherspoon's response to this question was equally direct: God expresses his intentions for us through the moral law.

Witherspoon subscribed to a conventionally Calvinist belief that God created and sustains the world through decrees that express God's intentions for the world. Part of this divine law is God's moral law, or the principles that govern

God's expectations of human behavior toward one another (and God). Followers of Calvin believed that God gave human beings the moral law at their creation as a covenant of obligation in which God promised to protect human beings if they lived according to divine expectations. After the Fall, human beings could no longer satisfy God's moral law perfectly, but it remained binding as a set of norms for our behavior, a "perfect rule of righteousness" (as the Westminster Confession put it) that God reiterated in the Ten Commandments.[6] Attention to the moral law constrains the more destructive tendencies of reprobate individuals and societies while giving Christians "clearer sight of the need they have of Christ" and "a rule of life," providing a target for moral aspiration by "informing them of the will of God and their duty."[7] Puritan divine William Ames claimed that we have access to these divine decrees, not just in the Decalogue, but in the "order in natural things," as a "law of nature" that ensures that the "common government" of all of creation follows God's designs.[8]

The "obligation of virtue," according to Witherspoon, was to live a life attuned to the requirements of this moral law. For Calvinists like Witherspoon, the Bible was the most reliable source for knowledge about God's law. "There is nothing certain or valuable in moral philosophy," he assured, "but what is perfectly coincident with the scripture."[9] In fact, he claimed that "the excellence of the scripture doctrine" is that "it contains the greatest and most powerful motives to duty, and the fittest to work on our hopes and fears." He assumed that "the principles of duty" articulated in the Bible "are more clearly and fully enforced by the proper authority, than any where else," and that they have "an evident tendency to promote holiness in all who believe and embrace [Scripture]."[10] And what does the Bible tell us are the fundamental obligations of the moral law? The glory of God is our fundamental duty, declared Witherspoon, and "the good of others is the great object of duty."

Service to God and others is how we glorify God from a biblical perspective, and Witherspoon believed that these priorities were reflected in a number of scriptural texts, especially the Ten Commandments. The first table of the Decalogue commends fealty to God, while the second table outlines broad parameters for our relationships with other people. Witherspoon acknowledged that much of Old Testament law was particular to the circumstances of Israel and its covenantal relationship with God; still, he maintained that the Ten Commandments were a universal and timeless encapsulation of God's law. "The moral law published upon Mount Sinai," he declared in his *Lectures on Divinity*, is "a publication or summary of that immutable law of righteousness, which is the duty of creatures, and must accompany the administration of every covenant which God makes with man."[11] This law is an "unalterable rule of duty to creatures" that preceded and served as the foundation of the legal codes of all historical social communities. In fact, Witherspoon argued, "the moral law as it requires obedience to the will, and conformity to the nature of God, was binding on the Angels before the creation of the world; and will be the duty of holy angels and redeemed sinners after the resurrection."[12]

In his focus on the Ten Commandments as the obligation of virtuous duty, Witherspoon was simply carrying on a Calvinist family tradition. Calvin identified "obedience that is paid to God" as "the mother and guardian of all virtues, sometimes their source."[13] The requirements of obedience are determined by God's law, specifically (though not exclusively) as it is represented in the Decalogue.[14] According to Calvin, "the law points out the goal toward which throughout life we are to strive. In this the law is no less profitable than consistent with our duty."[15] He understood the ultimate purpose of God's law to be the cultivation of dispositions of character, and in fact, to Calvin's mind, this encouragement of character was what distinguished God's law from human law. Human law, said Calvin, is primarily concerned with discrete actions and the restraint of evil, whereas God's law is concerned with actions but more broadly with making us better people. Adherence to God's law demands and stimulates inward "righteousness" and "purity of heart" in the committed Christian, whereas dispositions like "lust, anger, hatred, coveting a neighbor's possessions, deceit, and the like" are signs of a departure from God's law.[16] As we saw in the last chapter, to Calvin the commandments did not just outlaw stealing, disrespectful actions, and killing; they also encouraged virtuous character traits like trust, honor, gratitude, mutual concern, modesty, justice, and veracity.[17]

Similar to Calvin, Ames believed virtue is shaped by commitment to "the written law of God."[18] Ames too gave special attention to the Ten Commandments, which he read not as a minimal list of prohibitions but as a summary of virtue that develops through the pursuit of duty. Out of the sixth commandment's prohibition on murder, for instance, Ames drew the virtue of respect for humanity, which he argued "is the virtue by which we are inclined to preserve the life of our neighbor and his tranquility through lawful means." Ames thought that this humanistic virtue was cultivated by the performance of specific duties, namely "supplying things helpful and preventing things hurtful" in the lives of others whom we can affect. From respect for humanity, Ames argued, derives a host of secondary virtues, like patience, long-suffering, forgiveness, concord, benevolence, courtesy, affability, and equanimity.[19] All of these virtues are part of the broader commitment to respect for humanity, which Ames believed was habituated by adherence to God's moral law.

This synthesis of law, duty, and virtue was reflected in Witherspoon's explanation of "the obligation of virtue," as was his Calvinist confidence in the Bible as a representation of the divine law behind our understanding of duty. In his moral philosophy lectures at Princeton, though, he cautioned students not to overestimate what the Bible can tell us about our particular obligation in any specific circumstance. He admitted that scripture was "perfectly agreeable to sound philosophy; yet certainly it was never intended to teach us every thing."[20] He noted the moral performance of non-Christians and asked how we explain their fulfillment of the obligation of virtue if mining scriptural source material is the only way to know one's moral responsibilities.

Instead of assuming that the Bible was our only source for knowledge of God's law, Witherspoon appealed to an idea with deep roots in Western classical and Christian moral thought: natural law. In Christian theology, the idea went generally like this: the universe operates according to divine law, which includes God's expectations of human beings in the moral law. The priorities of the divine moral law, to honor God and do good for others, are reflected in biblical imperatives, but they are also embedded in human nature and imprinted on every human heart, providing all normally functioning human beings with a natural moral compass. All human beings can know at least the general contours of what God desires for us and for human community through the exercise of reason and the testimony of conscience, which (as William Ames would put it) "is the intelligent creature's self-judgment in his subjection to God's judgment."[21]

To Calvin, Ames, Witherspoon, and others, the natural law internalized in conscience is the same moral code reflected in the Ten Commandments. Calvin argued that "it is a fact that the law of God which we call the moral law is nothing else than a testimony of natural law and of that conscience which God has engraved upon the minds of men."[22] But Calvin was quite clear that the Fall leaves us unable to perfectly satisfy the requirements of the natural law, so that this conscientious access to God's standards of right simply "deprives men of the excuse of ignorance" of their failures, and "proves them guilty by their own testimony."[23] Sin renders us too susceptible to self-indulgence to adequately satisfy our duty to love God or other people with the whole hearts that the moral law requires. One of the purposes of the law, then, is to offer perspective, a mirror by which we become aware of the distance between ourselves and God's intentions for us.²⁴ The law judges our moral failures, tempers our pride, convicts us of our sin, and (Calvin hoped) opens us to our need for grace. Once "it is clear that by our wickedness and depravity we are prevented from enjoying the blessed life set openly before us by the law," said Calvin, "the grace of God, which nourishes us without the support of the law, becomes sweeter, and his mercy, which bestows that grace upon us, becomes more lovely."²⁵ In its accusatory form, the law prepares the way for God to save us in grace.

Despite Calvin's insistence that no one can perfectly satisfy the law, he still recognized a constructive purpose beyond its negative accusatory function. The law reminds us of our moral deficit, but it also provides parameters, boundaries, and constructive targets for our behavior. By creating a moral baseline culture to which social pressures and punishments can be ascribed, God's law protects human communities from people whose behavior is inadequately restrained by the needs and concerns of others (or the expectations of God).²⁶ In other words, natural law provides a foundation for the content and coercive function of social and civic law, defining the limits to acceptable behavior within a society. But among Christians, Calvin thought the law offered even more, namely, "the best instrument for them to learn more thoroughly each day the nature of the Lord's will to which they aspire."²⁷ Calvin does not say that Christians are miraculously equipped to live the requirements of the law perfectly, therefore earning their way into God's graces. Instead, he argues that God's grace empowers Christians to struggle toward God's expectations as encapsulated in the law. The pilgrimage of moral improvement—of honoring God and loving others more fully—is the content of the Christian life, says Calvin, and the precepts of the moral law give Christians constructive signposts toward which to aspire. He celebrated this function of the law even though we cannot satisfy it perfectly because he believed that in the grace of Christ, God promises to complete our struggle to live to the law.

In fact, Calvin talked about the natural law mainly in the context of salvation and the Christian life. Before the experience of grace, the law readies us for grace by laying bare our need for God, and then after the experience of God's conversion, the law educates the Christian in ways to better satisfy God's intentions. His theological descendants shared Calvin's concern for the salvific significance of the law, but some of them made much more of the wider social significance of natural law than he did. Calvin suggested that the restraining function of the law served as a basis for civil law and punishment, and seventeenth-century Puritans agreed. For the Puritans, natural law provided a standard of evaluation by which to measure the legitimacy of human laws—and lawgivers. In the English Civil War, they justified overthrowing King Charles in part by arguing that his reign had abandoned principles of right embedded in the natural law.[28] In New England, they constructed bodies of civil law not primarily on specific Deuteronomic prescriptions from the Bible but from basic precepts in the natural law as they understood it.[29] The Puritans' conception of natural law as the legal and moral bedrock for civil society would inform later Enlightenment political philosophy, and this idea of natural right would become one of the conceptual bases for the American colonies' Declaration of Independence from Britain.[30]

Witherspoon believed in the reality of natural law, as he made clear at the start of his *Lectures on Moral Philosophy*.[31] He never abandoned the Bible as an authoritative moral source, nor did he imply that human beings can know everything they need to know about moral obligation through the exercise of their own rational functions. Witherspoon the Calvinist insisted that sin had left its mark on human beings' moral capacities. But the idea of a natural law imprinted on the conscience and at least moderately accessible to rational deliberation and judgment was an essential foundation upon which he could make broader public appeals for moral conduct in and around the war. His *Lectures on Moral Philosophy* were meant to orient his students to this moral project, that "we ought to take the rule of duty from conscience enlightened by reason, experience, and every way by which we can be supposed to learn the will of our Maker, and his intention in creating us such as we are."[32] That included the Bible, but not just the Bible.

Sometimes Witherspoon equated conscience with that universal moral sense the Scottish sentimentalists were so fond of discussing. Hutcheson's moral sense, Witherspoon claimed, "is precisely the same thing with what, in scripture and common language, we call conscience. It is the law which our Maker has written upon our hearts, and both intimates and enforces duty, previous to all reasoning."[33] In connecting conscience to the moral sense, however, he critiqued the sentimentalists' insistence on making moral virtue all about affection, at the expense of a role for reason and moral deliberation. The moral sense is about character *and* duty, he argued, about heart and head, affection and reason. Both his co-opting of the idea of moral sense and his critique of it illustrate the distinct fusion of Calvinism and Scottish moral philosophy in Witherspoon's ethics. By identifying conscience with moral sense, Witherspoon invoked his Calvinist moral tradition to translate a popular idea from contemporary philosophy. At the same time, he introduced a connection between this human moral experience and biblical authority by insisting that the exercise of conscience represents our reasoned deliberations on the moral law of God. His Calvinist corrections to this philosophical idea reflected the tandem relationship he saw in the performance of moral duty and the cultivation of virtue.

The Duties of Virtue

Unlike the sentimentalists, then, Witherspoon was not comfortable with describing virtue as just "an approbation of a certain class of actions as beautiful." From his Calvinist point of view, conscience was the heart of virtuous character formation because it was the foundation of rational deliberation on moral duty. "The moral sense implies also a sense of obligation, that such and such things are right and others wrong; that we are bound in duty to do the one, and that our conduct is hateful, blameable, and deserving of punishment, if we do the contrary."[34] By tapping into God's law, conscience helps us recognize our duty, and from habitual "compliance with duty or supposed obligation" develops virtue. In fact, the fulfillment of moral duty is the heart of our attraction to virtue: "It is not duty because pleasing, but pleasing because duty," he reminded.[35] What we recognize as attractive in someone of good character is a commitment to moral obligation, for such a commitment is essential to cultivating character in individuals and a society. But duty to what, or better yet, to whom?

Witherspoon began his discussion of the obligations of virtue with our duties to God, unsurprisingly since the will and intentions of God are the basis for the moral law itself. But noteworthy is Witherspoon's implication that our relationship to God is a *moral* obligation. We often confine the idea of moral obligation to other people, or more expansively to other created beings, but by its inclusion in the lectures on moral philosophy Witherspoon indicated his belief that religious obligations to God are themselves moral, insofar as they are the obligations of *relationship*. Witherspoon identified our duties to God as consisting of external obligations (i.e., worship and religious practice) and internal obligations, though he focuses mostly on internal obligations, by which he means the internal dispositions of love, fear, and trust.[36] Again we see Witherspoon's synthesis of duty and virtue at work when he defines our moral obligations to God largely in terms of habitual attitudes we should cultivate. The dispositions of love and fear toward God are not only responsibilities themselves, but they also serve as motivation for us to discharge our moral duties to ourselves and others.

Witherspoon believed that fear of divine punishment and hope for divine favor were appropriate motivators for moral action, though he acknowledged a certain amount of philosophical debate around this point. He asserted that the expectation of sanction implied the reality of moral law as well as accountability to a lawgiver, both ideas that were unsatisfyingly missing (to his mind) in sentimentalist accounts of virtue as natural aesthetic sense.[37] He did not think you could talk about the cultivation of virtue without explaining where virtue gets its moral content. What makes character actually *good*? Virtue's content comes from the moral law, but if the law is real, it must have an origin and there must be a lawgiver to whom we are accountable, which means we must expect that there will be positive and negative consequences to our conformity to or deviance from the moral law. To Witherspoon, rejection of the idea of rewards and punishment implied a rejection of the reality of the moral law (or, in the case of someone like Hume, the denial of the lawgiver), which he feared rendered moral virtue nothing more than aesthetic sensibility or cultural convention.

This theme of divine rewards and punishment also played a role in Witherspoon's understanding of our moral duty to ourselves. Witherspoon believed we had moral obligations to ourselves, but not the kind of self-care and self-respect that we prioritize in our time. Instead, Witherspoon taught that we have an obligation to improve ourselves in both piety and moral virtue. He referred to the improvement of our religious lives as a duty of "self-interest," to attend to "our relation to the Divine Being" and to work at "procuring his favor." Our duty to morally improve ourselves he referred to as the project of "self-government," meaning the cultivation of character. Witherspoon advocated for the moderation of "desires and affections" to ensure that they did not interfere with our duties to God and others, as well as the development of "virtues of humility, contentment, patience, and such as are allied to them."[38] His assumption that the cultivation of moral character was an "obligation of virtue" we owe ourselves represents another layer of connection between virtue and duty in Witherspoon's vision of the moral life.

The final category of moral duties Witherspoon identified was, of course, our duties to other people, but if we go to his lectures looking for a laundry list of specific obligations, we stand to be disappointed. Witherspoon did not commend any specific duties, but rather summed up our responsibility to other people as "love to others, sincere and active." For him, "the great law of love to others" is a moral obligation that requires us to have the "greatest and best interest" of others in mind, "wishing doing them good in soul and body." Our obligation to others consists of whatever contributes constructively to another's real needs in a particular moment. Even though elsewhere he objects to the sentimentalists' tendency to dissolve all virtue into benevolence, he was comfortable claiming that "benevolence . . . is the principle and sum of that branch of duty which regards others." Benevolence represents an admirable character trait and the range of duty we have to the interests of others.

The duty to love others and pursue their best interests as much as we are capable should govern our relationships with specific people, argued Witherspoon, and as an example, he lifted up friendship—in the process, pushing back on contemporary critics who thought Christianity emphasized disinterested love so heavily as to undermine the moral value of friendships. Quite the opposite, argued Witherspoon. There is such a thing as a Christian friendship, and it can be an arena in which to regularly discharge our duty to love others and desire their best interests. The obligations of loving other-regard extend beyond our friendships, however, and Witherspoon included in "the law of love" a broader duty to people we do not know intimately and to the common good. He cited approvingly the story of the Good Samaritan, arguing that its expansion of the "neighbor" to whom we are obligated "is one of the greatest beauties in moral painting any where to be seen."[39] Witherspoon imagined the duty to love others as "a calm and deliberate good-will to all," an obligation that, when practiced consistently, creates in people a disposition of concern about the specific needs of others.

Witherspoon cited patriotism as another example of the law of love in action. A year before the colonies' Declaration of Independence, the Synod of New York and Philadelphia issued to its member congregations a letter about the rising political tensions. In the letter, which was to be read from every pulpit in the synod, Witherspoon (its chief author) encouraged his fellow Presbyterians to maintain their commitment to piety and patriotism in troubled political times. He defined patriotism as a "generosity of spirit, or benevolence of heart" that compels a person to "offer himself as a champion in his country's cause."[40] His letter called on his fellow colonists to stay committed to one another: all "should be united together as servants of the same matter, and the experience of our happy concord hitherto in a state of liberty should engage all to unite in support of the common interest."[41] Proper patriotism was an expression of benevolence, love for one's fellow citizens that prompts unity and courageous sacrifice for the collective good. Witherspoon's celebration of patriotism as a discharge of our duty to benevolence helps to explain the moral good he saw in Americans' collective investment in the revolution, as he celebrated in his lectures and public addresses "those who have sacrificed private case and family relations" for the cause of independence. For Witherspoon, patriotic zeal was a specification of our broader duty to others, dictated by God's moral law.

At the same time, Witherspoon recognized that love of country can distort our obligations to the "law of love," particularly our duties to people beyond our nation. In his philosophy lectures, he took care to subordinate patriotism to the "love of mankind," which he argued is "greatly superior." In fact, he warned that some version of "attachment to country appears in a littleness of mind, thinking all other nations inferior, and foolishly believing that knowledge, virtue and valor are all confined to themselves." He emphasized that the celebration of patriotism should not be confused with jingoistic fervor, a point he made in his *Dominion* sermon too. His assumption that the duties of benevolence extend beyond one's fellow citizens informed his concern for the treatment of prisoners of war on both sides of the Revolution, and it prompted his commitment to respectful public rhetoric for the king, parliament, and British forces throughout the war.[42] Love of country and one's fellow citizens was good, but that love should not eclipse the duty to respect the rights and well-being of people beyond one's nation, even in times of war.

As is clear in his recommendation and critique of patriotism, a charitable and humble "public spirit" was essential to Witherspoon's understanding of the political character necessary for the health of his new nation. Such character was what Witherspoon had in mind when he implored the hearers of his *Dominion* sermon to attend to piety and virtue in the execution of the war. Witherspoon assumed that the cultivation of virtue was directly served by the performance of our duty to others as dictated by God's moral law, specifically the duty to attend benevolently to the needs of other individuals and to the common good.

Calvinism and Rights

At first glance, it might seem that Witherspoon has traveled a lot of conceptual miles to end up somewhere similar to the contention of the sentimentalists, that virtue consists of a spirit of—and the practice of—benevolence to others. But

Witherspoon argued that we need the language of duty and commitment to the moral law to improve on thinkers like Hutcheson in a couple of ways. First, making the dictates of divine law the "obligation of virtue" roots his conception of the virtuous life theologically: virtue is the habituation of a commitment to doing God's will. Second, Witherspoon's insistence on the idea of duty to describe moral and political character reminds us that our behavior and our character are inextricably tied; fulfilling our moral obligations develops moral character, and moral character inspires us to do our duty to God and others. Finally, Witherspoon's synthesis of duty and virtue allowed him to connect his understanding of political character to a priority on natural human rights.

Like many other leaders of the American Revolution, Witherspoon thought the conflict was principally about the protection of natural rights. In his *Dominion* sermon, he asserted that the war was justified as a defense of the colonists' rights, particularly religious liberty. In an *Address to the Natives of Scotland Residing in America*, meant to convince members of that constituency to side with the patriotic cause, Witherspoon summarized the colonies' "complaint" with the charge that Britain "will not suffer us to enjoy our ancient rights."[43] In a treatise he called a *Memorial and Manifesto of the United States of North-America* and directed primarily to European witnesses to the war, Witherspoon claimed that the colonies had long endured Britain's encroachment on their rights to economic self-direction and free trade out of an affection for "their parent country," until Britain exploited that bond beyond its strength with "the famous stamp act" and tea taxes.[44] Even then, said Witherspoon, the colonists' first recourse was to issue "addresses and petitions" that argued for "the security and preservation of our rights," because "reconciliation to Britain . . . was the wish of every soul."[45] Only when those petitions of rights were met with hostility did the colonists reluctantly declare their independence.

Witherspoon's focus on the independence movement as a defense of natural rights put him in broad company among defenders of the Revolution. The Declaration of Independence itself claimed that it was "self-evident" that human beings have "unalienable Rights" that were threatened by British imposition. Those rights famously included "Life, Liberty, and the pursuit of Happiness," but the list of complaints in the Declaration also implies rights to political representation, economic freedom, and due process. The defense of rights is the responsibility of government, says the document, and when those rights are jeopardized, the people also have the right to resist and remake their government.

Much of the popularity of rights language during the Revolution marked the influence of John Locke's political theory, particularly as it was refracted by men like Thomas Jefferson, the chief author of the Declaration. Knud Haakonssen observes that, generally speaking, the concept of natural rights was not as fundamental to the Scottish Enlightenment that shaped Witherspoon as it was to Dutch and English writers like Hugo Grotius and Locke. David Hume had no use for the concept of rights, perhaps because the language insinuated a deity as the origin of such rights. Francis Hutcheson acknowledged a set of natural rights that later influenced Witherspoon, though he subordinated the concept of rights to his primary concern, benevolence.[46] Thomas Reid emphasized natural rights as the manifestation of our duties to others as indicated by natural law.[47]

Witherspoon was influenced by philosophical considerations of rights in Britain and America, of course, but he did not need the advent of the Enlightenment to discover natural rights, because the idea had a long history in the moral traditions of Western Christianity and, more specifically, Calvinism. Implicated in the execution of the religious dissident Michael Servetus in 1553, Calvin hardly seems like the right starting place for discourse on human rights, but throughout his career in Geneva, Calvin was concerned with liberty, especially religious liberty. Calvin's commitment to religious liberty began as a typical Protestant rejection of medieval church overreach; he argued against the church's micromanagement of Christians' individual spiritual lives, distinguishing between essential matters of faith and the many discretionary aspects of piety for which Christians should enjoy the freedom to follow the dictates of conscience. Furthermore, he objected to the forced physical submission or persecution of non-Christians in the name of the faith.[48] At the same time, Calvin also recognized an individual's right to conscientiously disobey political authorities who usurped God's prerogative by dictating religious duties, or whose rule significantly violated God's moral law, though he was reluctant to invest a right of collective political resistance in the people themselves.

Liberty of conscience, then, took the form of a human right for Calvin, a claim of freedom rooted in the prerogatives of one's direct relationship with God, a claim that precedes rather than derives from governmental authority, and in fact a claim that represents restrictions on any governmental authority. Admittedly, Calvin's respect for individual liberty was always careful and conservative, bound by hefty concern for law and order (in both church and state). His concern with order only intensified over time, so much so that late in his Genevan career, Calvin wrote more often about citizens' duties to church and state than he did about religious or political liberties. In fact, Calvin grew increasingly fond of asserting the prerogative of the church as a governing institution over a great deal of the religious lives of its members, and of the government in enforcing proper worship and piety.[49] This collusion between church and civil government severely limited the range of religious liberty Calvin was willing to entertain in Geneva, and it was during this later period in Calvin's life that Servetus had his ill-fated encounter with the Protestant reformer. Yet Calvin never completely abandoned the idea of religious liberty, and through his career he also acknowledged (if unsystematically) other liberties too—of citizenship, property, due process, and self-protection.[50] Calvin recognized many of these rights as correlatives to the civic duties with which he was more occupied.[51]

Some of Calvin's followers teased out the promise in his theology for a more robust commitment to natural rights. In response to intense religious persecution (most infamously represented in the St. Bartholomew's Day Massacre of 1572), French Calvinists like Theodore Beza (1519-1605) turned Calvin's freedom of conscience into an aggressive right of resistance. Calvin had cast the right of conscience mostly as a duty to passively disobey political obligations that transgressed one's understanding of God's will, but in the hands of thinkers like Beza, conscientious conviction could now justify active resistance against tyrants whose rule violated God's moral law, especially as it was represented in the Decalogue. And contrary to Calvin's conservative reliance on other political entities for relief from tyranny, Beza and others argued that freedom of conscience empowered the people themselves to reject godless tyranny.[52]

In the English Civil War, Protestant clergy preached a freedom of conscience and right to disobedience when rulers encroached upon their spiritual freedom. As William Haller noted, they rooted this right in God's law "revealed in conscience and the scriptures, a law which they claimed took precedence over all other commands."[53] The preachers' invocation of rights aligned with parallel arguments that English lawyers like Sir Edward Coke were making in common law, which asserted the prerogative of law over even the will of kings. Kings too were subject to the common law, which in turn was rooted in the natural law derived from conscience and reason, which in turn was a derivation of God's moral law, meant for God's glory and the good of God's people.[54] Both law and government were ultimately meant for the protection of citizens' rights, and when government abandoned that end, it was ripe for reform in God's name.

The assertion of rights against the king that fed the English Civil War eventually became a debate among competing factions in parliament, as

Presbyterians and Independents clashed in their different understandings of the balance between religious freedom and maintenance of ecclesiastical (and social) control. Presbyterians represented the cautious and conservative side of Calvin's teachings, arguing that a strong church authority with a tight regulation of religion was important for both church and state. Independents—a caucus of low-church groups that included some extreme parties, like the Levellers—took Calvin's thoughts on religious liberty to their eventual conclusion, arguing for an extensive right to freedom of conscience, beyond the jurisdiction of the state to control. In arguing for religious liberty, they also argued for a right to expression (speech) and, by extension, a right to a free press. In fact, the Levellers went so far as to compose a series of documents called "Agreements of the People" that, as David Little points out, called for "full-fledged constitutional democracy, with provisions for equality before the law, division of powers, judicial reform, the prohibition of religious tests for public office, and a revolutionary doctrine of the freedom of religion and conscience."[55] From an initial assertion of religious rights came a robust constellation of natural rights—self-defense, conscientious conviction, speech, press, and assembly—all rooted in the authority of natural law.

During this same period, Puritan master teacher William Ames was utilizing the idea of rights to talk about economic justice. While he never explicitly used the term "rights" in his *Marrow of Theology*, Ames offered the raw materials for a conception of rights in that influential Puritan textbook, arguing that a "feeling of equality toward others" is at the heart of justice claims. This "feeling of equality" or "equity," which he claimed was the ultimate "end" of the law, underwrites people's entitlement to fair treatment.[56] In his later work, *Conscience, and the Cases Thereof*, Ames explicitly identified the principle of equity as a matter of "common and moral right," a "natural right," and the central principle of God's law as articulated in the Decalogue and known by the conscience.[57] Equity is the foundational obligation of God's law, he said, meaning that it represents the basic entitlement to be regarded as equal to other human beings.[58] Extrapolating from the Decalogue's prohibition on theft, he claimed that the right to equity requires a social commitment to distributive, "emendative," commutative, corrective, and criminal rights. Ames identified economic rights of property acquisition, ownership, transfer, and distribution, "founded, not only on human, but also on natural and divine right."[59] He understood these basic economic rights to be rooted in a natural equality afforded to all people, not by government deference, but by the moral law of God.[60]

The protection of rights was also at the heart of the *Body of Liberties*, an encapsulation of basic rights for citizens of the Massachusetts Bay Colony, the culmination of a decade-long process of defining the limits of that colony's government enacted into law in 1641. Few (if any) of these rights were the invention of the New England Puritans, but they embraced them as consistent with the moral demands of "humanitie, Civilitie, and Christianitie" and identified them as the legal bedrock of the colony.[61] Primarily the work of pastor and lawyer Nathaniel Ward, the *Body of Liberties* focused mostly on a right to due process, extensively outlining the circumstances in which citizens could be lawfully detained, what prerogatives they could expect in legal procedures, and what recourse to appeal they would enjoy. Other rights identified in the document included prohibitions on arbitrary seizure of property, restrictions on (though not the abolition of) torture, protections from domestic violence for women and children, rights to humane treatment for servants, and a prohibition on animal cruelty. Interestingly, the *Body of Liberties* went so far as to outlaw slavery in the Puritan colonies in most circumstances: "There shall never be any bond slaverie, villinage, or Captivitie amongst us unless it be lawfull Captives taken in just warres, and such strangers as willingly selle themselves or are sold to us."[62]

What the *Body of Liberties* did not explicitly identify as a human right was religious liberty or freedom of conscience, perhaps unsurprising for a colony established as a "city on a hill" to institutionalize proper piety as a social compact. The Puritan bill of rights included extensive protection for churches to govern their own affairs, but it said little about individual rights of conscience.[63] It guaranteed individuals the freedom to register dissent in any public decision pertaining to religion or morals, but it did not condone civil noncompliance, and it certainly did not excuse disobedience.[64] In fact, even the right to dissent was strictly limited, the document insisting that "the dissent only be entered with the reasons thereof, for the avoiding of tediousness." Register your dissent and sit down, it seemed to say, and beyond this allowance, the *Body of Liberties* offered citizens no other liberties of conscience.

In fact, the document codified the collusion between church and state that was the hallmark of Massachusetts governance. It declared that "Civil Authoritie hath power and libertie to see the peace, ordinances and Rules of Christ observed in every church according to his word, so it be done in a Civill and not in an Ecclesiastical way."[65] What exactly distinguished a civil enforcement of religion from an ecclesiastical one the document does not say, but the Puritans' attempt to separate the jurisdictions of church and state while ensuring that civil and religious institutions and leaders cooperate in protecting both public order and the health of religion has all the markings of Calvin's collusion of church and state in Geneva. In a move toward theocracy, the *Body of Liberties* ends by enumerating twelve capital offenses derived directly from the Ten Commandments—false worship, witchcraft, sexual deviance, stealing, and murder were all civil offenses worthy of death.[66]

Roger Williams would have been unsurprised by the absence of any robust protection of religious rights in the *Body of Liberties*, given that he was a victim of that intolerance, banished from Massachusetts in part because he harped on the freedom of conscience and separation of church and state. Arguing for religious freedom, Williams invoked his theological heritage on religious rights, but he extended it in directions that few of his fellow Calvinists would have considered proper. Williams argued that the freedom to follow one's conscience in religious matters, without interference or punishment from civil government, was a fundamental right necessitated by the nature of religious belief, because conscience is impervious to coercion and malleable only by persuasion. He also thought religious freedom was a proper reflection of conventional English understandings of civil jurisdiction, and even of the teachings of Christianity itself.[67] He underscored how injurious a violation religious persecution was by comparing it to physical rape: "The forcing of a woman, that is, the violent action of uncleanness upon her body against her will, we count as a rape. By proportion, that is a spiritual or soul rape which [forces] . . . the conscience of any person to acts of worship."[68] He made clear that he considered religious rights to cover both profession and practice, and he argued that punishment for nonparticipation in established religion is as oppressive as punishment for the "deviance" of what a person actively says and does in the name of their beliefs.[69]

Given his circumstances, it is no surprise that Williams was most concerned with religious rights, but he occasionally nodded to a broader conception of rights. In a tract he contributed to parliamentary debates on freedoms in 1644, Williams identified the preservation of civil rights as the primary responsibility of political power, especially in the context of religious pluralism and in circumstances of social upheaval.[70] Elsewhere he referred to church members as being no more deserving of the protection of "natural and civil rights and liberties" than other citizens.[71] In neither case did he explain what he meant to include in those invocations of rights, but his regular reference to the jurisdiction of magistrates as the protection of "the bodies and goods" of their citizens implies certain rights to life and property.[72] Similarly, to the extent that Calvinists understood rights and duties to be in a correlative relationship, his assignment of "civil order, peace, and civility" to the obligations of political authority can be read as an implicit acknowledgment of a right to peace, freedom from molestation, and even protection against slander.[73] And his endorsement of the Calvinist doctrine of rule by popular consent, along with his support of the Puritan revolution against King Charles, signaled agreement with a right of resistance being articulated by his fellow Calvinists in that war.[74]

The Puritans represent one manifestation of concern for natural rights in the British Calvinist tradition, but the figure most closely influential on Witherspoon's understanding of rights was perhaps Gershom Carmichael (1672–1729). Carmichael, who taught moral philosophy at the University of Glasgow (as Hutcheson's immediate predecessor), is credited with introducing the natural rights tradition to the Scottish universities, on the doorstep of the Scottish Enlightenment.[75] His work, taught in most Scottish universities when Witherspoon would have been a student, put Roman law in conversation with Christian theology and the philosophies of Grotius, Pufendorf, and Locke. The parallels between Carmichael's moral philosophy and Witherspoon's are remarkably close, so much so that it is safe to assume that Witherspoon knew Carmichael's work well and appreciated his own synthesis of Calvinism and early modern philosophy.[76]

Like Witherspoon, Carmichael insisted that a central concern for moral philosophy was the elucidation of duty, defined by the requirements of the natural law.[77] Carmichael argued that God's law includes duties to God, ourselves, and others, and our duty to ourselves and others is rooted in the value all persons have as reflections of the *imago Dei*.[78] Also like Witherspoon after him, Carmichael summed up our duties to other persons as the obligation of benevolence:

> The sum of these duties consists in this, that *each man should treat the universal system of rational creatures with benevolence subordinated to love and reverence for God; and therefore each man should attempt to promote the common good of these creatures so far as his strength permits, and so long as he has no knowledge that it may interfere with the illustration of the divine glory*.[79]

Carmichael identified as the "*second* fundamental precept of Natural Law" (the first being our duty to show reverence to God) the obligation to further "*the common good of the whole human race, and, so far as this allows, the private good of individuals.*"[80] He believed that these duties of benevolence were best pursued in the protection of rights. "We may infer then that the best method of defining the duties which apply to men with respect to other men is to set out the various *rights* which belong to men, jointly and separately, from which the corresponding *obligations* will become clear of their own accord."[81] In fact, Carmichael believed (again, like Witherspoon) that moral duty was simply the correlative to the reality of rights: "the same law which gives someone a right which is valid against others, also by that very fact imposes on those others the corresponding obligation."[82]

Among the rights Carmichael identified were the rights of life, liberty, "physical integrity," chastity, reputation, and property, all human rights that Witherspoon would later acknowledge.[83] His heavy emphasis on the rights of life, liberty, and physical integrity in particular had important implications for his negative view of slavery and his robust support for a right of self-defense and political resistance. Comparisons to Witherspoon on both of these fronts shed light on Witherspoon's support of the American Revolution, but they also prompt questions about his failure to follow Carmichael on the subject of slavery.

Carmichael centered duty and natural law so much in his moral philosophy that he left relatively little space for talking about virtue, and this lack of attention marks one of the few differences between him and Witherspoon, who, as we have observed, makes virtue the center of his understanding of the moral life. Despite this difference, we see continuity between the two, for Carmichael did not deny the importance of virtue so much as he believed that extensive attention to virtue and vice was simply unnecessary, given his assumption that virtue chiefly derives from adherence to the duties of moral law:

> I thought it plainly superfluous to enter into a more particular discourse on [virtue and vice], as if the doctrine of virtue were entirely distinct from the doctrine of duties. For anyone who understands what he should do in life, and what he should not do, cannot be ignorant of what should be classified as virtue and vice.[84]

Acknowledging the relative imbalance between his discussions of virtue and duty, Carmichael still had something to say about the former, and it sounded very similar to Witherspoon's later lectures at the College of New Jersey. Carmichael defined virtue as "*a habit tending toward obedience to the Divine Law*, that is, to doing actions prescribed by the law with the intention of doing so, and to omitting forbidden actions with that intention."[85] When we habituate our commitment to protecting the rights of others, said Carmichael, we make justice a virtue, for *"justice toward other men*, i.e., the habitual will to perform the duties which are due to them and to abstain from the contrary actions, assumes in the person for whom justice is to be done, some *right* or *facility afforded by law, of doing, having, or obtaining something from someone else*."[86] Though they placed their emphases differently, Witherspoon surely appreciated Carmichael's connection between a life of character and the habitual commitment to rights and duty.

Rights, Duty, and Virtue

When he invoked rights, Witherspoon was channeling this Calvinist tradition, but he also was participating in the political and philosophical debates of the day. His synthesis of religious rights talk and ideas from Enlightenment philosophers gave him a bilingual vocabulary for commending rights as the object of public benevolent character. Witherspoon's commitment to natural rights fit seamlessly into his larger emphasis on character, thanks to the role he gave to the performance of duty in the life of virtue. As we have seen, Witherspoon identified "the great law of love" as our primary obligation to others. He defined that obligation as attention to the needs of others, "their greatest and best interest" and "doing them good in soul and body." He then connected the obligations of benevolence to respect for and defense of natural rights. Rights represent "the supreme law of moral duty," he lectured, because "whatever others have a just right and title to claim from me, that is my duty, or what I am obliged to do to them." Duty and rights are "correlative terms," said Witherspoon, so that the protection and fulfillment of rights represent the chief "application" of our "particular duties" of benevolence to others. All of this is to say that an essential requirement for fulfilling our obligations to the law, and thus to God's wishes for human community, is the protection of rights. And a habitual commitment to honoring and protecting rights contributes fundamentally to a life of virtue.

Witherspoon believed that the fundamental obligation of a nation of benevolent character is respect for natural human rights. In his elucidation of natural rights, he distinguished between perfect and imperfect rights, a distinction going back at least as far as Grotius and Locke. Perfect rights are entitlements so fundamental to being human that it is incumbent on government to protect them when threatened, by force if necessary. For instance, Hutcheson identified the right to life, labor, and self-determination as perfect rights.[87] These rights, he wrote, are ones "that the universal Violation of [them] would make human Life intolerable," and thus he argued that the forceful protection of them "seems exceedingly advantageous to the Whole, by making every one dread any Attempts against the perfect Rights of others."[88] In the same vein, Witherspoon identified the following as perfect rights: a right to life and liberty, the right to protect one's life and to determine what causes constitute a good reason to risk it, the right to things held in common (air, water, and earth are his examples), the right to the yield from one's own talents and labor, the right of "private judgment in matters of opinion," the right to associate (in which he includes a right to voluntary marriage), and the right to protection against slander and defamation, what he calls a "right to character."[89] Witherspoon's list bears close resemblance to Carmichael's summary of perfect natural rights.[90]

For Witherspoon, what made these rights natural is that they are not dispensations awarded to us by civil authority but entitlements we possess by virtue of being human. Like Carmichael before him, Witherspoon understood rights to be a reflection of our value as rational creatures made in the image of God, and their force was rooted in the imperatives of divine law. Rights are the articulation of God's expectations for our treatment of one another, which we experience as entitlements to certain behaviors (or to protection from behavior).[91] In this argument, Witherspoon distinguished himself from Hutcheson's justification of natural rights. Hutcheson subordinated rights to utilitarian calculations of benevolence, arguing that what we call rights are really practices that we have recognized over time result in maximizing the public good: "whenever it appears to us, that a Faculty of doing, demanding, or possessing any thing, universally allow'd in certain Circumstances, would in the whole tend to the general Good, we say that any Person in such Circumstances, has a Right to do, possess, or demand that Thing."[92] For Hutcheson, the more public good that stands to be gained by a general sense of entitlement, the stronger a claim to right, but Hutcheson's logic means that rights are secondary to, and defined by, instrumental calculations of beneficent effect.

By contrast, Witherspoon thought that the power behind natural rights was the authority of God's law, and perfect rights were so essential to the expectations of God's law that they demanded protection and enforcement.[93] Chief in importance among all of the perfect rights for Witherspoon was the right to religious belief, or freedom of conscience. Witherspoon thought liberty of conscience was the most fundamental right a person could hold because it represents the intimacy of a person's relationship with God, with which no other human being has the authority to interfere. Witherspoon's concern for religious rights was not surprising for a Calvinist, for as we have seen, the Calvinist commitment to natural rights began conceptually with a defense of religious rights against the encroachments of both church and state. Witherspoon shared this priority, and in his *Dominion* sermon, he expressed his fear that the loss of religious rights would be the ultimate cost to the colonies' continued submission to the crown: "There is not a single instance in history in which civil liberty was lost, and religious liberty preserved entire. If therefore we yield up our temporal property, we at the same time deliver the conscience into bondage."[94] Other human rights may be justifiable grounds for resisting an encroaching state, but Witherspoon feared the violation of other rights was a slippery slope to losing the most sacred right of all: the right to determine one's own beliefs. For Witherspoon, the defense of rights in the Revolution was primarily a fight for what William Lee Miller called "the first liberty," religious liberty.[95]

Besides perfect rights like religious liberty, Witherspoon talked about imperfect rights, a category of entitlements that are not necessarily enforceable by the coercive power of the state. Some examples Witherspoon gave are the expectation of charity and compassion in times of dire need, entitlement to gratitude for charity bestowed, and the fair and reliable exchange of property and goods.[96] It is important to note here that the expectations in this category are still rights, meaning we are entitled to their provision and protection, and other people (or society) have a corresponding obligation to honor them. But, as Witherspoon says, "the very definition of an imperfect right is such as you cannot use force to obtain" it.[97] Provision for an imperfect right is an obligation on someone, and the refusal to protect or provide for an imperfect right is a moral crime. In fact, Witherspoon says that "the violation of an imperfect right is often as great an act of immorality as that of a perfect right."[98] While the moral failing involved in ignoring our responsibility to another person's imperfect rights is real, it is not correctable or punishable by the coercive power of the legal system.

Because "human laws reach only, in ordinary cases, to the perfect rights," Witherspoon referred to the enforcement of perfect rights as *justice*, while he called the obligations we have to imperfect rights *mercy*, perhaps misleadingly given our modern association of acts of mercy with voluntary charity. "Justice consists in giving or permitting others to enjoy whatever they have a perfect right to—and making such an use [sic] of our own rights as not to encroach upon the rights of others."⁹⁹ Mercy, he explained, is "a readiness to do all the good offices to others that they stand in need of, and are in our power, unless they are opposed to some perfect right, or an imperfect one of greater moment." But while the obligation to protect and provide for imperfect rights cannot be enforced by coercion or law, it is a real moral obligation, "strongly binding on the conscience and absolutely necessary to the subsistence of human society." Thus, the failure to meet our obligations to people's imperfect rights is a serious defect of moral character.[100]

Besides the categories of perfect and imperfect, Witherspoon distinguished between alienable and inalienable rights. To designate rights as inalienable, as the Declaration of Independence does, is to claim that they are nontransferable, that is, they are rights that we cannot yield control over to others. Some rights, even perfect rights, may be alienable, meaning that we can voluntarily transfer control of them to others. Among alienable rights, Witherspoon cited self-defense, which he thought was the chief right people transfer to the state (at least substantially, if not entirely) when they engage in the social compact. Importantly, as we will see, Witherspoon believed that the right to self-defense could be reclaimed from a government that fails to meet its responsibility to be the protector of the people.

The pursuit of justice in property exchanges was also for Witherspoon an alienable right, a responsibility we cede to civil authority. Witherspoon justified private property as a right in a couple of ways. Certainly, his inclusion of a right to the yield from our labors implied a right to both property and work. Other times he justified a right to private property in terms of sustenance, arguing that it is a "confessed and exclusive right to a certain portion of the goods which serve for the support and conveniency of life." In other places, Witherspoon justified his interest in private property in more consequentialist terms, arguing that the "community of goods" held together in a modern society was unrealistic and that "public utility" required private property as an institution of a "civil society fully formed" in order to "compel universal industry." He even believed the unequal distribution of goods in a society was not only a reality to accept but also good, for it created the occasion for people to exercise "the noblest affections of the human mind," such as charity and compassion, and "active virtues" like ingenuity, diligence, and patience.

By contrast to alienable rights, inalienable rights are fundamental liberties that no one but we ourselves may control. Among these rights, Witherspoon highlighted a "right to self-preservation" and "provision," freedom of thought and opinion, and "matters of religion." These rights are so fundamental to the protection of one's own person, including one's mind and conscience, that control cannot be ceded to another party. Witherspoon observed that "some say that liberty" itself broadly construed "is unalienable, and that those who have even given it away may lawfully resume it." In fact, Witherspoon believed that the preservation of the inalienable right to personal liberty is the whole purpose of a social compact. We form societies for protection and collective provision in order to preserve our individual liberty. When a society fails that protection, it calls into question the efficacy and legitimacy of the social compact. As we will discuss, Witherspoon's adoption of the idea of inalienable rights to life and liberty had clear consequences for his justification of resistance against Britain, but it also had implications for his beliefs on human slavery—whether he recognized that connection or not.

Rights and the Common Good

In our time, the invocation of rights sometimes sounds like an assertion of individual prerogative against the collective, implying that individual rights and the common good travel in opposite directions. But Witherspoon thought that a commitment to natural rights *was* an investment in the collective good, because the defense of citizens' rights was an essential expression of a "public spirit" of benevolence. Protection of natural rights is how a virtuous society shows concern for its members, and respect for rights is how individual members of a society fulfill their duties to each other, to themselves, and ultimately to God. A commitment to natural rights is "the obligation of virtue" that best serves the common good.

But Witherspoon also thought that society as a whole has rights. In modern human rights discourse, community rights or group rights are often pitted against individual rights. Some critics of Western human rights language argue that a preoccupation with the rights of individuals is an imposition of European norms on other world cultures and societies. They argue that in some cultures, the protection of the group is more primary than the articulation of individual liberties. So, for instance, some global critics of UN rights language reject the emphasis put on liberty of conscience or an individual's freedom to exit a religious group, arguing that the focus on individual freedom puts at risk the integrity and survivability of religious and cultural communities. Instead, they prefer to talk about the right of groups to maintain their own moral and cultural traditions, even if some of those traditions impinge on the individual rights of persons in the group (traditional religious restrictions on women's autonomy are the most obvious example). The contest between individual rights and group rights is a major point of contention in modern human rights discourse.

Witherspoon thought that individual rights and social needs were more compatible than some of the modern rhetoric suggests. He recognized that there are moments in which the assertion of natural rights conflicts with social expectations. He established the authority of rights in natural law, prior to any obligation society places on us, arguing that natural rights are not subject to the whims of political authority. At the same time, Witherspoon was no libertarian, for he assumed that human beings are fundamentally social creatures and that our membership in society comes with certain obligations to the rights and well-being of others and to the whole. In other words, natural rights cannot simply be elaborations of a fundamental right to be left alone, as long as we exist within the context of a community of persons with rights claims of their own.

Based perhaps on a Calvinist appreciation for social covenants, Witherspoon connected concern for the common good to his understanding of rights. In fact, this is what Witherspoon thought a social compact was, an agreement "to deliver up or abridge some part of their natural rights, in order to have the strength of the united body, to protect the remaining, and to bestow others."[101] For Witherspoon, my rights are defined by the obligation society has to my needs and entitlements, and my obligations to the common good correspondingly represent restrictions on my rights. Rights and duties are correlative, in that my duty to others is sometimes defined by their rights (and vice versa), but also because the pursuit of my rights sometimes is justifiably limited by the needs of others. In acknowledging the need for adjudication between appeals to individual rights and the social good, Witherspoon reflected a tension inherent in rights talk, including in Calvinist political theology.[102]

Witherspoon referred to society's rightful expectations of its citizens to contribute to the collective good as "common rights." One of those common rights was the expectation of "diligence," by which he meant society's right to expect each member to contribute productively to the social good. Interestingly, Witherspoon interpreted this common right to diligence not just as a compulsion to be "useful" but also as the basis for a prohibition against suicide, which robs society of our utility. Another common right Witherspoon identified was society's right to the "discovery of useful inventions," though he also suggested that inventors be compensated for ideas they contribute to the common good. A third common right for Witherspoon was respect for the "dignity of human nature," by which he seems chiefly to have in mind respect for corpses, but he also may have meant to imply a broader respect for people's bodies. All of these ideas represent attitudes and actions that society has a right to expect from its citizens, said Witherspoon, which of course creates corresponding duties on citizens to fulfill them.

Another interesting example of how the rights of citizens define and limit others' rights in Witherspoon's moral outlook is his endorsement of the "right of necessity." The right of necessity, which goes back at least as far as Grotius, is the belief that in moments of dire need a person is entitled to use someone else's property without their permission. In moments of intense starvation or exposure, for instance, one person's right to the means of survival overrides another's right to property protection. Among British philosophers, one issue of debate—besides whether the right of necessity exists at all—was whether it represented an exception to natural rights. Some, like Samuel Pufendorf, argued that the right of necessity was not a natural right but an expression of mercy, but Gershom Carmichael insisted that the right of necessity was itself a specification of natural right. In fact, Carmichael claimed that it was a perfect right (meaning enforceable by civil authority), because in life-threatening situations, the right of necessity is simply a manifestation of the incontestable right to life.

Witherspoon agreed with Carmichael's assertion that the right of necessity is a perfect natural right. He explained that the right of necessity was the liberty to do what one needs to do to ensure "self-preservation" and "provision," to protect one's own life or the life of another, ideas that Witherspoon included among perfect rights. He imagined the right of necessity not only justified the seizure of another person's property but also, say, the apprehension of an assailant in defense of an innocent victim (including oneself). Whether the claim of necessity was invoked to allow the violation of property rights or personal liberty, Witherspoon granted that the interest of survival, as an expression of a right to life, could trump other social norms, even other rights, in emergency situations. In fact, he indicated that a right of necessity, as a perfect right, justified not only the taking of private property without permission but also, if necessary, the taking of it by force.[103]

Witherspoon anticipated the objection that a right of necessity represented an "exception" to moral law that opened the floodgates for all kinds of other exceptions, thereby diluting the authority and effectiveness of the law. He responded, however, in a manner similar to Carmichael, that a right of necessity is not so much an exception to the moral law as a more binding specification of the law. He reminded his students that any right to personal property "is to be held only in such manner, and to such a degree, as to be both consistent with, and subservient to, the good of others. And therefore these extraordinary cases are agreeable to the tacit or implied conditions of the social contract."[104] In other words, with the proper motive and legitimate need, the invocation of a right of necessity was consistent with the fundamental obligation of benevolence behind all rights and the moral law itself, sometimes more so than a blanket appeal to property rights. In arguing this way, Witherspoon demonstrated his belief that rights claims, like invocations of other moral principles, had to be interpreted and applied to particular circumstances. In the case of emergency circumstances, the right of necessity could be the most binding expression of benevolent duty to the moral law.

Witherspoon therefore invoked rights as a way of highlighting the fundamental duties society and its members have to individuals, but he also found the language of rights useful to talk about the moral duties members of a society have to the society as a whole. It is important to note that Witherspoon was quite reluctant to invoke social needs as a curtailment of individual natural rights. While acknowledging the possibility of conflicting rights claims in a society (or conflicts between individual rights and the common good), he insisted that the origin and authority of natural rights lie deeper than any social compact, because rights are rooted in the protections afforded by God's moral law. This made Witherspoon much more protective of rights than thinkers in the earliest generations of the Calvinist tradition, for whom concerns about social order frequently trumped individual liberties. For Witherspoon, a robust defense of natural rights was in the best interest of individuals and the common good, for it signaled a commitment to benevolence as the satisfaction of our "obligation of virtue" to God.

Practical Wisdom

Whether referring to rights claims or other moral principles, Witherspoon recognized that the general duties of the natural moral law do not tell us immediately and exhaustively what we should do in a particular case. Interpreting and applying the moral law to specific circumstances requires skill in ethical reasoning and deliberation. Likewise, the affirmation of natural rights does not automatically clarify what that respect for rights requires of us in specific circumstances, especially in scenarios in which the rights of one person impinge on the rights of another, or the rights of an individual conflict with the common good. Interpreting and applying moral principles and adjudicating competing rights claims require thoughtful deliberation. In the moral law, Witherspoon pointed out, there are things that we are commanded to do, things we are forbidden to do, and things that are morally indifferent, but these categories exist at a general level. He suggested that interpreting general principles in context was necessary to determine whether a specific act is commanded or prohibited. He talked about the role of intention in the evaluation of a moral act, cautioning that an evil act cannot be made good by a righteous intention, and a good act can be ruined by a suspect intention. Intention mattered to his moral calculus, but it did not on its own determine the morality of an act.[105] As we have seen, he recognized the reality of circumstances in which the needs of individuals or the common good may justify the cautious limitation of individual rights expression. Finally, in a discussion of moral law in his divinity lectures, Witherspoon demonstrated a sophisticated distinction between acts of commission and omission, arguing that the latter is not always "less heinous" than the former.[106]

Witherspoon recognized that moral deliberation about rights and duties was a difficult responsibility requiring skill and commitment, both for individuals and for a nation. In an interesting address delivered after the war to a society in Philadelphia, called "Observations on the Improvement of America," Witherspoon elaborated on the importance to the new nation of wise discernment.[107] Discussing the factors that would contribute to the country's prosperity, Witherspoon insisted that a moral foundation was essential—in particular, a commitment to the principle of justice. He argued that an investment in "equity and liberty," liberty of conscience, and the fair "partition of property" would establish a society built on a fundamental respect for its citizens and a commitment to principles of fair opportunity. But he acknowledged that building such a nation would be hard, in part because of the wisdom needed to translate general moral commitments like justice and equality into concrete public policy. "It is extremely difficult," he said, "after you depart from general principles to discover what particular regulations will be for the interest of a country. It requires a very comprehensive mind, and a thorough knowledge of the course of trade and [policy] in general."[108] Looking ahead, Witherspoon anticipated the need for political leaders with considerable practical wisdom to convert the moral ideals on which the nation was founded into a system of concrete legal and policy structures.

This is not the only occasion when Witherspoon invoked the idea of practical wisdom, or what was often called prudence. While he hesitated to call it a virtue, Witherspoon emphasized the importance of practical wisdom to the life of character.[109] He used the term to refer to mature wisdom, critical reasoning, attention to detail, and patience, virtues necessary to understand what is happening in the moment and how the general strictures of moral law apply. To do the right thing and be a good person or society requires understanding the right and good in particular circumstances, and the translation of general moral obligation into actual duties often requires nuanced consideration. Moral principles and competing rights claims need to be interpreted to determine what specific course is right in a particular moment, and the ability to do that careful interpretation of the moral moment is itself a sign of necessary character, for both the individual moral life and the well-being of an ethical society, as Witherspoon's remarks to the Philadelphia society made clear.

Witherspoon's emphasis on prudence reflected a priority placed on practical wisdom by other Calvinist thinkers before him. To William Ames, prudence was the disposition "whereby all the force of reason is used to find out what is right and to apply the means of reason rightly. It alone discerns those things which belong to doing right and possess the force of understanding, knowledge, and wisdom."[110] Ames argued that prudence involves the application of biblical principles, not just the exercise of a natural capacity for sound judgment. He insisted that "what is called right reason [prudence], if it is to lead to absolute rectitude, is nowhere else to be discovered than where it is—in the Scriptures."[111] Prudence requires "a general comprehension of good and evil" as reflected in biblical principles as well as an ability to relate that understanding "as it applies to individual things considered in the circumstances by which they are surrounded."[112] In other words, prudence is the capacity to discern and interpret the relevance of biblical law to real-life situations as they occur.

As such, Ames argued that prudence includes the capacity to exercise "circumspection, caution, and due diligence," for the application of biblical principle to concrete decisions and cases requires a person to investigate the moral implications of the moment and relate them to competing moral claims carefully and wisely. It often requires distinguishing between "greater duties" and "lesser" in order to determine moral priority, and it requires that the prudent thinker recognize that not every circumstance requires the same moral zeal, so that they must determine "in every duty the proper measure of desire and intensity of strength" that is necessary to do what is right.[113] In his attribution of prudence to God, Ames described it as the capacity to recognize "fit," what is the right thing to do in a specific circumstance, and his description of the corresponding human trait also carried this connotation.[114]

We see the priority on practical wisdom and discernment in the mammoth works of another English Calvinist, Richard Baxter (1615–91). Baxter was a nonconformist during the Civil War, whose long career as a preacher and theologian saw him suffer regular persecution after the restoration of the monarchy in 1660. Witherspoon was apparently a devoted reader of Baxter's works, many of which are extended exercises of this capacity for practical judgment. In 1673, Baxter published *A Christian Directory*, an enormous casebook of practical concerns for which he provided theological and moral guidance.[115] The *Directory* spans issues in domestic relations, individual moral decision-making, social and political responsibilities, and other arenas. Throughout the volume, Baxter intermingles the language of duty and virtue as Witherspoon did, arguing that "uprightness of heart and life" is the epitome of the life of virtue, but defining that uprightness as being "devoted and subjected unto God," God's laws, and the teachings of Jesus.[116]

If the upright life consists of daily fidelity to God's will, Baxter acknowledged such a commitment would require considerable practical wisdom to discern what God required in any particular moment. Like Ames, Baxter insisted that the Christian must have a "large understanding" of the will of God, by which he seems to have meant a comprehensive account of biblical principle, but we also must be capable of interpreting and applying that principle to specific situations. That requires subtle discernment of circumstances, of competing moral claims, and of grades of good and evil.[117] Baxter acknowledged that the rightness of some actions is obvious but that in other cases, "the good of some actions is but little discernible any where," and that a prudent Christian would have to trust in the rightness of their discernment of duty. The prudent Christian would need to be a serious student of the moment, but must avoid myopic preoccupation with just the present, maintaining "an eye to posterity, and not only to the present time or age," to understand the long-term implications of any decision.[118] The evaluation of duty also required humility, self-criticism, and a willingness to inconvenience oneself to serve God's intention in a particular circumstance, again a fusion of duty and virtuous disposition not unlike Witherspoon's moral vision. Baxter's voluminous *Christian Directory* commended this practical wisdom and modeled it in its detailed consideration of hundreds of cases of conscience. For Baxter, as with Ames, the application of biblical moral principle to life choices was no easy or straightforward task. Both men believed that the exercise of prudence was essential to the application of God's will, expressed in general principle in the Bible and conscience, to the daily realities people face.

Witherspoon's emphasis on practical wisdom followed the example of his theological forerunners, though he arguably allowed more room to imagine its natural exercise among the unredeemed than Ames or Baxter offered. Witherspoon's understanding of practical wisdom as a necessary part of healthy political character also reflected his synthesis of duty and virtue in the moral life. In prudence, character and duty mutually support one another, as the habituation of wise deliberation on moral duty becomes a sign of good character. Doing one's moral duty becomes as much a part of who that person is as the actions they perform or decisions they make. At the same time, the performance of duty depends on a foundation in virtue, making a person more inclined to recognize a moment of obligation, to interpret their duty properly, and to follow through with what is required of them. Prudence, then, is both disposition and duty.

In his fast day sermon, in his training of students, and in his public leadership throughout the Revolution, Witherspoon commended a wise and benevolent "public spirit" as essential to the health of the new American republic. The political implications of that moral character can be summarized in four maxims: (1) virtuous citizens and leaders are essential to healthy politics; (2) virtue is necessarily tied to respect for and adherence to moral law; (3) the most fundamental expression of a society's commitment to moral law is the protection of natural rights; and (4) the purpose of moral law, rights, and virtue is to bind us to one another and to the common good, in benevolent mutual regard. Witherspoon believed that a society that aspires to this public spirit must intentionally cultivate constructive political character in its citizens and leaders. In the next chapter, we will examine how Witherspoon thought this cultivation might happen through the institutions he faithfully served in his career in America: church, family, and college.

Notes

1. Witherspoon, LMP, Lecture V, *Works*, III:389.
2. Mt. 7:12, NRSVUE.
3. Witherspoon, LMP, Lecture IV, *Works*, III:383.
4. Witherspoon, LMP, Lecture IV, *Works*, III:383.
5. Witherspoon, LMP, Lecture IV, *Works*, III:385.
6. "The Westminster Confession of Faith (1646)," in *Creeds of the Churches*, ed. John Leith, 3rd ed. (John Knox Press, 1982), 213–14.
7. "Westminster Confession," XIX, in Leith, *Creeds of the Churches*, 214.
8. Ames, *Marrow of Theology*, 108–9. Westminster also referred to "the light of nature" that testifies to God's expectations for us enough "as to leave men inexcusable" for their transgressions against God's intentions. See "The Westminster Confession in Leith," 193.
9. Recapitulation of the *Lectures on Moral Philosophy*, 470.
10. Witherspoon, LD, Lecture IV, *Works*, IV:30.
11. Witherspoon, LD, Lecture XVII, *Works*, IV:117.
12. Witherspoon, LD, Lecture XVII, *Works*, IV:118.
13. Calvin, *Institutes*, II.8, 372. In talking about the connection between duty to God and virtue, Calvin was invoking Augustine.
14. See *Institutes*, II.7, 348, for an example of this broader reference for "the law." By contrast, in the very next chapter of his *Institutes*, Calvin embarks on an extended explication of the requirements of the moral law by focusing specifically on the Ten Commandments.
15. Calvin, *Institutes*, II.7, 362.
16. Calvin, *Institutes*, II.8, 372.
17. Calvin, *Institutes*, III.7, 692–3.
18. Ames, *Marrow of Theology*, 226.
19. Ames, *Marrow of Theology*, 314–15.
20. Witherspoon, LMP, "Introduction," in *Works*, III:368.
21. Ames, *Marrow of Theology*, 111.
22. Calvin, *Institutes*, IV.20, 1504.
23. Calvin, *Institutes*, II.2, 282.
24. Calvin, *Institutes*, II.7, 355.
25. Calvin, *Institutes*, II.7, 356.
26. Calvin, *Institutes*, II.7, 358.
27. Calvin, *Institutes*, II.7, 360.
28. David VanDrunen, *Natural Law and the Two Kingdoms: A Study in the Development of Reformed Social Thought* (Eerdmans, 2010), chapter 4.

29 John Witte, *The Reformation of Rights: Law, Religion, and Human Rights in Early Modern Calvinism* (Cambridge University Press, 2007), 294–308.
30 See David Little, *Essays on Religion and Human Rights: Ground to Stand On* (Cambridge University Press, 2015), chapter 7, for one representation of this lineage.
31 In the introduction of the *Lectures on Moral Philosophy*, Witherspoon referred to "some there are, and perhaps more in the present age than any former age, who deny the law of nature, and say, that all such sentiments as have been usually ascribed to the law of nature, are from revelation and tradition" (367). Attributing the rejection of natural law to followers of Hutcheson, Witherspoon cast his lot with thinkers like Gershom Carmichael and Samuel Clarke, the latter of whom he identified as "one of the greatest champions for the law of nature."
32 Witherspoon, LMP, Lecture IV, *Works*, III:387.
33 Witherspoon, LMP, Lecture III, *Works*, III:378.
34 Witherspoon, LMP, Lecture III, *Works*, III:380.
35 Witherspoon, LMP, Lecture III, *Works*, III:381.
36 Witherspoon, LMP, Lecture VII, *Works*, III:401–2.
37 Specifically, Witherspoon was responding to an objection he attributed to Shaftesbury, that the idea of divine reward and punishment made moral performance "mercenary." See LMP, Lecture V, *Works*, III:389–91.
38 Witherspoon, LMP, Lecture IX, *Works*, III:409.
39 Witherspoon, LMP, Lecture VIII, *Works*, III:405.
40 John Witherspoon, "Letter from the Synod of New-York and Philadelphia," in *Works*, III:10.
41 Witherspoon, "Letter from the Synod of New-York and Philadelphia," in *Works*, III:12.
42 I trace how this commitment to benevolent virtue shaped Witherspoon's understanding of proper conduct in war in Chapter 5.
43 Witherspoon, *Works*, III:51.
44 Witherspoon, *Works*, IV:367.
45 Witherspoon, *Works*, IV:368.
46 Knud Haakonssen, "Natural Jurisprudence and the Theory of Justice," in *The Cambridge Companion to the Scottish Enlightenment*, 2nd ed., ed. Alexander Broadie and Craig Smith (Cambridge University Press, 2019), 204–6.
47 See Scott Philip Segrest, *America and the Political Philosophy of Common Sense* (University of Missouri, 2010), 55–7, and Haakonssen, "Natural Jurisprudence," 204–6.
48 See Witte, *Reformation of Rights*, 46–7.
49 Witte, *Reformation of Rights*, 72–3.

50 Little, *Essays on Religion and Human Rights*, 225–9. See also Witte, *Reformation of Rights*, 57–8.
51 Witte, *Reformation of Rights*, 61.
52 See Witte, *Reformation of Rights*, chapter 2.
53 William Haller, *Liberty and Reformation in the Puritan Revolution* (Columbia University Press, 1955), 70.
54 See Haller, *Liberty and Reformation in the Puritan Revolution*, 69–78. See also Little, *Essays on Religion and Human Rights*, 185.
55 Little, *Essays on Religion and Human Rights*, 186.
56 Ames, *Marrow of Theology*, 306–7; *Conscience*, V.II, 111.
57 Ames, *Conscience*, Book V.LV, 221. See also V.I, 100.
58 Calvin too talks about equity, by which he means a principle of responsibility to honor people's rights and to respond to people's basic needs as we are able. Little, *Essays on Religion and Human Rights*, 226–7.
59 Ames, *Conscience*, V.XLI, 222–23; *Marrow of Theology*, 321–4.
60 Ames, *Marrow of Theology*, 110–11.
61 *Body of Liberties*, in *Puritan Political Ideas*, ed. Edmund S. Morgan (Bobbs-Merrill, 1965), 182.
62 *Body of Liberties*, 196.
63 *Body of Liberties*, 199–201.
64 *Body of Liberties*, 193.
65 *Body of Liberties*, 190.
66 *Body of Liberties*, 197–9.
67 For Williams on the nature of belief (and why coercion does not yield genuine religious conformity), the parameters of civil authority, and the incompatibility between Christianity and religious persecution, see James Calvin Davis, *On Religious Liberty: Selections from the Works of Roger Williams* (Harvard University Press, 2008).
68 *On Religious Liberty*, 205.
69 See, for instance, *On Religious Liberty*, 94 and 181.
70 *On Religious Liberty*, 242.
71 *On Religious Liberty*, 207.
72 For instance, see Williams's preface to *The Bloody Tenent of Persecution* in *On Religious Liberty*, 87.
73 *On Religious Liberty*, 119. Late in his life, Williams participated in a series of debates with Quakers in Rhode Island, whom he regarded as agitators of public order. Nonetheless, his engagement with them in these public occasions modeled a right to free expression (though Williams was willing to limit that right when speech became excessively slanderous or threatening). Williams provided a

laborious account of his debates with the Quakers in *George Fox Digg'd out of His Burrowes*.
74 For Williams's adoption of the Puritan doctrine of rule by popular consent, see *On Religious Liberty*, 125, 132, and 149.
75 James Moore and Michael Silverthorne, eds., *Natural Rights on the Threshold of the Scottish Enlightenment: The Writings of Gershom Carmichael* (Indianapolis, IN: Liberty Fund, 2002), x.
76 As an indicator of Carmichael's prominence in the eighteenth-century educational landscape in Scotland, Francis Hutcheson explicitly acknowledged his intellectual indebtedness to Carmichael (Moore and Silverthorne, *Gershom Carmichael*, xv).
77 Moore and Silverthorne, *Gershom Carmichael*, 11–12.
78 Moore and Silverthorne, *Gershom Carmichael*, 47.
79 Moore and Silverthorne, *Gershom Carmichael*, 47.
80 Moore and Silverthorne, *Gershom Carmichael*, 48.
81 Moore and Silverthorne, *Gershom Carmichael*, 213.
82 Moore and Silverthorne, *Gershom Carmichael*, 39.
83 Moore and Silverthorne, *Gershom Carmichael*, 77–8.
84 Moore and Silverthorne, *Gershom Carmichael*, 18.
85 Moore and Silverthorne, *Gershom Carmichael*, 42.
86 Moore and Silverthorne, *Gershom Carmichael*, 43.
87 Hutcheson, *Beauty and Virtue*, 183.
88 Hutcheson, *Beauty and Virtue*, 182.
89 Witherspoon, LMP, Lecture X, *Works*, III:416.
90 Moore and Silverthorne, *Gershom Carmichael*, 77–8.
91 Witherspoon, LMP, Lecture X, *Works*, III:415–16; Moore and Silverthorne, *Gershom Carmichael*, 44.
92 Hutcheson, *Beauty and Virtue*, 182.
93 Witherspoon, LMP, Lecture VIII, *Works*, III:406.
94 Witherspoon, DPPM, *Works*, III:36.
95 William Lee Miller, *The First Liberty: America's Foundation in Religious Freedom, Expanded and Updated* (Georgetown University Press, 2003).
96 Witherspoon, LMP, Lecture X, *Works*, III:417.
97 Witherspoon, LMP, Lecture X, *Works*, III:417.
98 Witherspoon, LMP, Lecture VIII, *Works*, III:407.
99 Witherspoon, LMP, Lecture VIII, *Works*, III:408.
100 Witherspoon, LMP, Lecture VIII, *Works*, III:408.
101 Witherspoon, LMP, Lecture X, *Works*, III:417.
102 Even an ardent defender of human rights has to admit that occasionally membership in a collective will pit rights against one another and against the

common good. For instance, at great personal cost, Roger Williams spent the bulk of his early career in New England arguing for the inviolable right of free conscience, suffering the penalty of banishment as a result. Later in his life, however, when he was chief officer of the colony of Rhode Island, he was confronted with fellow residents who objected to tax practices and militia conscription in the name of conscientious conviction. Williams and others instituted these social obligations for the good of the colony. Taxes were needed to fund all of the travel to England to resist antagonists in Massachusetts and Connecticut (and even some residents of Rhode Island) who were trying to steal the colony's charter and claim its land for themselves. The militia was necessary to protect the colony from the increased threat of indigenous tribes, whose hostility the manipulative practices of Massachusetts' leaders were stoking. Invoking Williams's commitment to freedom of conscience, some residents of Rhode Island argued that they did not believe in taxes or armed service and should not be forced to contribute. Williams's response was to deny that the appeal to rights can ever be absolute within a society. Sometimes the good of society trumps the right of the individual. For Williams, there could be no "conscientious objection" to taxes or military service because such an assertion of liberty puts a disproportionate burden on others and threatens the collective good. See Davis, *On Religious Liberty*, 33–8.

103 Witherspoon, LMP, Lecture XVI, *Works*, III:466–8.
104 Witherspoon, LMP, Lecture XVI, *Works*, III:466.
105 Witherspoon, LMP, Lecture IX, *Works*, III:412–13.
106 Witherspoon, LD, Lecture XV, *Works*, IV:99.
107 *Observations on the Improvement of America* is notoriously difficult to date precisely, but the reader can infer from the brief argument that it was delivered near or after the conclusion of the war. Students of Witherspoon from the early nineteenth century onward agree, however, that Witherspoon was the author of the address, confirmed by both the argument and style.
108 *Observations on the Improvement of America*, in *Works*, IV:385.
109 In Lecture IX of the *Lectures on Moral Philosophy*, Witherspoon appears to question whether prudence is actually a virtue, as Aristotle claims. His problem with the Greek understanding of prudence is that it seems too concerned with a kind of Aristotelian balance as the definition of virtue, rather than (as Witherspoon would prefer) a conformity with moral law. William Ames makes exactly the same objection in his *Marrow of Theology*, 230.
110 Ames, *Marrow of Theology*, 228.
111 Ames, *Marrow of Theology*, 225. Ames objected to Aristotle's insinuation that a natural capacity for prudence is the foundation of virtue. This is part of his

larger objection to the philosophical distinction between theology and ethics, the latter allegedly concerned only with human society and this life. Instead, Ames assumed that Christian ethics flowed from theological convictions and that ethical responsibility consisted of the application of biblical principles to Christian living. In fact, unlike the Aristotelian tradition, Ames did not consider the cardinal virtues discrete virtues at all, but "four conditions necessarily required in the disposition that deserves the name of virtue," which he ultimately defines as the character to discern and satisfy the will of God (228).

112 Ames, *Marrow of Theology*, 228.
113 Ames, *Marrow of Theology*, 229. Ames represents practical wisdom as one way that human beings reflect the image of God.
114 In his discussion of the attributes of God, Ames identifies prudence as one part of the character of God, expressed potently in creation itself, "whereby [God] knows the fittest occasion for all things." See *Marrow of Theology*, 97.
115 Richard Baxter, *A Christian Directory*, 1673, Reprint (Soli Deo Gloria Publications, 1990).
116 Baxter, *Christian Directory*, 737-8.
117 Baxter, *Christian Directory*, 739.
118 Baxter, *Christian Directory*, 740.

4

Schools of Character

As a preacher and a public figure, John Witherspoon identified good political character as the habituation of benevolence, the impulse to serve the needs of others and contribute to the common good of society. He thought that individuals of a benevolent character pursued the good of others as a reflection of their duty to God, whether that sense of duty was communicated to them through the Bible or through the natural moral law that resides in every human conscience. He assumed that a benevolent society exhibited a strong concern for natural rights, and he was certain that the defense of individual rights contributed constructively to the collective good. And he insisted that the social project of cultivating political character, a "public spirit," as he called it, was essential to the health of the new United States.

But if this project of cultivating character was so important, how was it to be done? How does a society encourage in its citizens the maturation and habituation of this benevolent attitude? Witherspoon assumed that three institutions played key roles in developing political character: religion, family, and college.

"Virtue and Piety Are Inseparably Connected"

As we have seen already, Witherspoon did not think that good political character was the possession of Christians alone. His belief in natural law and conscience gave him theological reason to be confident that the unredeemed could tap into at least a basic understanding of God's expectations for human beings. Through this natural capacity for moral discernment, all citizens could develop some semblance of constructive character and contribute to the good of others and society. This guarded optimism about political character in a religiously diverse country did not mark a departure from his Calvinist tradition. He sometimes borrowed Scottish philosophical language to talk about the "moral sense" he thought was widely available to citizens regardless of their piety, but his belief in a certain level of natural moral capability was at home in his theological tradition.

At the same time, Witherspoon was clear that he believed the Christian religion was an important source of inspiration for public virtue. He believed that the experience of "real religion"—meaning an evangelical commitment to Christian faith—made possible a higher capacity for moral living, because in the redeemed Christian the natural capacity for morality is augmented by the sanctifying power of the Holy Spirit. Because true piety brought with it the promise of deeper moral character, Witherspoon thought that the spread of Christianity was advantageous to society. The greater the number of pious Christians the nation could boast, the better their collective character. He also thought religion had a positive influence on the unredeemed in that the pious served as moral exemplars for society, and the prevalence of Christian preaching made the moral lessons of Christianity known beyond the church.

We should pause to acknowledge the obvious, that when Witherspoon extolled the benefits of a public presence for religion, he was talking specifically about Protestant Christianity. He was aware, of course, that the colonies hosted a fair amount of religious diversity. While Protestants may have dominated the colonies, Witherspoon knew that Catholics and Jews counted among the Americans who would fight for independence and live in the new nation. In addition, he knew that many of the men with whom he labored in the struggle against Britain held peculiar religious views that deviated significantly from his orthodox Calvinism. Witherspoon knew the colonies were not a religious monolith, and nowhere do we have evidence of him peddling in the anti-Jewish, anti-Muslim, or anti-Catholic rhetoric that would have been commonplace among Protestants of his time. Nowhere do we have evidence of Witherspoon disparaging the eclectic religious convictions of his revolutionary colleague Thomas Jefferson, his good friend Benjamin Rush, or his former pupil James Madison. Yet he remained stalwart that orthodox Christianity, because of its prevalence but also because of its singular grasp of truth, was a positive force in the moral health of the nation. Thus, when Witherspoon talked up the usefulness of public piety, Protestant Christianity is what he had in mind.

As a result, throughout his career in Scotland and America, he argued for the public encouragement of Christian religion. In his *Dominion* sermon, before laying out the character he thought would be required to win the coming war, he began with an appeal to every person in the audience to exhibit "a sincere concern for his own soul's salvation."[1] He did so because he thought it was his primary duty as a preacher, but also because he believed an increase in piety would contribute significantly to the character that would be necessary in the conflict to come. In fact, Witherspoon declared that "he is the best friend to American liberty, who is most sincere and active in promoting true and undefiled religion, and who sets himself with the greatest firmness to bear down profanity and immorality of every kind."[2] He ended his sermon with the confident claim that "it is in the man of piety and inward principle, that we may expect to find the uncorrupted patriot, the useful citizen, and the invincible soldier. God grant that in America true religion and civil liberty may be inseparable."[3]

A year before, the Synod of New York and Philadelphia issued that letter to its member congregations on the occasion of a similar fast day, called to reflect on the hostilities with the mother country. The letter, which Witherspoon surely wrote, hits the same themes. It calls on American Presbyterians to "look beyond the immediate authors either of your sufferings or fears, and to acknowledge the holiness and justice of the Almighty in the present visitation." It suggests that the conflict "is a proper time for pressing all of every rank, seriously to consider the things that belong to their eternal peace"—in other words, attend to the health of your religion. The letter tells its readers that attending to their salvific state will also prepare them to contribute to the collective good, for an improvement in piety will bring an infusion of character necessary for the brewing conflict.[4]

Witherspoon clearly thought that Christian zeal contributed positively to political character, so that giving "attention to the public interest of religion" was a legitimate social priority.[5] In encouraging piety as a social good, Witherspoon was right in step with both his Calvinist tradition and broader eighteenth-century assumptions about religion's public importance. Calvin assumed that good religion contributed positively to the health of the state, which is why he oversaw such close cooperation between the church and civil government in Geneva. Calvin simply assumed that "no government can be happily established unless piety is the first concern."[6] The encouragement of piety ensured a moral compass for the civil realm, so Calvin entrusted the support of religion to the civil magistrate. Inspired by Romans 13, he taught that "civil government has as its appointed end . . . to cherish and protect the outward worship of God, to defend sound doctrine of piety and the position of the church, to adjust our life to the society of men, to form our social behavior to civil righteousness, to reconcile us with one another, and to promote general peace and tranquility."[7] And he was certain that the first two responsibilities in this list were essential to guaranteeing the others.

Calvinists like Massachusetts minister John Cotton (1585–1652) followed this logic. Cotton asked rhetorically, "is it not the proper work of the civil magistrate to preserve the civil peace, and to prevent or reform the disturbance of the tranquility or peace of any such societies in whose peace the peace or weal of the city or society is concerned?"[8] Assuming this responsibility, Cotton argued that peace could not be successfully protected without maintaining a level of piety in civil society. Thus, he argued, "civil governors, though to them be chiefly committed the bodies and goods of the people (as their adequate object), yet, in order to [accomplish] this, they may, and ought to, procure spiritual helps to their souls and to prevent such spiritual evils as that the prosperity of religion among them might advance the prosperity of the civil state."[9]

It is important to note that Calvinists of the early modern period were not of one mind on this issue. Roger Williams expressed more than a little skepticism about the Puritan assumption that good religion was a necessary ingredient for a healthy civil society. In his *Bloody Tenent of Persecution*, Williams famously opposed the civil enforcement of religious compliance in the name of public order. He admitted that the "ordinances and disciplines of Christ Jesus, though wrongfully and profanely applied to natural and unregenerate men, may cast a blush of civility and morality upon them."[10] But he argued that the cost of this civil enforcement of religious adherence outweighed whatever appearance of order it provided. He worried that nonvoluntary religion hardened the hearts of the unregenerate against God and religion or misled them into thinking they were saved when they were not. Public enforcement of religion was bad for religion, and it was unnecessary for public order. On this last point, Williams was sure that history bore him out: "So many stately kingdoms and governments in the world have long and long enjoyed civil peace and quiet, notwithstanding their religion is so corrupt as that there is not the very name of Jesus Christ amongst them. And this every historian, merchant, [and] traveler in Europe, Asia, Africa and America can testify."[11]

Williams notwithstanding, Witherspoon's assumption that Christian piety brings something vital to social health was standard fare in his Calvinist tradition. That religion was beneficial and necessary to healthy public life was a widely shared assumption in the eighteenth century beyond orthodox Calvinists as well. Civic republicans like George Washington, John Adams, Benjamin Rush, and John Jay assumed that religion was an essential source of public virtue. They were deeply committed to a citizen's right to practice the particulars of their own religion, but they also advocated for public support of a general religious ethos in society, believing that public morality would be sustained by this encouragement of religion in its varied forms. As John Witte and Joel Nichols describe it, "Civic Republicans urged that society needs a fund of religious values and beliefs, and a body of civic ideas and ideals, that are enforceable both through common law and communal suasion." They cite Benjamin Franklin's invocation of the "Publick Religion" of America as an example of this foundational moral resource that "taught a creed of honesty, diligence, devotion, public spiritedness, patriotism, and obedience; love of God, neighbor, and self; and other ethical commonplaces taught by various religious traditions at the time of the founding."[12] To civic republicans, reliance on religion as a source of public virtue was not incompatible with a commitment to religious liberty.

Still, not everyone in the eighteenth century was of the mind that traditional Christianity was a guarantor of social health. Devotees of certain kinds of Enlightenment thinking insisted not only that religion was a matter of private "opinion" (as Jefferson famously referred to it), but that organized religion was more likely to carry with it political collusion and autocracy than public virtue.[13] Weighing in on the effort to legalize tax assessments for supporting church clergy and teachers in Virginia, James Madison observed that "more or less in all places," the civil establishment of religion resulted in "pride and indolence in the Clergy, ignorance and servility in the laity, [and] in both, superstition, bigotry and persecution."[14] Even some deeply religious spokespersons, particularly among minority dissenters, emphasized the personal dimension to religious belief over its public function. Baptist preacher John Leland declared that "government has no more to do with the religious opinions of men than it has with the principles of mathematics," and that the public's only relationship to religion should be the protection of free exercise.[15]

Among those who did think that the public encouragement of Christianity was a social good, there was nonetheless disagreement about just how formal that encouragement ought to be. In other words, the belief that religion is a constructive public influence does not necessarily lead to the conviction that religion (or one particular religion) ought to be established as a legal preference or receive state support. Certainly, some in the eighteenth century (and beyond) believed that the formal establishment of religion was appropriate and good for social health, which is why state establishments and tests for office survived for so long. Patrick Henry led the charge for state support of Christian education in Virginia, arguing that the nonsectarian funneling of state taxes to churches would provide an infrastructure for public virtue and order in the state, a movement that required the efforts of Jefferson, Madison, and a coalition of Presbyterians and evangelicals to defeat.[16] John Adams also trumpeted the benefits to public order of a "mild establishment" of religion, which led the people of Massachusetts to bake into the state constitution of 1780 both a commitment to liberty of conscience and state support for local churches.[17] New Hampshire, Connecticut, and Maine were still providing tax support for Congregational churches until about 1820. Massachusetts did not relieve itself of its church establishment until 1833.[18]

Witherspoon clearly thought Christianity was a positive public force. In his moral philosophy lectures, he argued that "If... virtue and piety are inseparably connected, then to promote true religion is the best and most effectual way of making a virtuous and regular people. Love to God, and love to man, is the substance of religion; when these prevail, civil laws will have little to do."[19] He also talked frequently about the role that ministers play as sources of moral edification and public officials as models of good piety. As Michael Sullivan observes, "Witherspoon believed that the educational role of the Church in a republican age was almost as important as its spiritual role," so he saw his preparation of divinity students as an investment in the health of the church in America but also as the training of social teachers of character.[20]

Witherspoon acknowledged that this close connection between virtue and piety raises a question: how far could the magistrate interfere in matters of religion? He responded with a reiteration of his commitment to religious liberty, which he believed to be a natural right. He limited the magistrate's involvement in religion to modeling piety and defending the rights of conscience. He endorsed the magistrate's right to enact and enforce laws principally about moral behavior, but not to prescribe particular religious beliefs. He accepted the government's "public provision for the worship of God," but he understood that provision within his broader commitment to protecting citizens' religious liberty, suggesting that any support for worship should be in the spirit of a "parent." Civil leaders have a "right to instruct," he argued, "but not to constrain." In other words, government could assume a pedagogical role when it came to piety and morality, but not a compulsory one.[21]

Despite his confidence in the public usefulness of religion, Witherspoon refused to call for the legal establishment of Christianity in the colonies. For him, true Christian piety could only be a result of true conversion, and that conversion could only come from a free acceptance of Jesus Christ. Witherspoon believed that Christian piety could make its constructive mark on public character only in an environment in which people could make free decisions about their religious lives. This is why he emphasized the theme of religious liberty so much in his calls for political independence from Britain. Only a society that promoted religious liberty and the freedom of conscience could expect religion to flourish, and therefore only a society that valued religious liberty would be one within which Christianity could benefit the moral character of the people.[22] His commitment to religious liberty and disestablishment is also why he was very reluctant to talk explicitly about politics from the pulpit, even back to his time in Scotland.[23]

Witherspoon acknowledged the argument "that in case any sect holds tenets subversive of society and inconsistent with the rights of others, that they ought not to be tolerated," and noted this was the basis for restricting Catholics in England. However, he expressed reservations about this "way of reasoning," arguing that "we ought in general to guard against persecution on a religious account as much as possible." He suggested that "such as hold absurd tenets are seldom dangerous," and when they are, it is often "when they are oppressed." He then cited Holland as an example of a society that permits Catholics to exist unmolested with no negative consequence.[24]

Witherspoon's advocacy for the public importance of religion in the colonies, rooted in a broader commitment to religious liberty, may seem inconsistent with his support of national Presbyterianism in Scotland. In another of his fast day sermons, this one preached ten years before he emigrated to New Jersey, Witherspoon sounded more like the Puritan jeremiads in his assumptions about church and state. The sermon was partially a lament of the "public strokes" that Scotland had endured in his time—economic scarcity, famine, and war—which he directly blamed on the impiety of the people.[25] He described Scotland "both as a nation, and as a church, exceedingly fallen and low," and he observed that "so great is the prevalence of irreligion, contempt of God, sensuality and pride, that many of the grossest crimes are not only practiced but professed, not only frequent but open, not only persisted in but gloried in and boasted of."[26] He argued that "the want of a public spirit" in the country proved "how negligent have we been of promoting, or praying for the interest of religion."[27] And he took a dig at the Moderates, arguing that "many have of late been ashamed of the cross of Christ, and the doctrine of the grace of God," and that their substitution of "a pliant and fashionable scheme of religion" for classical orthodoxy was nothing more than "a beautiful but unsubstantial idol, raised by human pride." As he observed in other European countries, so Witherspoon predicted for Scotland that the watering down of traditional Christian doctrine would be "the forerunner and brought last at its heels a deluge of profaneness and immorality in practice."[28]

For the younger Witherspoon in Scotland, declension in orthodox religion necessarily led to social evils, and the good of the nation depended on a restoration of Christian religion, so much so that he insisted, "we have no warrant to ask national prosperity without a revival of religion."[29] He ended that sermon with a rousing call for an evangelical awakening, when "religion shall rise from its ruins" for the good of church and state.[30] Even in this explicit call for revival, though, Witherspoon pulled up short of promoting the formal civil establishment of Christianity. In fact, Witherspoon's leadership of Popular Party Presbyterians in his home country was a pushback against a close collusion of church and state. Recall that one of the big issues between the Popular Party and the Moderates was the question of who should enjoy the prerogative to select local ministers. The Popular Party insisted that ministerial leadership should largely be up to the local congregation, with appropriate oversight by other ministers and churches in the presbytery. The Moderates argued that prominent patrons ought to have a say in selecting local clergy in proportion to their economic and political power. In making that claim for the power of patronage, Moderates were appealing to the Patronage Act of 1711, which awarded wealthy landowners just that kind of power in their local parishes. As James Foster points out, however, the wealthiest landowner in many parishes was the crown or its political allies, and the Moderates' proposal would "effectively put the ministry of hundreds of Scottish churches under English control."[31] Thus, in the context of the Scottish Kirk, Witherspoon's leadership of the Popular Party aligned him with a kind of separation of church and state.

Witherspoon's 1758 sermon also reflected the reality that in Scotland the Presbyterian Church was the official Kirk, and thus both a religious and a political institution. After a decade in the very different religious environment of the colonies, Witherspoon's perspective on church and state seems to have reconciled with the greater religious pluralism in his new home. His call for religious recommitment in the *Dominion* sermon does not have the flavor of an orthodox revival sermon, the way his text from the 1758 fast day did. Instead, he talked about good religion in more general terms, perhaps as an attempt to appeal to his less homogeneous audience. "True religion," he states in *Dominion*, "is nothing else but an inward temper and outward conduct suited to your state and circumstances in providence at any time."[32] He emphasized the moral performance associated with Christianity more than any kind of doctrinal conformity, and in fact, he clarified in the sermon that he did not "mean to recommend a furious and angry zeal for the circumstantials of religion, or the contentions of one sect with another about their peculiar distinctions. I do not wish you to oppose any body's religion, but every body's wickedness."[33] In his deference to denominational differences among colonial Christians, he even admitted that "there are few surer marks of the reality of religion, than when a man feels himself more joined in spirit to a true holy person of a different denomination, than to an irregular liver of his own." The Synod Letter from 1775 also took for granted the relative unimportance of denominational "circumstantials" to the health of public life, emphasizing instead the moral formation possible by different flavors of Christianity. "The denomination or profession which shall take the most effectual care of the instruction of its members, and maintain its discipline in the fullest vigor, will do the most essential service to the whole body," meaning the public good.[34] While Witherspoon never retreated from his subscription to orthodox Calvinism, when it came to his commendation of religion as a resource for political character, he seemed satisfied with the moral teachings of Christianity rather than insisting on doctrinal orthodoxy.

Another clue to Witherspoon's thinking about the public role of religion may be found in his work on the American revision of the Westminster Confession of Faith. Composed in 1647 as a shared statement of faith for the short-lived alliance between British Puritans and Scottish Presbyterians during the English Civil War, the Westminster Confession reflected the dominant view of church–state relations in post-Reformation Europe. It proposed that the civil authority in a given region had a responsibility to protect and promote good faith and doctrine:

> The civil magistrate may not assume to himself the administration of the Word and Sacraments, or the power of the keys of the kingdom of heaven: yet he hath authority, and it is his duty to take order, that unity and peace be preserved in the Church, that the truth of God be kept pure and entire, that all blasphemies and heresies be suppressed, all corruptions and abuses in worship and discipline prevented or reformed, and all the ordinances of God duly settled, administered, and observed.[35]

Elsewhere, the Confession warned that resistance to civil or church authority "upon the pretense of Christian liberty" was susceptible to punishment by civil authorities.[36]

Well before Witherspoon got to the colonies, American Presbyterians adopted the Westminster Standards as an encapsulation of their doctrine and discipline, but they increasingly ignored the portions of the Confession that awarded the civil magistrate authority over religion. In 1788, the Presbyterian Church in the United States of America explicitly revised the Confession, and nearly all of their changes targeted the discussions of church–state collusion. They removed the phrase that gave civil authority power to punish religious dissent, and they significantly revised the above paragraph from Chapter 23:

> Civil magistrates may not assume to themselves the administration of the Word and sacraments; or the power of the keys of the kingdom of heaven; or, in the least, interfere in matters of faith. Yet, as nursing fathers, it is the duty of civil magistrates to protect the church of our common Lord, without giving the preference to any denomination of Christians above the rest, in such a manner that all ecclesiastical persons whatever shall enjoy the full, free, and unquestioned liberty of discharging every part of their sacred functions, without violence or danger. And, as Jesus Christ hath appointed a regular government and discipline in his church, no law of any commonwealth should interfere with, let, or hinder, the due exercise thereof, among the voluntary members of any denomination of Christians, according to their own profession and belief. It is the duty of civil magistrates to protect the person and good name of all their people, in such an effectual manner as that no person be suffered, either upon pretense of religion or of infidelity, to offer any indignity, violence, abuse, or injury to any other person whatsoever: and to take order, that all religious and ecclesiastical assemblies be held without molestation or disturbance.[37]

Gone was the language of entrusting the health of orthodoxy to civil authority, and in its place was an acknowledgment of religious pluralism and civil government's responsibility to defend religious freedom. Protecting religious liberty was how the "nursing father" of the state could most appropriately encourage piety. The revision of Westminster was (like all matters among Presbyterians) the work of a committee, but it undoubtedly reflected one person's disproportionate influence on the Presbyterians' constitutional convention: John Witherspoon.

Witherspoon believed that freedom of conscience was a natural right, so it should not surprise us that he showed no real appetite for state compulsion of a particular doctrinal agenda. He made clear that, to his mind, religious liberty was the central issue at stake in the Revolution: "There is not a single instance in history in which civil liberty was lost, and religious liberty preserved entire. If therefore we yield up our temporal property, we at the same time deliver the conscience into bondage."[38] Thus he declared in the Synod Letter that "the greatest service which magistrates or persons in authority can do with respect to the religion or morals of the people, is to defend and secure the rights of conscience in the most equal and impartial manner."[39]

For Witherspoon, religious freedom required more than the *tolerance* of religious diversity. Tolerance implied that the freedom of religious dissenters to practice their faith without interference was a practical dispensation by those in authority. Such dispensation theoretically could be revoked at any time, reinforcing the idea that the state holds ultimate power and prerogative over religious matters.[40] Instead, Witherspoon insisted on religious *liberty*, a natural right to religious belief and exercise and the only condition in which people of piety could practice their faith with integrity. Unlike John Locke and more like his Calvinist forefather Roger Williams, Witherspoon believed that everyone has a right to government noninterference in their religion, including groups widely distrusted among the Protestant majority (including Catholics, atheists, and Muslims). As Foster observes, "Witherspoon . . . never endorsed the persecution of atheists, encouraged the toleration of Roman Catholics, treats freedom of conscience as a matter of right, and opposed any form of establishment following his move to America."[41]

Witherspoon's belief in the importance of religion to public character was again on full display in a sermon preached around the conclusion of the war. Witherspoon exhorted his audience to give thanks to God "for the goodness of his providence to the United States of America," and in the sermon he rehearsed some of the ways that God had blessed the republic in the war.[42] The sermon served as a fitting bookend to his oratorical leadership during the war because it followed much the same course as his *Dominion* address. He began with the same disclaimer he offered back in 1776, "that it has never been my practice, for reasons which appear to me to be good, to intermix politics with the ordinary service of the sanctuary."[43] But this day of national celebration, he argued, called for pious attention to the ways that God had ensured their victory. He began with a scriptural exegesis of the doctrine of Providence, followed by a lengthy litany of the signs of Providence in the war, especially the fact that "our most signal successes have generally been when we had the weakest hopes or the greatest fears."[44] He reminded them how low their prospects looked at the end of 1776, only to be turned around by the patriot victory in Princeton. He mentioned their victories against the formidable British fleet despite their reliance on a hodgepodge of private ships. He pointed out the surprising victory over Burgoyne at Saratoga, the table-turning alliance with the French, and of course the leadership of General Washington, "his characteristic qualities . . . so perfectly suited to our wants, that we must consider his appointment to the service, and the continued health which he has been blessed, as a favor from the God of heaven."[45] He saw the Providence of God in the surprising miscalculations of the British army and the persistent unity the colonies maintained throughout the ordeal.

The providential hand of God has blessed the United States, declared Witherspoon, and acknowledging that divine blessing should evoke a corresponding sense of responsibility. So the last third of his sermon emphasizes the importance of piety and virtue to a nation beholden to God for its very existence. "It is our duty to testify our gratitude to God," preached Witherspoon, "by usefulness in our several stations, or in other words by a concern for the glory of God, the public interest of religion, and the good of others."[46] As he first warned on that fast day in 1776, so he cautioned his hearers on this day of thanksgiving in 1782, that "the manners of the people in general, are of the utmost moment to the liability of any civil society. When the body of a people are altogether corrupt in their manners, the government is ripe for dissolution."[47] Civil laws provide moral stability, but even the law cannot ensure the survivability of a nation whose people are not united in a deeper commitment to character. "Civil liberty cannot be long preserved without virtue," he warned. "A republic once equally poised, must either preserve its virtue or lose its liberty, and by some tumultuous revolution, either return to its first principles, or assume a more unhappy form."[48]

"The teachers and rulers of every religious denomination," he said, "are bound mutually to each other, and to the whole society, to watch over the manners of their several members," thus providing communities of character formation that contribute to the common good of the nation as a whole.[49] The encouragement of religion was not just a responsibility of religious leaders, but also an ideal trait in political leaders. "I hope it will be no offence in speaking to a Christian assembly," he said, "if I say that reverence for the name of God, a punctual attendance on the public and private duties of religion, as well as sobriety and purity of conversation, are especially incumbent on those who are honored with places of power and trust."[50] Witherspoon the Calvinist preacher, believed that a Christian sense of duty—to glorify God and serve others—ideally produced civic leaders of good character, and that kind of leadership was essential to the health of the nation. To our ears, it may sound like Witherspoon was implying a religious litmus test for political leadership, and to a certain extent it is true that he considered the ideal civic leader to be one of good Christian piety. As we have seen, however, Witherspoon's encouragement of public piety took for granted a political context in which religious freedom was protected as a natural right. He believed that only a political environment that allowed citizens to practice religion freely would successfully encourage that voluntary practice. Witherspoon's concern was clearly public character, not doctrinal uniformity, and he thought that the public support of voluntary religion was one way to deepen that commitment to character among the people. After all, we must remember what he ultimately considered good public piety to be: a commitment to the glory of God discharged through an investment in the good of others.

It was in this spirit that Witherspoon called for pious public leadership. He urged citizens to select "to places of trust, men of inward principle," arguing that "the people in general ought to have regard to the moral character of those whom they invest with authority, either in the legislative, executive, or judicial branches, such as are so promoted may perceive what is and what will be expected from them."[51] The people ought to select leaders on the basis of their character, leaders who understand that "they are under the strongest obligations to do their utmost to promote religion, sobriety, industry, and every social virtue, among those who are committed to their care." His chief concern for public society was its moral character—a commitment to "order, industry, frugality . . . modesty and self-denial." If the people selected leaders "without personal integrity and private virtue," then they would "soon pay dear for their folly."[52]

"Wisdom and Prudence in the Religious Education of Children"

Witherspoon thought ministers and magistrates, as public servants, played important roles in the cultivation of a publicly beneficial piety, but at the end of his 1782 sermon, he indicated his belief in another significant locus for moral formation: the family. Witherspoon ended that sermon with a call for families to double down in raising their children in good religion, "to sow the seeds which may bear fruit in the next generation." Those seeds he imagined were a "vigor" for the good of the republic, for "whatsoever state among us shall continue to make piety and virtue the standard of public honor, will enjoy the greatest inward peace, the greatest national happiness, and in every outward conflict will discover the greatest constitutional strength."[53]

Within Calvinism, the family was an important site for educational and moral formation. The English and American Puritans, for instance, believed that parents should educate their children as a part of their care for their religious welfare. As Edmund Morgan observed, "The Puritans sought knowledge, therefore, not simply as a polite accomplishment, nor as a means of advancing material welfare, but because salvation was impossible without it."[54] Children would need to be able to read in order to study the Bible and understand Calvinistic doctrines. Reading would also open them to the testimonies of saints who could serve as devotional role models. This kind of religious literacy prepares a child to hear God's call to salvation and enter into a life of true piety. Besides reading and writing, family education included training in moral discipline, and, at the proper age, an exploration of vocation. In good Reformation fashion, the Puritans believed that every person was called to make a specific contribution to society, and that God provided talents and interests to direct a person to their social role. "By thus yoking together in name the business of earning a living and the duties of religion the Puritans emphasized the sacredness of every man's work in the world."[55] The family was the locus for this spiritual, intellectual, moral, and vocational preparation.

Like his Calvinist kin, Witherspoon thought that instruction by parents was key to the cultivation of piety and thus a socially useful morality. In a sermon he preached in 1789 at Old Presbyterian Church in New York City, Witherspoon used the gospel tale of Jesus welcoming children (Mk 10:13–16) as a springboard to talk about the importance of bringing children up in the faith. Youth, he said, was "the fittest and best time for instruction."[56] The instruction he had in mind was religious Catechism, and his primary concern was for the eternal state of children. Witherspoon took Jesus' welcome of children as affirmation "that children may, even in infancy, be the subjects of regenerating grace, and thereby become *really* holy."[57] Pushing back on conventional wisdom that young children are too young to understand religious teachings, Witherspoon argued that piety is like language in that children are capable of picking it up at a young age when they are immersed in it through their parents. If families prioritize religious instruction, "it is not impossible that some of those young children might recollect and be affected with the majesty and condescension of Jesus of Nazareth, and the impression be attended with happy fruits."[58]

While Witherspoon was concerned with creating environments for children to discover a redeemed relationship with God, he also assumed that part of this religious instruction would be moral formation. In his discussion of family matters even more so than with politics, we see Witherspoon's intimate association of religion with moral growth. The "graces of the spiritual life" that he thought children should learn from their parents included "humility, gentleness, teachableness, sincerity, and easiness to be reconciled."[59] All of these virtues Witherspoon judged to be "frequently lost or vitiated by growing years," making the argument all the more compelling to establish them in children as early as possible. Speaking directly to young people in his audience, he asked them to be open to instruction by their parents and other authority figures, to disavow "rude and boisterous passions," and to attend to their relationship with God.

Like other virtue theorists, Witherspoon assumed that moral character needed to be habituated and internalized until it becomes who we are. He argued that the earlier this moral training began, the better, because children are pliable enough to absorb these lessons in a way that will shape the adults they become. Using a botanical analogy, he observed that "you may bend a young twig and make it receive almost any form: but that which has attained maturity, and taken its ply, you will never bring into any other shape than that which it naturally bears. In the same manner those habits which men contract early in life, and are strengthened by time, it is next to impossible to change."[60] He also argued that this habituation is most successful when it is modeled by others, so he charged parents to constantly set an edifying example for their children. "If children naturally form their sentiments, habits and manners, by imitation of others in general, how much more powerful must be the example of parents, who are every hour in their sight, whom nature teaches them, and whom duty obliges them to love, and when it comes recommended by the continual intercourse, and the endearing services that flow from that intimate relation."[61]

Witherspoon provides another look at his vision for the family in two series of letters he wrote on education and marriage respectively, which found themselves to press in *Pennsylvania Magazine* in 1775 and 1776.[62] The overall image of the family he offers is one that is earnest and disciplined but decidedly cooperative and loving. He urged parents to "rejoice" in their children as "the gift of a gracious God." Consistent with his moral philosophy, he declared that "all persons young and old, love liberty," and that it is healthy for children to exercise freedom within the bounds of safety.[63] Let your children "romp and jump about as soon as they are able," he advised. It will make them physically healthier and emotionally happier.[64] Witherspoon recommended, in a sense, that parents let their children be children. He obviously thought it was important for children to learn to respect authority, but he cautioned against parents imposing their authority in a "savage and barbarous" way, which only serves to make children rebellious.[65] Instead, he recommended that parents be firm but compassionate with their children; he discouraged physical punishment, and he recommended that parents be willing to admit to their children when they themselves have been wrong. With this character, parents model the kind of persons their children should want to be. "There is no opposition at all," he wrote, "between parental tenderness and parental authority."[66]

In imagining the ideal family life, Witherspoon had a decidedly nonhierarchical understanding of the relationship between husband and wife. This is a clear deviation from the arc of his Calvinist tradition, where gender hierarchy within the family was a treasured reflection of the orderliness of God's creation. For the Puritans, for instance, women were expected to defer to their husbands' authority in all matters, despite the considerable responsibilities wives often had for the governance of the household (including finances).[67] By contrast, Witherspoon acknowledged that it was far from a given that husbands were always the intellectual or moral superiors to their wives, so he argued that whoever in a relationship has greater gifts in those areas should, in a sense, call the shots. "Wherever there is a great and confessed superiority of understanding on one side, with some good nature on the other, there is domestic peace. It is of little consequence whether the superiority be on the side of the man or woman, provided the ground of it be manifest."[68] In the letter, he anticipated that this advice would open him up to ridicule for encouraging husbands to be "henpeckt," but he argued that there is nothing wrong—and a lot that is right—about men deferring to wives who are clearly wiser than they are. He also observed that women are often better than their husbands at negotiating these differences. Regardless of who is considered to be in charge, he counseled parents to present a united front to their children, suggesting that a "husband and wife ought to conspire and cooperate in everything relating to the education of their children; and if their opinions happen, in any particular, to be different, they ought to examine and settle the matter privately by themselves."[69] A reader cannot help but suspect that these letters reflected Witherspoon's own experience of family life with Elizabeth and their children.

A controversial occurrence (somewhat humorous, in retrospect) during Witherspoon's time in Paisley offers yet another illustration of how important he thought the family was to the formation of public character. One Saturday night in February 1762, a group of young men was caught throwing a raucous dinner party in which they made fun of the sacrament of the Lord's Supper, as well as the minister who would administer it the next day. They invoked the Lord's name in vain, mockingly recited Scripture and Christ's words of institution, and even included a pilfered communion token as a prop in their play-acting. In the eighteenth-century Scottish kirk, ministers distributed tokens to parishioners whose knowledge of the faith and uprightness of life were suitable enough to warrant entrance into the sacrament; no one was invited to the Lord's Supper without a token. One of the young men apparently pocketed one, and after having a bit of fun with it, included it in a note to a local girl, inviting her to join their festivities. (No one knows for sure what the note said, but it was apparently scandalous enough that when the authorities got involved, the boy who sent it made sure to retrieve and destroy it.) Their mockery was so boisterous that it was overheard on the street outside the residence where they gathered, and eventually they were brought before Witherspoon and the church elders to answer for their profanity.

After an investigation, Witherspoon preached a sermon called "Seasonable Advice to Young Persons," in which he made direct commentary on the episode, though he referred to none of the boys by name. Nonetheless, the boys' families soon accused Witherspoon of public slander, and to refute the charges, Witherspoon gave his own written account of the incident to the town council, along with a script of his sermon. Crafted around the image of "walking in the counsel of the ungodly," taken from Psalm 1, Witherspoon's sermon was a dissertation on the insidious and contagious nature of vice, especially among young people. He described vice as the perfect opposite of virtue, a negative character rooted in sinful habits, encouraged by bad company, and fueled by ill-directed affections and passions. Most of the sermon was a warning to the young people of his congregation to avoid vice, but he included plenty of admonition for parents too, imploring them to commit to "wisdom and prudence in the religious education of children." Keep them from "the company and conversation of profane persons," he advised, and provide them good moral examples, for "children are formed by imitation, in their temper and manners."[70] Witherspoon used the sermon to remind parents that the formation of positive moral character is built on the instruction and modeling they receive at home. But he ended the sermon with a message for the broader community. Evidently disappointed that some in the town had failed to take the incident as seriously as he had, he reminded them that

> when vice rears up its head, . . . it is of great importance what treatment it meets from the public. If it passes without notice, we may conclude that corruption hath deeply infected the whole mass. If men are afraid or ashamed to express their indignation at it, we may conclude the conspiracy is formidable; and that the interest of truth and piety is greatly on the decline.[71]

The cultivation of character begins at home, preached Witherspoon, and its absence in the family is a "sensible injury to the public." The home is where intellectual and vocational training began and where religious instruction laid its foundation; thus, the building blocks of public character depended on parents teaching and modeling virtue to their children.

Cultivating Character in "The Union of Piety and Literature"

Witherspoon did not think that moral education ended in the home, of course. Training in moral character also formed the purpose of what we now call higher education, the experience of college. As is the case today, college education was not a universal experience in the colonies in the eighteenth century. Women and non-white males were rarities as students in the colonial colleges, nonentities as graduates, and while institutions made efforts to open the opportunity to young men from lower-class backgrounds, entrance to college remained a luxury predominantly available to the economic elite. Roger Geiger, a historian of American higher education, observes that "the estimated 721 students attending American colleges in 1775 represented 1 percent of an age cohort of white males. A quarter century later, in 1800, about the same proportion attended colleges." These numbers indicate that "as a social institution, the colonial colleges never transcended a narrow social base, and the same conditions persisted well into the nineteenth century."[72]

It is widely assumed that the colonial colleges, many of which were started by religious groups, were mainly concerned with training ministers. In reality, while candidates for the clergy made up the majority of college students in the early generations of Harvard, Yale, and Princeton, the curricula of those institutions (and other colonial colleges to follow) were never designed solely for divinity students. From their start, for instance, Harvard and Yale were institutions meant to train men for civic leadership in Puritan society, including ministers but also lawyers and magistrates. As Charles Dorn notes, a responsibility to the public good was a common conviction in the American colonies, and it informed the popular assumptions about higher education. Colonial colleges existed not just for ministerial training, but "to serve society by producing intellectually enlightened and morally disciplined graduates."[73] Students of the era who pursued higher education no doubt did so as a means of self-improvement, but the cultural notion of self-improvement included increasing one's capacity to contribute constructively to society. "That institutions of higher education . . . promoted this behavior as the ideal for their graduates is hardly surprising, for it fit well with the prevailing social ethos."[74]

The College of New Jersey was no different. Its beginning in 1746 was the inspiration of primarily New Light Presbyterians, who needed an institution to train ministers, one that was more in line with their commitment to Christian revivalism than the stodgy orthodoxy of Yale or the rationalism of Harvard. But it was never meant to be just a seminary, and from the start civic leaders in New Jersey were invested in its success, including financially. The board included laymen as well as ministers, and the charter request committed the school as "a means of raising up men that will be useful in other learned professions [besides the ministry]—ornaments of the State as well as the Church."[75] The student body in the college's first decades was dominated by young men bound for church leadership, but by Witherspoon's time, those students were a distinct minority, outnumbered by young people with political, judicial, and economic aspirations in the new nation.[76] The Princeton curriculum included tracks for divinity students, requiring them to take the higher levels of Hebrew and Greek necessary for biblical exegesis, but the overall course of study was designed to provide the intellectual and moral foundation necessary for public leaders of many sorts. All students were required to study classical literature, English poetry, philosophy, geography, logic, mathematics, and modern science as well as religious texts. Witherspoon himself emphasized the importance of rhetoric, ethics, and aesthetics.[77] With this curriculum, the college would turn out well-rounded and learned men suitable for public service.

The American expectation that liberal arts education was as much about character formation and social usefulness as it was about learning vocational skills was shaped by the Puritan philosophy of Harvard and Yale, but also by the legacy of George Turnbull (1698–1748), the leading voice on liberal education to come out of the Scottish Enlightenment. Educated at Edinburgh, as

Witherspoon later would be, Turnbull was a student of Shaftesbury's writings, a teacher of Thomas Reid, and the most notable Scottish writer on the civic good of education. Influenced by classical writers and Locke's treatise on education, Turnbull's *Observations upon Liberal Education* (1742) offered a vision for liberal education as training for the moral improvement of human beings. All parts of a liberal education, including science and the arts, contributed to advancing the "natural furniture" God has placed in the human mind, including the conscience, reason, imagination, and affections. Turnbull believed that learning contributed to personal liberty, and true liberty positioned people to care for their own happiness and the common good. Turnbull's *Observations* were widely appreciated in Scotland and America, where his most prominent fan was none other than Benjamin Franklin.[78]

Turnbull insisted that education has a moral purpose: "Good education must of necessity be acknowledged to mean proper care to instruct early in the science of happiness and duty, or in the art of judging and acting aright in life." A liberal education prepared "youth for choosing and behaving well in the various conditions, relations, and incidents of life" by acquainting them deeply with the world, the human condition, and our responsibilities in human society.[79]

What does such a curriculum look like? Science was an important part of that curriculum, for Turnbull maintained that curiosity about the world and the human condition is a natural gift from God, to be cultivated and directed toward the good: "One of the chief excellencies of man, and one of the main ends for which he is framed an intelligent creature, is to improve his understanding, and enrich his mind with knowledge, by satisfying this curiosity, and enquiring diligently with them into the reasons and uses of things."[80] He believed that "natural philosophy, or instruction in the wisdom and goodness of the works of creation and providence" (i.e., natural science and mathematics) "is therefore the first step in teaching and recommending virtue."[81] Turnbull also advocated for a priority on history, for teaching history provides examples of virtue and industry.[82] History demonstrates the importance of "the character of the benevolent man, who is capable of discovering readily what the interests of society require at his hands, and steadily pursues the public good, and is therefore not flattered with mere lip-praise, but sincerely and cordially loved and honored," especially when studied in contrast with a historical figure "who, contracted within himself, thinks of no other end but the gratification of some one or other of his own sensual, selfish appetites."[83] The study of history is meant to give students ample examples of these two kinds of character, so that they may be better at distinguishing them and modeling their own behavior after the right one.

Turnbull rejected a preoccupation with classical languages as "the main part of education," preferring studies that could more immediately prepare students "for the duties and business of life."[84] Classical language study was central to eighteenth-century British education, but Turnbull recommended reducing the emphasis on Latin and Greek to make more time for other disciplines he thought contributed to an appropriately broad education. He preferred the inclusion of modern languages to a sole focus on classical ones, allowing that the study of language was obviously important for its communicative function, "as means of getting into acquaintance with the knowledge of those who went before us, or who speak different languages from our own; or for the sake of communicating what we know to others."[85] Language study also cultivates the imagination by improving our facility with images and metaphors and deepening our capacity for analogical thinking, which Turnbull argued is useful for discerning moral responsibility.[86]

Ethics, poetry, and the history of law should be part of liberal education, said Turnbull, as well as politics and government, rhetoric and oratory, and music.[87] Art was important for study because it is a language of moral expression, said Turnbull, reflecting the close relationship between aesthetics and virtue emphasized by Scottish Enlightenment thinkers: "The pursuit of virtue is nothing else but the pursuit of order in the government of the affections, and of order in the frame and government of society"—and virtue as an appreciation for order is cultivated by, among other things, the study of order, beauty, and proportion in nature and the arts.[88] He emphasized the importance of leisure, rest, and exercise in his vision of a liberal education.[89] Interestingly, Turnbull got to religion's role in liberal education somewhat late, but he did include it, primarily for its usefulness to the study of morality.[90]

The moral formation that happens in liberal education requires more than informational accumulation. Liberal education develops in students the dispositions and capacities that make them more responsible, sensitive, useful, and benevolent citizens and leaders. Education should teach young people to entertain "the great and important questions" of our existence.[91] It should habituate interest in the human condition and train students to exercise command over their affections.[92] "Imagination" gives us an appreciation for "truth, proportion and harmony, and is nearly allied to virtue." It allows us to make connections between the things we love and the desires and needs of others.[93]

Curiosity helps us respect the natural law and have a deeper appreciation for the beauty of order.[94] The industry necessary for well-ordered societies and the "self-command" that develops in us "the deliberative habit" of thinking and learning before we make choices are important virtues for public life, since to Turnbull's mind "the foolish choices and pursuits of men, are not so much owing to false judgments, as to the habit of acting precipitantly, and without examining our fancies and appetites."[95] Ultimately, Turnbull believed that the end of education was freedom and happiness, but happiness defined as "a hearty disposition to promote the greater good of mankind, and a large capacity for usefulness in society."[96] Turnbull believed that "the great lesson in life, is that virtue alone is true honour and solid durable happiness," and "it is not till this persuasion is deeply rooted in the heart, that one can be said to be well instructed, educated or formed."[97] Therefore, he wrote, "what ought to be the first and most early care in education [is] the formation of a right temper, by carefully nursing and cherishing good dispositions in young minds."[98]

Given the popularity of Turnbull's take on liberal education, it is reasonable to assume that Witherspoon knew the work, and the similarities between the two men's educational philosophies are more than coincidental. Witherspoon also enjoyed a long friendship with Benjamin Rush, the Princeton alum responsible for finally convincing the Witherspoons to come to America and an advocate in his own right for the civic importance of liberal education. Younger than the college president, it is possible that Rush's convictions regarding education's constructive contribution to the health of a republic developed in part by observing what Witherspoon was doing at the College of New Jersey. Like Witherspoon at Princeton, Rush would go on to recommend a practical college education for students headed to careers in the church, government, law, or commerce, a holistic course of study that included classical studies while also making ample room for work in the English language, science, law, politics, and history. Like Witherspoon, he affirmed the benefit of music and physical recreation for the health and development of young people. With Witherspoon, Rush insisted that a "useful education" must include religion and the study of the Bible as a foundation for character formation, for "religion teacheth him that no man 'liveth to him self,'" though Rush more than Witherspoon allowed that "every religion that reveals the attributes of the Deity, or a future state of rewards and punishments" would do as a source for moral education.[99] One place Rush was ahead of Witherspoon was in his strong advocacy for the education of women. Recognizing that women played important civic roles too, as property stewards, domestic economists, parents, and marital partners, Rush developed an educational plan for women that bore close resemblance to what he recommended for men.[100]

Witherspoon clearly recognized the vocational diversity in the student body he oversaw, and while he (and others) may have lamented the decrease in young men preparing for church ministry during his presidency, he embraced the social charge of preparing future civic leaders for public service. Prepare them he did, for out of Witherspoon's classes came a US president, four continental congressmen, seventeen members of the US Congress, nine governors, an attorney general, and a Supreme Court justice, not to mention numerous ministers, state judges and legislators, and other useful civil servants. Witherspoon improved the curriculum and raised the college's colonial reputation considerably on the strength of his own, by recruiting well beyond the Middle Colonies (many of the graduates important to the Revolution came from the South), and by improving academic resources. He acquired scientific apparatus, including a widely admired orrery, and augmented the library single-handedly by bringing over three hundred books with him from Scotland, including texts from his Scottish philosophical contemporaries.[101]

That Witherspoon acknowledged and embraced the college's civic mission is clear in his benedictory address of 1775. Witherspoon began that address by pointing out how graduation marked the students' entrance into public life, and he commended religious and moral character to them for the public roles they would soon assume. Throughout, he asked them to hold on to the pillars of religion and the liberal arts (or "literature," as he sometimes abbreviated it) to shape their character:

> Your education in a seminary of learning, is only intended to give you the elements and first principles of science, which should whet your appetite for more, and which will enable you to proceed with an assured hope of success. It hath been generally a favorite point with me, to recommend the union of piety and literature, and to guard young persons against the opposite extremes. We see sometimes the pride of unsanctified knowledge do great injury to religion; and on the other hand, we find some persons of real piety, despising human learning, and disgracing the most glorious truths, by a meanness and indecency hardly sufferable in their manner of handling them.[102]

This combination of piety and the liberal arts was something he emphasized at the start of his divinity lectures as well, saying that "piety, without literature, is but little profitable; and learning, without piety, is pernicious to others, and ruinous to the possessor."[103] Speaking about ministers in a way that would extend to all his students, Witherspoon declared that "there is no branch of literature without its use. If it were possible for a minister to be acquainted with every branch of science, he would be more fit for public usefulness. The understanding which God has given us, and every object that he hath presented to it, may be improved to his glory. A truly good man does grow both in holiness and usefulness, by every new discovery that is made to him; therefore learning in general is to be esteemed, acquired, and improved."[104]

Witherspoon insisted that "grammar, mathematics, astronomy, oratory, history, law, physic, poetry, painting, statuary, architecture, music; nay, the subordinate divisions of some of these sciences, such as, anatomy, botany, chemistry, are all of them sufficient to employ a life, to carry them to perfection." He expressed some concern that inordinate focus on any one of these fields could make it likely that a person would be insufficiently learned in the others, so he recommended that "to make what the world calls a learned man, or a great scholar, requires a very general knowledge of authors, books and opinions of all kinds." He reminded his students that the idea of "a great scholar, or a man of erudition" formed in the liberal arts "always carried in it the idea of much reading." Included in his vision of the liberal arts was literacy in the "pretty large circle of the sciences . . . taught in our schools and colleges," which allowed that "something of the principles of the whole may be understood by a person of capacity and diligence." This scientific literacy was essential for public life: "a man may not be a mathematician or an astronomer, and yet understand something of the true system of the universe. He may understand many sciences so far as to comprehend the reasoning of those more deeply skilled."[105]

A Princeton education, then, was not restricted to the training of ministers, and it was more than a chance to cultivate the self in some kind of humanistic individualism. Witherspoon led the College of New Jersey with the conviction that higher education had a public and social purpose. That public purpose was a moral mission, in at least two senses. First, Witherspoon thought that he was preparing students to serve society with their skills, talents, and knowledge, and that doing so allowed them to live into their specific obligations to general benevolence. If, as we have seen, moral character for Witherspoon consisted largely in the discharge of one's duties to the good of others and the common good, then preparing students to serve society rather than just themselves was an education in benevolence. In this way, Witherspoon reflected his Calvinistic understanding of vocation.[106] The Puritan sense of vocation was the axis of education at both Harvard and Yale (at least in their early days), and Witherspoon thought of a Princeton education in that same way.

Witherspoon understood the moral mission of college in a second way, too. Besides vocational preparation, college was an opportunity to cultivate and deepen the virtues that make a person committed to the responsibilities of benevolence. The study of human nature allowed students to be both practical and empathetic in their relationships with others in society. Investment in languages deepened one's capacity for effective communication. An appreciation for art, literature, and aesthetics contributed to a citizen's appreciation for beauty and virtue. The development of the imagination improved one's ability to connect and communicate across experiential differences. The study of rhetoric depended on and deepened the piety of a future minister and prepared him to productively appeal to experience, simplicity in expression, productive passion, and precision in preaching and teaching.[107] Education in law required and encouraged the habituation of integrity: "There can be no doubt that integrity is the first and most important character of a man, be his profession what it will; but I have mentioned it here because there are many not so sensible of the importance of it in the profession of the law, and think it is necessary to make a good man, but not a good lawyer."[108] Preparation for a public career in the law also required intellectual nimbleness and interpersonal "delicacy," as well as "extensive knowledge in the arts and sciences, in history and in the laws."[109] Similarly, future legislators would need the dignity and discernment encouraged by a liberal arts education imbued with Christian morality, but also "a necessity of knowledge of the most liberal kind, that is, the knowledge of men and manners, of history, and of human nature."[110]

Witherspoon knew that neither knowledge nor aesthetic appreciation alone substituted for virtue. He believed that "education and manner have a sensible effect upon men in general," but he also acknowledged that learning can be used "by men of vicious disposition."[111] He admitted that a "bad man" can marshal the advantages that education gives him for sinister ends, and that when that happens, it "is unspeakably pernicious, and that very thing has sometimes made weak people against learning."[112] He rejected the suspicion of education based on its openness to abuse, however, arguing that education can be directed toward public benefit "by assisting the good in the cultivation of their powers." When intellectual and aesthetic education is complemented by character formation, "then the same weapons will be used in defense of truth and virtue, with much greater advantage, than they can be in support of falsehood and vice."[113] Knowledge and aesthetic appreciation inform and deepen character, thought Witherspoon, but they alone do not create it.

Another indication of Witherspoon's conviction that it takes character to learn character occurs in an amusing moment in his first rhetoric lecture, where Witherspoon betrayed a preference for students of moderate innate intelligence over natural genius. Education can fail to produce much yield in someone with very limited intellectual capacity, he confessed, but geniuses seldom make the best students either. "A very great genius," he commented, "is often like a very fine flower, to be wondered at, but of little service either for food or medicine. A very great genius is also often accompanied with certain irregularities, so that we only consider with regret, what he might have been, if the lively sallies of his imagination had been reined in a little, and kept under the direction of sober judgment."[114] Students of great natural talent can be idiosyncratic, unfocused, and less useful than students of moderate ability who have just enough intelligence to be motivated to make themselves better by the application of industry. "In the middle regions of genius, there are often to be found those who reap the greatest benefit from education and study. They improve their powers by exercise and it is surprising to think what advances are to be made by the force of resolution and application."[115] One wonders if Witherspoon was describing himself in this category. If so, his public contributions proved his own point, that "persons of the middle degrees of capacity, do also, perhaps generally, fill the most useful and important stations in human life."

Beyond the curriculum, Witherspoon believed that residency at the college was an exercise in moral education, as students (ideally, at least) would discipline their behavior by living cooperatively with each other and under the watchful eye of their tutors and president.[116] Alas, this formative function of residential education was not as effective as Witherspoon might have liked, as reflected in amusing disciplinary anecdotes biographers and historians have collected from his time as president.[117] But the students did learn valuable intellectual and moral skills while living, learning, and debating together. As Princeton historian Thomas Jefferson Wertenbaker put it,

> The Princeton undergraduate of the eighteenth century had his regular allotment of the classics, philosophy, and science and had to do his share of memorizing, but more important for his future were the discussions with fellow students and instructors over this phase of his work or that, his debates or his orations. It was

this which gave him practice in exercising his creative ability. In after years when the graduate, now in his state legislature, or a justice of the supreme court, or a member of his state constitutional convention, was called upon to solve some important problem, he not only could draw upon the experience of other ages but could think the matter out for himself.[118]

The social contribution of his former students bears out the success of President Witherspoon's vision for liberal education.

As virtue theorists remind us, virtue is taught, practiced, and habituated in formative communities. Witherspoon believed that the family, church, and colleges all served as communities of moral formation, schools of character on which a healthy civil society depended for citizens and leaders of virtue. Only with investment in public character, he predicted, would a benevolent nation emerge from the fires of revolution and war.

Notes

1 Witherspoon, DPPM, *Works*, III:31.
2 Witherspoon, DPPM, *Works*, III:41.
3 Witherspoon, DPPM, *Works*, III:45.
4 Witherspoon, "Letter from the Synod of New-York and Philadelphia," in *Works*, III:9–14.
5 Witherspoon, DPPM, *Works*, III:40.
6 Calvin, *Institutes*, IV.20.9, 1495.
7 Calvin, *Institutes*, IV.20.2, 1487.
8 As quoted in Irwin H. Polishook, *Roger Williams, John Cotton, and Religious Freedom: A Controversy in New and Old England* (Prentice-Hall, 1967), 98.
9 Polishook, *Religious Freedom*, 74.
10 *On Religious Liberty*, 130.
11 *On Religious Liberty*, 133.
12 John Witte, Jr. and Joel A. Nichols, *Religion and the American Constitutional Experiment*, 4th ed. (Oxford University Press, 2016), 37.
13 Witte and Nichols, *Constitutional Experiment*, 34–5.
14 James Madison, "Memorial and Remonstrance against Religious Assessments, [ca. 20 June] 1785," *Founders Online*, National Archives, https://founders.archives.gov/documents/Madison/01-08-02-0163. [Original source: *The Papers of James Madison*, vol. 8, *10 March 1784—28 March 1786*, ed. Robert A. Rutland and William M. E. Rachal. The University of Chicago Press, 1973, 295–306.]

15 As quoted in Frank Lambert, *The Founding Fathers and the Place of Religion in America* (Princeton University Press, 2003), 207–8.
16 For a useful summary of the struggle for disestablishment in Virginia, see Lambert, *Founding Fathers*, 225–35.
17 Lambert, *Founding Fathers*, 221–3.
18 Lambert, *Founding Fathers*, 225.
19 Witherspoon, LMP, Lecture XIV, *Works*, III:447.
20 Michael Sullivan, "John Witherspoon: Religious Educator to the American Founding Generation," *Religious Education* 117:1 (2022), 85.
21 Witherspoon, LMP, Lecture XIV, *Works*, III:449.
22 Sullivan, "John Witherspoon: Religious Educator," 81–2.
23 James Foster, "Of the Civil Magistrate: John Witherspoon's Doubly Religious Toleration," *Global Intellectual History* 5:2 (2020), 271.
24 Witherspoon, LMP, Lecture XIV, *Works*, III:448.
25 Witherspoon, Sermon 40, *Works*, II:470.
26 Witherspoon, Sermon 40, *Works*, II:471.
27 Witherspoon, Sermon 40, *Works*, II:473.
28 Witherspoon, Sermon 40, *Works*, II:472.
29 Witherspoon, Sermon 40, *Works*, II:462.
30 Witherspoon, Sermon 40, *Works*, II:476.
31 Foster, "Civil Magistrate," 267.
32 Witherspoon, DPPM, *Works*, III:45.
33 Witherspoon, DPPM, *Works*, III:41.
34 Witherspoon, Letter from the Synod of New-York and Philadelphia, *Works*, III:13.
35 "Westminster Confession of Faith (1647)," chapter XXIII, in *Creeds of the Churches: A Reader in Christian Doctrine from the Bible to the Present*, 3rd ed., ed. John H. Leith (John Knox Press, 1982), 220.
36 Leith, *Creeds of the Churches*, 216.
37 "The Constitution of the Presbyterian Church in the United States of America" (Philadelphia, PA: Thomas Bradford, 1789), Internet Archive, http://archive.org/details/const00pres.
38 Witherspoon, DPPM, *Works*, III:36.
39 Witherspoon, Letter from the Synod of New-York and Philadelphia, *Works*, III:13.
40 On this point, he agreed with Thomas Paine's insistence that "toleration is not the opposite of intoleration, but is the counterfeit of it. Both are despotisms. The one assumes to itself the right of withholding liberty of conscience, and the other of granting it." Thomas Paine, *The Rights of Man* as quoted in Witte and Nichols, *Constitutional Experiment*, 33.

41 Foster, "Civil Magistrate," 273.
42 John Witherspoon, Sermon 45: Delivered at a Public Thanksgiving after Peace, *Works*, III:61–84.
43 Witherspoon, Sermon 45, *Works*, III:61.
44 Witherspoon, Sermon 45, *Works*, III:66.
45 Witherspoon, Sermon 45, *Works*, III:67.
46 Witherspoon, Sermon 45, *Works*, III:79.
47 Witherspoon, Sermon 45, *Works*, III:81.
48 Witherspoon, Sermon 45, *Works*, III:81.
49 Witherspoon, Sermon 45, *Works*, III:81.
50 Witherspoon, Sermon 45, *Works*, III:83.
51 Witherspoon, Sermon 45, *Works*, III:82.
52 Witherspoon, Sermon 45, *Works*, III:82.
53 Witherspoon, Sermon 45, *Works*, III:84.
54 Edmund S. Morgan, *The Puritan Family: Religion and Domestic Relations in Seventeenth-Century New England* (Harper & Row, 1966), 89.
55 Morgan, *Puritan Family*, 71.
56 John Witherspoon, Sermon 31: On the Religious Education of Children, *Works*, II:249–62.
57 Witherspoon, Sermon 31, *Works*, II:251.
58 Witherspoon, Sermon 31, *Works*, II:252.
59 Witherspoon, Sermon 31, *Works*, II:255.
60 Witherspoon, Sermon 31, *Works*, II:254.
61 Witherspoon, Sermon 31, *Works*, II:258.
62 John Witherspoon, *Letters on Education*, *Works*, IV:125–59; *Letters on Marriage*, *Works*, IV:159–82.
63 Witherspoon, *Letters on Education*, *Works*, IV:126.
64 Witherspoon, *Letters on Education*, *Works*, IV:127.
65 Witherspoon, *Letters on Education*, *Works*, IV:133.
66 Witherspoon, *Letters on Education*, *Works*, IV:138.
67 Morgan, *Puritan Family*, 43–5.
68 Witherspoon, *Letters on Marriage*, *Works*, IV:167.
69 Witherspoon, *Letters on Education*, *Works*, IV:125.
70 Witherspoon, Sermon 41, *Works*, II:502–3.
71 Witherspoon, Sermon 41, *Works*, II:505.
72 Roger L. Geiger, *The History of American Higher Education: Learning and Culture from the Founding to World War II* (Princeton University Press, 2015), 76.
73 Charles Dorn, *For the Common Good: A New History of Higher Education in America* (Cornell University Press, 2017), 17. Dorn here is talking specifically

about Bowdoin College, but he argues that Bowdoin's establishment was typical of colonial and early republic institutions.

74 Dorn, *Common Good*, 28. See also Geiger, *American Higher Education*, 90–1.
75 As cited in Thomas Jefferson Wertenbaker, *Princeton: 1746–1896* (Princeton University Press, 1946), 19.
76 George Marsden notes that during Witherspoon's presidency, the proportion of Princeton graduates heading into the ministry fell from about one in two to one in eight. See *The Soul of the American University Revisited: From Protestant to Postsecular* (Oxford University Press, 2021), 59–60.
77 Wertenbaker, *Princeton*, 92–102.
78 For this summary of Turnbull importance, I am indebted to Terrence O. Moore's introduction of his edition of *Observations upon Liberal Education* (Liberty Fund, 2003), xi–xviii.
79 Turnbull, *Observations*, 171.
80 Turnbull, *Observations*, 182.
81 Turnbull, *Observations*, 326. Turnbull reflected the deep investment in science characteristic of the Scottish Enlightenment, which Witherspoon also inherited.
82 Turnbull, *Observations*, 331.
83 Turnbull, *Observations*, 175.
84 Turnbull, *Observations*, 243.
85 Turnbull, *Observations*, 323.
86 Turnbull, *Observations*, 247–8.
87 Turnbull, *Observations*, 332–6, 373, 401.
88 Turnbull, *Observations*, 382. See also 194.
89 Turnbull, *Observations*, 293–7.
90 Turnbull, *Observations*, 350–1.
91 Turnbull, *Observations*, 173.
92 Turnbull, *Observations*, 174–5.
93 Turnbull, *Observations*, 402–3.
94 Turnbull, *Observations*, 188.
95 Turnbull, *Observations*, 185, 191–2.
96 Turnbull, *Observations*, 175.
97 Turnbull, *Observations*, 363.
98 Turnbull, *Observations*, 206. "For whatever is the occasion or means of more affectionately uniting a rational creature to his part of society, and causes him to prosecute the public good, or interest of his species with more zeal and affection than ordinary, is undoubtedly the cause of more than ordinary virtue in such a person." (325)

99 "A Plan for the Establishment of Public Schools and the Diffusion of Knowledge in Pennsylvania; to Which Are Added, Thoughts upon the Mode of Education Proper in a Republic" (Philadelphia, PA: Thomas Dobson, 1786).
100 "Thoughts upon Female Education, Accommodated to the Present State of Society, Manners, and Government, in the United States of America. Addressed to the Visitors of the Young Ladies Academy in Philadelphia, 28th July 1787, at the Close of the Quarterly Examination, by Benjamin Rush, M.D.," *The Universal Asylum and the Columbian Magazine*, April 1790 (Philadelphia), 209–13; May 1790, 288–92.
101 Marsden, *Soul of the American University*, 73.
102 Witherspoon, *An Address to the Students of the Senior Class*, *Works*, III:104.
103 Witherspoon, LD, Lecture I, *Works*, IV:11.
104 Witherspoon, LD, Lecture II, *Works*, IV:16.
105 Witherspoon, LD, Lecture II, *Works*, IV:17.
106 See Chapter 1.
107 For the connections between the liberal arts and the cultivation of public virtues of benevolence, see Witherspoon's *Lectures on Eloquence*, especially Lectures XIV–XVI.
108 Witherspoon, LE, Lecture XV, *Works*, III:569.
109 Witherspoon, LE, Lecture XV, *Works*, III:571.
110 Witherspoon, LE, Lecture XV, *Works*, III:574.
111 Witherspoon, LE, Lecture VI, *Works*, III:514.
112 Witherspoon, LE, Introduction, *Works*, III:475.
113 Witherspoon, LE, Introduction, *Works*, III:475.
114 Witherspoon, LE, Introduction, *Works*, III:481.
115 Witherspoon, LE, Introduction, *Works*, III:481.
116 For more on the role of residential living in the overall public purpose of colonial colleges, see Dorn, *Common Good*, 18–19.
117 See for instance, Wertenbaker, *Princeton*, 76–7.
118 Wertenbaker, *Princeton*, 117.

5

The Character of Dissent

> We hold these truths to be self-evident, that all men are created equal, that they are endowed by their Creator with certain unalienable Rights, that among these are Life, Liberty and the pursuit of Happiness.—That to secure these rights, Governments are instituted among Men, deriving their just powers from the consent of the governed,—That whenever any Form of Government becomes destructive of these ends, it is the Right of the People to alter or abolish it, and to institute new Government, laying its foundation on such principles and organizing its powers in such form, as to them shall seem most likely to effect their Safety and Happiness.
> —The Declaration of Independence (1776)

In July 1776, John Witherspoon lent his vote to the Declaration of Independence from Britain.[1] The colonies had determined "to dissolve the political bands which have connected them" out of a perception that the mother country had consistently abused the rights "to which the Laws of Nature and of Nature's God entitle them." The Declaration provided the reasons for this assessment, citing a litany of transgressions that included ignoring the colonies' right to self-rule, representation, freedom in commerce, and access to due process. Witherspoon's signature on the Declaration, and his willingness to advocate publicly for independence in the months leading up to its dissemination, signaled his full agreement with the charges the colonies leveled against Britain. The Declaration's preamble, steeped in convictions about the purposes of government and the people's recourse when it fails them, closely aligned with Witherspoon's understanding of good political character. The cultivation of other-regarding virtues and the defense of natural rights were essential responsibilities of government, he believed, and when government abdicated its obligations, the same rights and virtues that characterized a healthy society could justify dissent, resistance, and even revolution.

Good Government

Like most of his fellow revolutionaries, Witherspoon believed that the legitimacy of government was rooted in popular consent and the idea of a social compact. Both of these concepts had been matters of debate among British intellectuals and politicians for at least a century. Thomas Hobbes and John Locke, for instance, believed that human society is based on a hypothetical social contract that compensates for deficiencies in the so-called state of nature, but they disagreed over what that compensation entails. For Hobbes, the state of nature is one of brutality, what Hobbes famously described as "war of all against all," where people represent threats to the lives and property of others. The social contract for Hobbes represented a deal between citizens and the leaders who ruled over them; citizens agreed to restrict their rights in exchange for protection from the worst inclinations of their neighbors.[2] Partially in response to Hobbes, Locke spun a more positive view of government, asserting that the state of nature was one of individual freedom rather than incessant war, and that government's responsibility was to protect citizens' rights and liberties rooted in the claims of the natural state. Protection required citizens to compromise some of their freedoms in the name of social cooperation and order, but for Locke, the ultimate purpose of government was the constructive support of basic freedoms like life, liberty, and property, in contrast to Hobbes' darker vision of civil magistrates as a check on human beings' penchant for violence.

On the subject of a social contract, Scottish political philosophers of the eighteenth century were all, one way or another, in conversation with Hobbes and Locke. Some of them, like David Hume, rejected the Lockean idea of a contract rooted in a state of nature, judging it excessively conceptual and divorced from the historical reality of human societies. Others, like Adam Ferguson, utilized the idea of a social compact not as an invention to protect some fundamental individualism, but as a reflection of the inherently social nature of humanity. For many Scottish intellectuals, one of the natural characteristics of the human species is that we desire community and relationships, something Locke seemed to imply was a compromise to our more inherent atomistic rationality. According to the Scots, the responsibility of government was to ensure conditions in which our social nature can survive and flourish.[3]

Related to the concept of a social contract is the notion of popular consent as the basis for government's legitimacy. This too was a contested idea in the seventeenth and eighteenth centuries. A long-standing theological position, rooted at least as far back as the medieval period, held that rulers derived their authority from God. A king is God's representative in the political realm, and his responsibility is to rule according to God's law. Of course, one corollary to this understanding of political power is that civil resistance is both a political crime and a religious sin because it challenges God's authority. In the seventeenth century, Puritan theologians and British lawyers argued that civil authority is rooted not in direct divine ordination but in popular consent. For the Puritans, this was not to deny the religious root of political authority, but it was to insist that the conduit of God's endorsement of a political leader was the will of the people. God communicated his choice of rulers through the consent of the people, and sometimes he expressed his displeasure with civil magistrates by removing popular support. With this understanding of popular consent as the measure of a ruler's legitimacy, political resistance need not necessarily be understood as a theological transgression. Sometimes the popular rejection of a leader may in fact be the means by which God applies a correction to rulers who have strayed from God's intentions.[4]

Witherspoon's views on government were shaped by these theological and philosophical debates, and in fact, he covered the range of views in his lectures on moral philosophy. In his tenth philosophical lecture, he provided an overview of the disagreements about the state of nature—whether there ever was such a thing, whether in our most natural state we are first and foremost individuals or inherently social, and whether avoidance of violence or the maximization of cooperation is the chief gain of the social contract. As he often did, Witherspoon found truth somewhere in the compromise of disparate positions. He agreed with Scottish philosophers that human beings are inherently social, or as he put it, "that our happiness and the improvement of our powers are only to be had in society."[5] He believed that human beings were created to naturally need relationships with other people, and his theological anthropology allowed him to declare confidently that "there is a real good-will and benevolence to others" built into us "as it is the work of God." The purpose of human society is to cultivate this cooperative spirit, but at the same time, Witherspoon's Calvinist subscription to the reality of sin inclined him to find truth in Hobbes' pessimism. Like Hobbes, he acknowledged that societies need governments that will protect individuals and the collective against the more destructive tendencies of other members. But Witherspoon insisted that government's social function included both the provision of protection and the cultivation of conditions necessary for citizens to flourish together.

His commitment to the negative and positive responsibilities of government, providing protection and encouraging cooperation, led him directly to a discussion of rights. Similar to Locke, Witherspoon argued that natural rights are a reflection of our natural state, and that a proper function of government is to cultivate respect for rights among its citizens. Our rights are also what is most in need of protection from others, so Witherspoon counted the defense of rights among the duties of government. The result is a vision of the social contract rooted in the concept of human rights. We agree to some limits on our rights in the social compact in order to protect most of them, and in fact, government facilitates the expansion of our rights by establishing a peaceful and cooperative environment in which human beings can live and work together. Because of the importance of natural God-given rights to Witherspoon's understanding of us as human beings, and because government both protects our rights and encourages in us a respect for others' rights, he ultimately rejected Hobbes's "contempt" for the idea of a constructive social compact. For Witherspoon, a society was "an association or compact of any number of persons, to deliver up or abridge some part of their natural rights, in order to have the strength of the united body, to protect the remaining, and to bestow others."[6]

Witherspoon believed that the social compact was rooted in the idea of consent, though he acknowledged that consent is often tacit rather than explicitly expressed by citizens. We indicate our consent to be a member of a society by remaining in it. That tacit consent includes our agreement to the "particular plan of government" under which we live, as well as the mutual obligation of subjects and rulers to one another.[7] Witherspoon argued that the human impulse to revolt from oppressive government confirms that government's legitimacy is rooted in popular consent: "When persons believe themselves upon the whole, rather oppressed than protected in any society, they think they are at liberty, either to rebel against it, or fly from it; which plainly implies that their being subject to it, arose from a tacit consent."[8] Subject and ruler understand themselves in a relationship of moral obligation that has the empowerment of social cooperation, the protection of rights, and the furthering of the common good as its ends: "The public good has always been the real aim of the people in general, in forming and entering into any society."[9]

For Witherspoon, then, the role of government included the protection of natural rights, the maintenance of law and public order, and the furtherance of the public good. But government had one additional purpose: the encouragement of political character among its citizens. "Good laws may hold the rotten bark some longer together," Witherspoon preached in a sermon at the war's end, "but in a little time all laws must give way to the tide of popular opinion, and be laid prostrate under universal practice."[10] Legal restrictions alone would never ensure the health and well-being of society; people will not commit to the common good just because of the threat of sanction. The parameters of law had to be coupled with the constructive cultivation of character in the people for the new nation to survive. "The moral causes of the prosperity of a country," he once wrote, "are almost infinitely more powerful than those that are only occasional." Ensuring the character of the nation was among the most fundamental duties of government, and "the moral causes arise from the nature of government, including the administration of justice, liberty of conscience, [and] the partition of property."[11] In its commitment to protecting rights and encouraging general benevolence, government can habituate a culture of character in its citizens.

Witherspoon also believed that virtuous leadership helped that project. In that sermon he preached near the end of the Revolutionary War, Witherspoon reminded his audience that "civil liberty cannot be long preserved without virtue." He went on to argue that the duty to cultivate virtue fell foremost on political leaders. "Those who are vested with civil authority," he preached, "ought with much care, to promote religion and good morals among all under their government."[12] The leaders of our government "are under the strongest obligation to do their utmost to promote religion, sobriety, industry, and every social virtue, among those who are committed to their care."[13] A healthy society both depends upon and promotes general benevolence and a respect for rights, he said, and cultivating that social commitment to character is among the chief responsibilities of political leadership.

In turn, citizens ought to entrust positions in government only to those who, in their personal constitution, are able to take on this responsibility. It was important for the people "to choose to places of trust, men of inward principle, justified by exemplary conversation." To Witherspoon, this was one of the major responsibilities of a society based on the authority of popular consent, that "the people in general ought to have regard to the moral character of those whom they invest with authority, either in the legislative, executive or judicial branches." Select for office those whose speech and manner of living reflect a healthy moral disposition, he warned, for "those therefore who pay no regard to religion and sobriety, in the persons whom they send to the legislature of any state, are guilty of the greatest absurdity, and will soon pay dear for their folly. Let a man's zeal, profession, or even principles as to political measures, be what they will, if he is without personal integrity and private virtue as a man, he is not to be trusted."[14] Witherspoon cautioned that character was even more important than political priorities in the selection of public leadership. "Whatsoever state among us shall continue to make piety and virtue the standard of public honor, will enjoy the greatest inward peace, the greatest national happiness, and in every outward conflict will discover the greatest constitutional strength."

When Witherspoon appealed to character as a public priority or a necessary criterion for political leadership, he often referenced piety as well, but as we have seen, this reflected more his assumption that religion contributed constructively to the morality of citizens than any desire for the state establishment of the Christian religion. Witherspoon was deeply committed to religious liberty, but he thought the encouragement of *voluntary* religion was the way religion could contribute to social morality. Citing a commitment to religious liberty, he appealed to religious institutions to serve the project of a virtuous society, arguing that the responsibility to contribute to public morality was an obligation that religious communities assumed in a social compact that guaranteed their liberty: "The teachers and rulers of every religious denomination, are bound mutually to each other, and to the whole society, to watch over the manner of their several members."[15] Religious communities are schools of virtue, he believed, and the cultivation of character among their adherents helped make those adherents moral members of the public, but religion would serve this purpose only if its practice remained voluntary.

Witherspoon developed his views on political government by studying British philosophers, but his political philosophy also reflected his Calvinist theological commitments, nowhere more obviously than in his synthesis of Scottish views of human nature and Hobbesian concerns about human depravity. As we have seen, Witherspoon's theological anthropology held together the stereotypical Calvinist realism about sin, especially as it manifests in tendencies toward selfishness and violence, with a cautious optimism regarding the potential of social cooperation that also has some precedent in Calvinism (particularly in someone like Roger Williams). This balance was reflected in his views on the purposes and responsibilities of government; it also influenced his understanding of the ideal structure of government. In his twelfth philosophical lecture, Witherspoon rehearsed the strengths and weaknesses of monarchy, aristocracy, and pure democracy. Like others before him, he recognized that monarchy brought a certain efficiency to government, but that efficiency also made it the likeliest to corrupt; the road from monarchy to tyranny was a short and direct route, he thought. A healthy aristocracy promised to put the ablest persons in positions of leadership, but it risked oligarchical hoarding and abuses of power. True democracy empowered the people themselves, the basis for government's legitimacy, but it also brought with it the very real threat of anarchy, as every citizen (even those of nefarious intent or modest intellect) would hold potential veto over measures to maintain law and order.

His overview of the advantages and disadvantages of each type of government was conventional enough, but more notable was the preference he signaled for a mixed form of government. Witherspoon's reasons for preferring mixed government were quintessentially Calvinist.[16] As much as he emphasized the societal importance of character among citizens and leaders, Witherspoon was not so idealistic to think that the cultivation of public virtue ensured social stability. Human beings are a mixture of benevolence and selfishness, cooperation and barbarity, so a form of government that internalizes checks and balances would accentuate the benefits of each type of government and mitigate their corruption. Witherspoon declared that "it is of consequence to have as much virtue among the particular members of a community as possible; but it is folly to expect that a state should be upheld by integrity in all who have a share in managing it. They must be so balanced, that when every one draws to his own interest and inclination, there may be an over poise upon the whole."[17] This appreciation for checks and balances, familiar to us now in the vernacular of American politics, was for Witherspoon rooted in his Calvinist assumptions about the constructive potential and the destructive tendencies simultaneously at home in the human condition.

Witherspoon's opinions about forms of government had a practical effect on his contribution to the structure of the new republic. He was a member of Congress in 1776 and 1777 during the debates over the kind of government that would bind the colonies together. What resulted from that first attempt was the Articles of Confederation, an arrangement that prioritized state power and committed the states to little more than a "league of friendship." By the end of the war, many prominent Americans recognized the weaknesses of a confederation that did not offer centralized authority to regulate interstate commerce, effectively raise taxes, or mount a realistic common defense.[18] Witherspoon was among those who believed something more was needed than the Articles offered. What was needed was a conception of government that would commit the states to a *collective* good. The Articles of Confederation, he feared, represented too little protection from the self-interest that would inevitably pit the states against one another. Without a commitment to a common national good, Witherspoon feared that the states would not do the substantial work of cultivating connective benevolence and mutual obligation. The eventual need for a constitutional do-over, one that began with a commitment by and to "We the People," seemed to bear out the wisdom in his skepticism.[19]

At the same time, Witherspoon's Calvinist moral realism made him believe that some connection between the states was better than none, so he eventually signed the Articles on behalf of New Jersey. In fact, in response to those who argued against the Articles because of their imperfection, he insisted that a government based on a minimal balance of power was better than leaving the states to nothing more than a destructive competition of interests. During the congressional debate, Witherspoon gave a speech on the proposed Articles in which he defended the effort, even while he privately harbored concerns that the proposed government was not strong enough to draw the states together in a relationship of mutual obligation. He stated that he was "none of those who either deny or conceal the depravity of human nature," and yet he implored his fellow members to endorse the proposed confederation rather than holding out indefinitely for a more perfect plan. Referring to the models offered by Switzerland and the Netherlands, Witherspoon assured his audience that a "well planned confederacy among the state of America, may hand down the blessings of peace and public order to many generations." He acknowledged that the Articles of Confederation may not be perfect, but he asked, "shall we establish nothing good, because we know it cannot be eternal?"

Of course, the confederation pulled up quite short of an eternal form of American government, and by 1787 the Constitutional Convention was looking for a new-and-improved plan for uniting the states of America. What began as an attempt to augment the Articles soon evolved into the development of a replacement. Because of other commitments to Princeton and to the nascent Presbyterian Church in America, Witherspoon could not participate in this effort, but the chief architect of the new Constitution did end up being a former pupil, James Madison. Unsurprisingly, given the source of his moral and political education, Madison oversaw the construction of a federal system that had a Witherspoon-like anthropology at its core, at once encouraging more benevolent cooperation than the Articles had, while incorporating checks and balances on citizens' and leaders' baser inclinations. It committed the states to a deeper level of cooperation in the project to form "a more perfect Union, establish Justice, insure domestic Tranquility, provide for the common defence, promote the general Welfare, and secure the Blessings of Liberty to ourselves and our Posterity." It made them mutually responsible to each other for the economic and military good of the whole. And it strengthened the central government to guard against regional rivalries and encourage a sense of collective identity.

The effect of Witherspoon on the architect of the Constitution is evident in several ways, including Madison's moral anthropology and the seriousness with which he took freedom of conscience.[20] Ralph Ketcham has argued that Christian religion was more important to Madison than his reputation sometimes allows, especially when we lump him together with his more blatantly unorthodox fellow Virginian, Thomas Jefferson. In reality, Madison purposely lingered in Princeton after his graduation to continue studies in religion and moral philosophy with Witherspoon, and during the early 1770s, he undertook a concerted study of biblical theology on his own. Evidence suggests that he was far from a theological traditionalist, but he took religion seriously, as his studies and his correspondence attest, and a number of Witherspoon's theological priorities may have rubbed off on him. Madison's zealous commitment to religious liberty, exemplified in his defense of the Virginia Bill Establishing Religious Freedom and his eventual leadership on the First Amendment, looks a lot like Witherspoon's priority on the same. And Witherspoon's moral anthropology, a mixture of cautious optimism in human beings' moral potential and realistic concern to rein in our most antisocial tendencies, also animated Madison's approach to politics and government. As Ketcham puts it, "Madison was thoroughly indoctrinated with a sense of awareness of an orderly, benevolent universe. Yet, his tough assessment of the frailty of man's nature, the finiteness of human understanding, and the occasional inclination of the world to be simply 'out of joint,' would have warmed the heart of Presbyterian John Witherspoon."[21] Actually, both parts of Madison's worldview would have resonated with Witherspoon, and as a result, his former teacher was much happier with Madison's second constitutional effort than he ever was with the Articles that preceded it.[22]

Good Resistance

Witherspoon believed that society was a cooperative venture in which people come together and give up some of their individual freedom in exchange for mutual protection, social connection, and an increase in collective flourishing.

Civil government was good when it offered protection for human rights, the maintenance of law and order, and an encouragement of general benevolence and the common good. When the government failed to deliver on these duties, citizens were within their rights to demand reform, and if leaders failed to adequately address the public's grievances, resistance and rebellion could be justified.

In its justification of rebellion, the Declaration of Independence acknowledged that "prudence, indeed, will dictate that Governments long established should not be changed for light and transient causes," and in his moral philosophy lectures, Witherspoon offered similar warnings. He cautioned his students that "resistance to the supreme power . . . is subverting the society altogether, and is not to be attempted till the government is so corrupt that anarchy and the uncertainty of a new settlement is preferable to the continuance of it."[23] For a while, Witherspoon (like many of his fellow colonists) may have hoped to find a diplomatic resolution to the impositions of the British government. Before Witherspoon emigrated from Scotland, Americans were already deeply concerned that the Sugar Act of 1764 and the Stamp Act of 1765 represented bold encroachments on the colonists' presumptions of self-government. Once he arrived in Princeton, Witherspoon heard the rumors that King George might send an Anglican bishop to American soil to enforce the official religion, raising serious concerns for the liberties of Witherspoon's Presbyterians and any other colonists who did not belong to the Church of England.[24] Nonetheless, a year before the Declaration, Witherspoon was still holding out for a solution short of war, if the tone of the Synod Letter he authored to his fellow Presbyterians that summer is an accurate indication of his views at that time.

A series of violent skirmishes in Lexington, Concord, Ticonderoga, and Bunker Hill, however, made independence a more popular option among Americans in 1776 than it had been before.[25] The calls for resistance and independence became louder, and many spokespersons for the movement were, like Witherspoon, clergy.[26] By the spring of 1776, Witherspoon clearly had concluded that British encroachment on the colonists' rights had reached a tipping point, for that April he discretely organized public discussions of independence among New Jersey leaders.[27] In May, he stood in his pulpit and declared publicly his belief "that the cause in which America is now in arms, is the cause of justice, of liberty, and of human nature," citing British threats to religious and civil liberties as his reason for supporting independence.[28] By July, as a representative of New Jersey, he formally endorsed the Declaration's insistence that the violation of fundamental rights was so egregious that the people had a "duty, to throw off such Government, and to provide new Guards for their future security." Soon thereafter he penned a letter to his fellow Scottish Americans, imploring them to support the war for independence as a legitimate response to Britain's decision to trample "our ancient rights."[29]

In another defense of the war, his *Memorial and Manifesto of the United States of North-America*, this time aimed at an international audience, Witherspoon made clear that the restoration of liberty and "the rights and privileges of freemen" was the original objective of American resistance, and only when their grievances were repeatedly ignored and mocked did they conclude that "it was impossible to preserve civil order any longer under the name and form of a government which we had taken arms to oppose," so "we found it absolutely necessary to declare ourselves independent of that prince who had thrown us out of his protection."[30] Political authority that abdicated its responsibility to protect basic liberties, adhere to moral law, further the public good, and encourage constructive character was no longer legitimate, and the people were within their rights to separate and form a new government.

At first glance, Witherspoon's embrace of revolution could appear to be a significant departure from his Calvinist tradition. Calvin described government as an "excellent and beneficial institution," the authority of which derives from God. Calvin's perception of political legitimacy as rooted in divine authority, coupled with his extreme anxiety about threats to social order, made him naturally conservative on the issue of resistance. Even if a specific ruler governs in a despotic way, wrote Calvin, normally the people did not have grounds to disobey, for Calvin assumed that rulers "never abuse their power by harassing the good and the innocent without retaining in their despotic rule some semblance of just government. No tyranny, therefore, can exist which does not in some respect assist in protecting human society."[31] Because political authority derives from God, "any who despise his power are striving to overturn the order of God, and are therefore resisting God Himself, since to despise the providence of the One who is the Author of civil government (*iuris politici*) is to wage war against Him."[32] As we saw in Chapter 1, Calvin occasionally opened the door for consideration of justified political resistance, but he certainly did not endorse the kind of popular revolt happening in America in the eighteenth century. Resisting even a corrupt or ineffective ruler still risked disrupting God's order, said Calvin, so normally the only appropriate recourse for a people suffering under a tyrant was to look to other legitimate political actors to intervene for relief or pray for God's deliverance in more miraculous ways.

A later Calvinist of whom Witherspoon was fond, the English Puritan Richard Baxter, echoed Calvin's conservatism. Baxter vigorously rejected the idea that political legitimacy was rooted in popular consent, arguing that "the people as people are not the Sovereign Power" for "the Power of Governing a Commonwealth is not a natural thing, but a Right that must come by Commission from a Superior; therefore it is not directly conveyed by mere nature: therefore the multitude have it not by nature."[33] For Baxter, the authority of a ruler comes from God, and like Calvin, he believed that the office maintained its divine authority even for unjust rulers. Baxter warned his readers to "take heed of those mistakes which confound sovereignty and subjection, and which delude the people with a conceit, that they are the original of power, and may [entrust] it as they please; and call their rulers to account."[34] No matter how despotic the ruler, he cautioned, "Let no vice of the person cause you to forget the dignity of his office. The authority of a sinful ruler is of God, and must accordingly be obeyed."[35]

Like Calvin, Baxter normally declined to endorse rebellion or civil war because he feared the anarchy that could result. He was inclined to think that even an unjust ruler still played an essential role in social stability. Living through the English Civil War and the Restoration, however, Baxter occasionally was willing to imagine circumstances in which a king's power could be challenged. Again like Calvin, he preferred that the challenge came from another entity with political authority, like the English Parliament, rather than a popular revolt. Occasionally he cautiously endorsed at least political disobedience, if not active resistance, on the part of citizens if royal power was inappropriately directed against God's values, the integrity of the law, or the common good of the people.[36] Normally, however, Baxter thought that the proper response to an unjust ruler was simply to endure: "Resist not, where you cannot actually obey: and let no appearance of probable good that might come to yourselves, or the church, by any unlawful means, (as treason, sedition, or rebellion,) ever tempt you to it. For evil must not be done that good may come of it."[37]

The Calvinist tradition is a wide express, though, and it hosts considerable theological and moral diversity. On the issue of political resistance, we must juxtapose Calvin and Baxter with some of the Calvinists in the English Civil War period, who argued explicitly for popular consent as the foundation of political legitimacy and resistance as a right of a people suffering under an unjust ruler. One such thinker was Scottish theologian Samuel Rutherford (1600–1661), who argued for a fundamental right to resistance based on the people's right to self-governance. Good Protestant that he was, he based his understanding of popular consent on the Bible, specifically in the precedent set by Old Testament monarchs:

> Mere conquest by the sword, without the consent of the people, is no just title to the crown, because the lawful title that God's word holdeth forth to us, beside the Lord's choosing and calling of a man to the crown, is the people's election (Deut. 17.15). All that had any lawful calling to the crown in God's word, as Saul, David, Solomon, &c., were called by the people, and the first lawful calling is to us a rule and pattern to all lawful callings.[38]

Rutherford appealed to the biblical idea of a covenant, in which both God's sanction and the endorsement of the people served to validate political power.[39] Political power derived its legitimacy from the commitment to defend God's law and protect the people, so that when a ruler abandoned one or both of those responsibilities, he violated the covenant on which his rule was validated, and his authority was no more: "A covenant giveth ground of a civil action and claim to a people, and the free estates, against a king, seduced by wicked counsel to make war against the land, whereas he did swear by the most high God that he should be a father and protector of the Church of God."[40]

The implications in Rutherford's political theology for King Charles were clear: "There be no mutual contract made upon certain conditions, but if the conditions be not fulfilled the party injured is loosed from the contract." For Rutherford, tyranny so represented the abandonment of God's charge and the good will of the people that a king who devolved into tyranny was by definition no longer a legitimate king: "If then any cast off the nature of a king, and become habitually a tyrant, in so far he is not from God nor any ordinance which God doth own. If the office of a tyrant (to speak so), be contrary to a king's offices, it is not from God, and so neither is the power from God."[41] And if a tyrant is no longer a king, then "the people have a natural throne of policy in their conscience to give warning, and materially sentence, against the king as a tyrant, and so by nature are to defend themselves," for political resistance is "an innocent act of self-preservation" to which all human beings have a fundamental right.[42]

The justifying rhetoric Witherspoon used for the American Revolution was more tempered in spirit than Rutherford's, but it exhibited similar roots in the insistence that popular consent was the conduit by which God awards rulers their authority. His philosophy lectures made that clear when he argued that "this doctrine of resistance . . . is essentially connected with what has been said on the social contract, and the consent necessary to political union. If it be asked who must judge when the government may be resisted, I answer the subjects in general, every one for himself. . . . Dominion, it is plain from all that has been said, can be acquired justly only one way, viz. by consent."[43] Again, he argued, "though people have actually consented to any form of government," he declared to them, "if they have been essentially deceived in the nature and operation of the laws, if they are found to be pernicious and destructive of the ends of the union, they may certainly break up the society, recall their obligation, and resettle the whole upon a better footing."[44] If the basis of political authority is popular consent, that consent could be revoked from a government that no longer served the interests of its people. Calvin would have been horrified by this bold assertion of popular power, but Calvinists like Rutherford would have found it compatible with their own political theology. In this way, Witherspoon's support of the war was quite consistent with at least a vein of his Calvinist tradition.

On a number of occasions, however, Witherspoon warned of the special dangers that accompanied civil war. As early as the Synod Letter of 1775, he warned his fellow Presbyterians that "civil wars are carried on with a rancor and spirit of revenge much greater than those between independent states."[45] He explained the depth of hostility that comes with civil war as a reflection of the harm that rebellion represents to the social identity and public order that once bound political kin together. "He who breaks the public peace, and attempts to subvert the order of the society of which he is a member, is guilty of the greatest crime against every other member, by robbing him of a blessing of the greatest value in itself, as well as essentially necessary to the possession of every other."[46] The venom is so great because the wound is so foundational to a peaceful society, and we regard those who threaten the civil order this way "as a felon, and a criminal breaking the law of God and man." We also experience civil war as an acute betrayal, said Witherspoon, a breach between people once bound by the sinews of citizenship. He called this bond of citizenship a kind of political "friendship" that is betrayed in civil war, the result being intense feelings of fear, hatred, and contempt by the other side.[47]

Witherspoon's preoccupation with the horrors of civil war in his lectures, sermons, and speeches may have reflected more than his anxieties over the conflict with the mother country. Eli Merritt reminds us that throughout the independence struggle, the colonies were in very real danger of breaking out into violent conflict with one another. Merritt documents how regional differences in culture, economic priorities, and political alliances threatened to divide the colonies into smaller confederations—New England, the Middle colonies, and the Southern bloc. A considerable amount of mistrust existed between these regional groups, and the temptation to pit their futures against one another hung in the air for the entire war. As a colonial leader convinced that the states would survive against Britain only by staying united, Witherspoon was deeply concerned about interstate rivalries. His numerous appeals to examples of the states working together in the war may have been psychological influences as much as a reflection of the war's reality. And his repeated references to the ills of civil war were probably attempts to remind his fellow colonists what they had at stake.

Witherspoon tried to capture the special tragedy of civil war in the warnings of his *Dominion* sermon. After going on about the horrors of war in general, for the living and the dead, he cautioned his congregation that civil war brings a special demonstration of our "depravity":

> But if this may be justly said of all wars between man and man, what shall we be able to say that is suitable to the abhorred scene of civil war between citizen and citizen? How deeply affecting is it, that those who are the same in complexion, the same in blood, in language, and in religion, should, notwithstanding, butcher one another with unrelenting rage, and glory in the deed? That men should lay waste the fields of their fellow subjects, with whose provision they themselves had often been fed, and consume with devouring fire those houses in which they had often found a hospitable shelter.[48]

To temper somewhat the high emotional and psychological costs of war, and to prevent the dissolution of the independence movement into regional conflicts, Witherspoon regularly asked his fellow Americans to commit to "a spirit of humanity and mercy" and "meekness and gentleness of spirit" toward both loyalists and their fellow patriots as the conflict unfolded.[49]

Despite the harm that civil war brings, Witherspoon thought the American Revolution was justified, and he articulated that justification in part through the language of rights, law, and duty that was so important to his understanding of political character. Specifically, Witherspoon referred to the rights of nations that derive from what he called the law of nations. In his philosophy lectures, Witherspoon taught his students that nations have rights analogous to individuals: "If there are any duties binding upon men to each other, in a state of natural liberty, the same are due from nation to nation."[50] Once the

American states declared themselves independent from England, then, it was reasonable for Witherspoon to suggest they possessed the same rights as any other nation. Earlier we noted that Witherspoon recognized perfect human rights to life, liberty, self-defense, self-determination, common-use resources, property (including one's labor), religious exercise, and other "opinions" of private judgment, and reputation.[51] Here Witherspoon insisted that nations enjoy rights to these same claims.

Witherspoon also argued that when one nation violated the perfect rights of another nation, that violation constituted grounds for justified war. "The violation of the natural rights of mankind being a transgression of the law of nature, and between nations as in a state of natural liberty, there being no method of redress but force, the law of nature and nations has as its chief or only object the manner of making *war* and *peace*."[52] To Witherspoon's mind, the Revolution was obviously about protecting the life and liberty of the colonies and their inhabitants from increasingly violent British suppression. As a response to what Gary L. Steward and others have called Britain's deliberate and alarming attempts to recalibrate the colonists' presumption of self-government (for instance, the Sugar, Stamp, and Declaratory Acts), the war was a reassertion of the colonies' rights to private property and self-determination. And Witherspoon was particularly clear that he thought religious liberty and the right to conscientious conviction were the ultimate concerns in the conflict. As he said in his *Dominion* sermon, "there is not a single instance in history in which civil liberty was lost, and religious liberty preserved entire. If therefore we yield up our temporal property, we at the same time deliver the conscience into bondage."[53] For Witherspoon, all of the other rights the budding nation fought to protect were in service to defending the right to religious exercise, the ultimate just cause for war.

In arguing this way, Witherspoon offered his own contribution to the so-called justified war tradition in Western political thought. The justified war tradition begins with the assumption that conflict between human collectives is inevitable and that sometimes a nation's duty to protect itself, its people, or innocent others will require violent engagement. War therefore serves as a regrettable but morally permissible course of action if it satisfies certain criteria. While different thinkers within the Western justified war tradition have had different views of the standards for measuring the morality of war, consensus has historically congealed around the following criteria: (1) there is a *just cause* that prompts the use of violence; (2) the war is not a private use of violence but is discharged by one in a position of *legitimate authority* to do so;

(3) war is employed as a *last resort*, after all reasonable alternatives have been exhausted; (4) there is a *reasonable chance of success* in using violence to achieve one's objectives; and (5) the decision to go to war is a *proportional response* to the hostility that prompts it. These so-called *jus ad bellum* criteria represent a framework for distinguishing a morally acceptable decision to go to war from a violent excursion that is illegitimate, frivolous, and unnecessarily dangerous.

Witherspoon would have been quite familiar with this kind of moral evaluation of war, given the Western justified war tradition's deep roots in Christian theology. With the conversion of Emperor Constantine in the fourth century, Christianity quickly shifted from an often-persecuted minority religion to the official religion of the Roman Empire. Correspondingly, Christian thinkers had to grapple with the compatibility between the religion of Jesus, with its "turn the other cheek" ethic and its nonviolent Savior, and the violence of a political arena that they now, in effect, controlled. The history of how Christian theology negotiated that seeming contradiction is deep and rich, but the short of it is that many thinkers determined that the *spirit* of Christian nonviolent love could shape a political ethic without requiring that a Christian political regime completely disavow violence as a coercive tool to maintain law and order. No thinker was more important to this reinterpretation of Christian political theology than Augustine. Augustine taught that Christians lived with a foot in each of two worlds, the realm of God's elect (what he called the "city of God") and the earthly realm of sin (the "city of man"), and their responsibility was to discharge their duties in the human realm with the heart and motivation of creatures whose ultimate end was God. This went for Christian magistrates and soldiers too, who must fulfill their responsibilities to defend their people and maintain social order, but in a way that reflected the spirit of love of God and neighbor.

Augustine believed that Christian rulers and soldiers should have peace as their ultimate end, but the reality of sin in the earthly realm sometimes required using force and violence to achieve that peace. To do so, ironically, made violence a tool of Christian charity, but only if it was used with peace as its end and neighborly love as its boundary condition. Augustine pressed this point in a letter to a Roman military leader, Count Boniface, who was wrestling with the compatibility of Christian faith with serving in the military. Augustine wrote to Boniface,

> Peace should be the object of your desire; war should be waged only as a necessity, and waged only that God may by it deliver men from the necessity and preserve them in peace. For peace is not sought in order to kindle war, but war is waged in order that peace may be obtained. Therefore even in waging war cherish the spirit of a peacemaker, that by conquering those whom you attack you may lead them back to the advantages of peace; for our Lord says: "Blessed are the peacemakers, for they shall be called the children of God."[54]

For Augustine, the use of violence as an instrument of peace dictated that domestic policing should be restrained and the invocation of war should only be done as a last resort response to a just cause (which he generally defined as defense of the political society or rescue of the weak or vulnerable). From Augustine's teachings about justified uses of violence in the name of peace and justice evolved a rich tradition—developed by thinkers like Thomas Aquinas, Francisco de Vitoria, and Francisco Suarez—of criteria by which we might measure the alignment of war with a Christian commitment to peace.[55]

Protestant Reformers like Calvin, a devotee of Augustine, worked within this same tradition on the morality of war, and Witherspoon was the heir of his thinking. Calvin too believed that war was only justified if the cause of war warranted the turn to violence, and he listed among the causes that he considered justified the defense of peace (what he called "common tranquility"), response to sedition, punishment of evil, defense of the rule of law, and intervention on behalf of oppressed innocents.[56] He insisted that war could be declared only by someone in a position of legitimate political authority and could be waged only for the public good, not on the basis of private grievances.[57] He articulated a principle of proportionality in his caution to magistrates against excessive "passion" (i.e., anger or hatred) in discharging their prerogative to war, and he articulated a principle of last resort when he advised them to "not accept the occasion [to war] when offered, unless they are driven to it by extreme necessity."[58]

Witherspoon's public remarks about the Revolutionary War reflect most if not all of the classic *jus ad bellum* criteria. The protection of rights and the public good are the fundamental duties of government, so to violate that obligation constituted a just cause for Witherspoon. His belief that government's legitimacy is rooted in popular consent underwrote his rejection of British rule and his support for the Americans' popular revolt. On a number of occasions, he outlined the steps the colonies had taken to request diplomatic adjudication of their concerns, arriving at war for independence only as a last resort and a response to violence first perpetrated by British soldiers. His belief in a reasonable chance of success is among the most tenuous of his commitments to the *ad bellum* criteria; while Witherspoon did not think the war frivolous and trusted in both the goodwill of Divine Providence and the skill of their leaders, he did admit (often in retrospect) that, on the face of it, the Americans were considerably outmatched by the skills and resources of the British army. Nonetheless, he believed the war to be a necessary and proportional response to the dire threat British rule represented to the colonists' fundamental rights and liberties, and one of his important roles during the Revolution was to repeatedly make the public case that this was a morally justified campaign.

Good War

Witherspoon was not only concerned about the moral rightness of the decision to go to war with Britain. He also thought it was important that the colonists conduct the war in a way that was as consistent as possible with moral virtue and principle. In other words, Witherspoon thought that good political character shapes *how* we go to war as much as *whether* and *why*.

Not everyone who believes that war can be justified agrees that the conduct in a justified war is therefore limited by moral parameters. In the Western history of war ethics, the insistence on moral boundaries for actions in war is what has distinguished a justified war from a crusade. From the perspective of the justified war tradition, war is a regrettable interruption of peace that may be judged necessary to protect innocent others, human rights, and a peaceful order. By contrast, a crusade is a holy war, a righteous battle with forces of evil. Crusaders tend to think in moral binaries: good versus evil, God versus Satan, godliness versus godlessness. Because the moral lines are so clear and the stakes are so high, crusaders tend to reject any limits to how they fight for what they perceive to be their righteous cause. A crusade against evil may employ any means necessary, and the objective is not just to win the battle but to annihilate the other, for our adversary is also the enemy of God. This attitude characterized the medieval crusades that the Holy Roman Church sponsored to reclaim the Holy Land from Islam, and a similar attitude sometimes characterized the rhetoric of the American Civil War, the World Wars, United States involvement in Vietnam, and the Cold War.[59]

By contrast, justified war thinkers insist that the moral parameters around war govern not only the decision to go to war but the actions we undertake to discharge the conflict. As James F. Childress puts it, the normal prohibition against killing, though overridden in the case of a justified war, nonetheless leaves "moral traces" or "residual effects" that dictate certain obligations and attitudes in conducting the war.[60] These moral traces manifest in what justified war thinkers have called the *in bello* criteria that govern war conduct. Historically, *in bello* criteria have included a principle of nondiscrimination that outlaws the intentional targeting of noncombatants and requires a commitment to minimizing the accidental death and destruction of innocents. A principle of proportionality also has been part of the *in bello* considerations, arguing that the tactics employed in a justified war should not extend significantly beyond what is necessary to accomplish the war's objectives. Finally, *in bello* criteria sometimes include attitudinal obligations, like a spirit of restraint, regret, humility, and respect for the humanity of one's enemy. All of these restraints on the conduct of war are reflections of the normal illicitness of taking life, a moral prohibition regrettably lifted in a war deemed necessary to accomplish the aims of peace.

This spirit of restraint normally does not accompany a crusader's mentality, and crusading rhetoric was rampant in the American Revolution, particularly among patriot clergy. Thomas S. Kidd offers Israel Evans as a powerful example. Evans was a former student of Witherspoon and served as a chaplain in Washington's army. Washington thought highly of his chaplain, and Evans worshiped the general. Evans clearly believed that the Americans' rejection of British rule was a divine calling and that God was at work in the efforts of the American army under Washington's leadership. He compared the colonists' emancipation from Britain with God's deliverance of the ancient Hebrew people from Egypt, and he saw the war as a conflict of both political and apocalyptic significance, saying that the colonies were fighting "the powers of Britain and of hell." The righteousness of the cause inclined Evans to baptize every means the colonial army employed, including brutal campaigns against the Iroquois of New York. The American troops were "instruments in the hand of GOD, for accomplishing so great a revolution, and extending the kingdom of his Son so far. Liberty and religion shall have their wide dominion from the Atlantic through the great continent to the western ocean."[61]

Evans was not alone in his view of the Revolution as a holy war or crusade. New York preacher Abraham Keteltas identified the war as the "cause of God" in the title of a sermon he preached in October 1777 at the Presbyterian Church in Newburyport, Massachusetts. Invoking the stories of God's interventions on behalf of Israel in the Old Testament, Keteltas hyperbolized the struggle against Britain as "the grand cause of the whole human race." He pronounced the war a timeless struggle for liberty, which he called the "parent of . . . every generous and noble purpose of the soul." He characterized the British as "the inveterate foes to mankind," the "cruel and bloody authors of this unjust, unnatural war," and the pawns of Satan in a cosmic battle with God's Providence. For Keteltas, the Revolutionary War was a contest between good and evil, and he had no doubt that God was on the side of the Americans.[62]

Six months later, Jacob Cushing used the anniversary of the British attack in 1775 to whip a Lexington gathering into a warring frenzy. Reminding his audience of the "singular and horrid scenes of that dismal and dark day," he lamented the loss of American lives, indicted the brutality of the British, and gave thanks to God that the damage from the skirmish was not more severe. He assured his hearers that the battle against the British begun that day was a holy endeavor. They were called to use their "swords as instruments of righteousness," to embrace the "important duty of shedding human blood" for the cause of liberty. Speaking directly to the local militia members, he proclaimed, "To arms! To action, and the battle of the warrior! Is the language of divine providence; and you have every motive imaginable to awaken, and excite you to be up and doing the work of the Lord faithfully." The soldiers should undertake their duties virtuously, he warned, but the virtues he had in mind were courage and "a martial spirit." Perfect the "art of war," he charged them, that they might "be helpful in vanquishing and subduing the enemies of GOD and this people."[63]

Kidd notes that "the framing of the war as the action of Providence could make it difficult for American leaders to maintain a critical perspective on the war or its tactics."[64] Chaplains, generals, and political leaders alike succumbed to this temptation to conclude that "if the cause was godly, then everything done in the name of the cause seemed godly too." Kidd points out that Americans have always been susceptible to this temptation, warning that "using God's might and right to justify one's cause can easily obscure the complexity or injustice of war." To his mind, "providentialism was the most morally problematic religious principle of the Revolution."[65]

Witherspoon was not shy about invoking the Providence of God in his view of the war either. After all, his rhetorical entrance into public support for the conflict was a sermon called *The Dominion of Providence over the Passions of Men*. But that sermon and his other public remarks about the war reflected a more careful, chastened assessment of God's role in the conflict than the crusaders around him allowed. The point of the *Dominion* sermon was to remind his hearers of the ways God can move through human *unrighteousness*; rather than baptizing the violence of the conflict, he encouraged his congregation to look for the movement of God despite the sin and "wrath" human beings visited upon each other. And in that sermon, he was at great pains to encourage his fellow Americans to conduct the war as virtuously as possible. He rejected demonizing talk of the king, Parliament, or other British leaders. He implored the colonists to approach the war with pious intentions, with humility and moderation. The intent of the entire back half of the sermon was the importance of maintaining good character in the conduct of the war.

In other public remarks, Witherspoon extended the relevance of character beyond the righteousness of cause to the conduct in war. In the 1775 Synod Letter, he insisted that war should be a last resort, conducted with restraint after all other reasonable measures had been exhausted: "That man will fight most bravely, who never fights till it is necessary, and who ceases to fight as soon as the necessity is over."[66] He rejected demonizing rhetoric, cautioning his readers to "desire the preservation and security of those rights which belong to you," and not to peddle in expressions of "disaffection to the king" or disparagement of the mother country.[67] Similarly, his *Memorial and Manifesto* ends with an acknowledgment that when we consider our adversaries to be "an enemy of God" (a particular temptation in civil wars, as he had cautioned), then it is no wonder that we are tempted to seek extraordinary vengeance on them. When a war is perceived to be a holy crusade against the forces of evil, it is not surprising that we cannot fathom coming to a moment of compromise to end the conflict. But Witherspoon recommended that his readers imagine that "the grounds of the quarrel are plausible on both sides," an act of empathetic imagination that may serve to helpfully complicate the conflict. He also instructed his readers to assume "the strictest honor and integrity" in the enemy, rather than attributing to them a level of inhumanity that makes it easier to justify boundless violence upon them. To respect our adversary, said Witherspoon, makes it easier to conform to our moral duty to exercise "humanity and mercy" to other human beings, even in times of war.[68]

In Witherspoon's concern with how the war was conducted, we see reflected what just war thinkers call *jus in bello* criteria, parameters for morally permissible conduct in war. Witherspoon was not naïve in his understanding of war. He recognized and accepted that nearly all means of "open violence" are considered justifiable in armed conflict. He also acknowledged that the casualties of war cannot be restricted perfectly to combatants; the other "people of the state" will necessarily suffer loss of life and property as well.[69] But he was unwilling to join the crusader in saying that all means are justified in a war with a just cause. Some means of violence remain immoral and unlawful, even in justified war, Witherspoon maintained. To this end, in the second of his *Druid* essays, Witherspoon offered this *jus in bello* principle, a commitment to moral conduct in war backed by the authority of both Christian religion and the natural law:

> That all acts of cruelty which have no tendency to weaken the resisting force, are contrary to reason and religion, and therefore to the law of nature and nations. The end of war is to obtain justice, and restore peace, therefore whatever tends to lessen or destroy the force of the enemy must be permitted. It is in this view alone that the capture of private property is allowed and justified. But to take lives without necessity, and even to treat prisoners with oppression or insult, above all to distress or torture the weaker sex, or the helpless infant, ought to be detested by every nation professing the gospel.[70]

Torture, the needless abuse of prisoners, targeting women and children, scorched-earth invasions, the use of poison, and other unnecessary inflictions of harm were all means of war that Witherspoon was unwilling to condone.

Maintaining a certain respect for the enemy was part of his instruction for maintaining moral character in war. The counsel to respect the enemy, however, did not prevent Witherspoon from calling out the immorality he saw in how the British were conducting the war, and his critique of British troops offers illustrations of his *jus in bello* principles in action. Indeed, Witherspoon was highly critical of the British for employing many of the tactics he abhorred, charging them publicly with the mistreatment of prisoners, the murder of noncombatants, and the unnecessary destruction of whole towns as they passed through the countryside.[71] In his sermon "Delivered at a Public Thanksgiving after Peace," he once again reflected on the lack of character among the British troops, including their "barbarous treatment of the American prisoners through the whole war." Witherspoon claimed that the contrast between American virtue and the British lack of it was on potent display every time there was a prisoner swap, for the British soldiers were "going home hale and hearty" while the American soldiers were clearly neglected and abused in the enemies' care. Witherspoon also mentioned the "abuse and contempt poured upon the inhabitants" of the colonies, the treatment of all "places of public worship (except those of the episcopal denomination) with all possible contempt and insult," and "the indiscriminate plunder of their property" as the British made their way through towns and territories. By Witherspoon's account, British troops regularly exhibited "insolence and cruelty," including in one case where they killed a noncombatant clergyman in the street.[72] All of these charges Witherspoon raised as violations of the moral expectations on proper behavior in war.[73]

Rejection of unnecessary violence and inappropriate targets was consistent with the way Witherspoon taught the ethics of war at Princeton. He instructed his students that a moral war is conducted proportional to its proper objective. "The duration of a war," he lectured, "should be according to natural equity, till the injury be completely redressed, and reasonable security given against future attacks." The initial "injury" that prompted the war should not be used as pretense for plundering the enemy: "the practice, too common, of continuing a war for the acquisition of empire, is to be condemned."[74] His lecture also featured commentary on the aforementioned tactics and targets he opposed, like torturing prisoners of war and targeting innocents. "All acts of cruelty and humanity . . . and all severity that has not an immediate effect in weakening the national strength of the enemy is certainly inhumanity."[75] Witherspoon allowed for deception in war, but consistent with his ethical priority on truth-telling, he minimized the frequency with which it would be truly justified. He ended his lecture on war with a reminder that even war is to be conducted with virtue, specifically generosity, magnanimity, integrity, and prudence.[76]

For Witherspoon, the American Revolution was not a crusade, but it was a moral endeavor, complicated by the existence of virtue and sin on both sides of the conflict. His insistence on moral parameters for the conduct of war was rooted in the broader importance he saw in political character as the bedrock of a healthy society. The character of a good society and its government depended on a commitment to the same ideals he emphasized when he focused on the character of good citizens: commitment to human rights, adherence to moral law, and the practice of benevolent virtue. The aggregate cultivation of this character in citizens makes for a good society, and maintenance of this character is one of the responsibilities of government. When government abandons this duty, it opens itself up to challenges to its legitimacy and makes itself vulnerable to dissent, rebellion, and reform. Even when a people engage in morally justifiable dissent and revolution, they must not abandon the principles of political character that inspire their dissent and represent the social compact they seek to reform. Respect for human rights, the moral law, and the collective good of the commonwealth constitute grounds for revolution, but they also serve as boundary conditions for how that revolution ought to be conducted. Throughout his public service to the American cause, Witherspoon was at great pains to remind his fellow patriots of the importance of character to the war itself, commending a chastened humility even when others were offering unnuanced warmongering.

Of course, the struggle for independence from Britain was not the only major moral crisis in which the colonies were invested. While white colonists asserted their rights against the British crown, they perpetuated a system of racial enslavement that deprived thousands of human beings of the very rights and liberties the independence movement held up as its ideal. Witherspoon was one of those revolutionaries with the guilt of racial enslavement on his hands, and in fact, the inhumanity of slavery touched rather close to home for him. One would think that his priority on political character, based on respect for human rights and a commitment to general benevolence, would compel him to stand indignantly against a system that violated those ideals. As we shall see, it did not.

Notes

1 Historians disagree about when exactly the document was signed. Most believe that the Declaration was approved and disseminated by Congress in July but signed by most members in August. A few of the names may have been added even later.
2 Thomas Hobbes, *Leviathan*. 1651 (J.M. Dent and Sons, 1973).
3 Christopher J. Berry, "Sociality and Socialisation," in *The Cambridge Companion to the Scottish Enlightenment*, 2nd ed., ed. Alexander Broadie and Craig Smith (Cambridge University Press, 2019), 234–47.
4 Belief in popular consent as the basis for political power was widely (though not universally) shared among the Puritans, but what they understood consent to legitimize varied. For some Puritans, rulers were appropriately chosen or endorsed by the people, but once selected enjoyed broad powers as the political representatives of God's authority. For other Puritans, the consent of the people not

only legitimized the choice of a ruler but also established the parameters of proper rule, and once a ruler stepped beyond those boundaries, he could be deposed and replaced. See Timothy H. Breen, *The Character of the Good Ruler: A Study of Puritan Political Ideas in New England, 1630–1730* (Yale University Press, 1970), 59–64.

5   Witherspoon, LMP, Lecture X, *Works*, III:417.
6   Witherspoon, LMP, Lecture X, *Works*, III:418.
7   Witherspoon, LMP, Lecture XII, *Works*, III:429.
8   Witherspoon, LMP, Lecture X, *Works*, III:418.
9   Witherspoon, LMP, Lecture X, *Works*, III:418.
10 Witherspoon, Sermon 45, *Works*, III:80.
11 Witherspoon, *Observations on the Improvement of America*, Works III:385. Thomas Kidd points out that this belief that good government fostered benevolent virtue in its citizens was fairly prevalent in eighteenth-century America, in part a reflection of the popularity of Montesquieu among the founders. See Thomas S. Kidd, *God of Liberty: A Religious History of the American Revolution* (Basic Books, 2010), 108–14.
12 Witherspoon, Sermon 45, *Works*, III:80.
13 Witherspoon, Sermon 45, *Works*, III:82.
14 Witherspoon, Sermon 45, *Works*, III:82.
15 Witherspoon, Sermon 45, *Works*, III:80.
16 Calvin himself preferred a mixture of aristocracy and democracy because he thought it best minimized the dual threats of tyranny and anarchy. See *Institutes*, IV.20, 1493.
17 Witherspoon, LMP, Lecture XII, *Works*, III:434.
18 Nicholas P. Miller, *The Religious Roots of the First Amendment: Dissenting Protestants and the Separation of Church and State* (Oxford University Press, 2012), 133. Witherspoon was not the only leader at the time who worried that the Articles were too weak to encourage a collective commitment to the common good of the United States. See Kidd, *God of Liberty*, 209.
19 Kidd argues that public virtue was an aim of the new Constitution, and that aim was partially achieved by shifting the balance of leadership to elected men of virtue rather than the masses. See Kidd, *God of Liberty*, 214–18.
20 For more on the relationship between Witherspoon and Madison on the development of religious liberty in the United States, see Miller, *Religious Roots*, chapter 5.
21 Ralph L. Ketcham, "James Madison's Religion: A New Hypothesis," in *James Madison on Religious Liberty*, ed. Robert S. Alley (Prometheus Books, 1985), 192.
22 As an indication of Witherspoon's enthusiasm for Madison's work on the new Constitution, the College of New Jersey awarded him an honorary degree, and

at the ceremony, Witherspoon commented: "It has been my peculiar happiness to know, perhaps more than any of them [the trustees], your usefulness in an important station, on that and some other accounts, there was none to whom it [the honorary degree] gave more satisfaction than to [me]." As quoted in Ketcham, "James Madison's Religion: A New Hypothesis," 180.

23 Witherspoon, LMP, Lecture XII, *Works*, III:436.
24 See Steward, *Justifying Revolution*, 34–58 for a discussion of how the colonists interpreted these and other British maneuvers as ominous signs of future curtailment of their right to self-government and self-defense. Nicholas Miller also discusses the very real threat to religious freedom and civil liberties that Witherspoon and others saw in the imposition of a bishop in the colonies. See Miller, *Religious Roots*, 138–44.
25 Steward, *Justifying Revolution*, 109.
26 Steward, *Justifying Revolution*, 38; Kidd, *God of Liberty*, 6–9, 90.
27 Steward, *Justifying Revolution*, 115.
28 Witherspoon, DPPM, *Works*, III:36.
29 Witherspoon, "Address to the Natives of Scotland Residing in America," in *Works*, III:51.
30 Witherspoon, *Memorial and Manifesto*, *Works*, IV:370.
31 John Calvin, *The Epistles of Paul the Apostle to the Romans and to the Thessalonians*, vol. 8 of *Calvin's New Testament Commentaries*, ed. David W. Torrance and Thomas F. Torrance (Eerdmans, 1991), 282. Similarly, in his commentary on 1 Peter, Calvin wrote: "If anyone objects and says that we ought not to obey princes who, as far as they can, pervert the holy ordinance of God, and thus become savage wild beasts, while magistrates ought to bear the image of God, I reply that the order established by God ought to be so highly valued by us as to honour even tyrants when in power. There is yet another reply still more evident, that there has never been a tyranny, nor can one be imagined, however cruel and unbridled, in which some portion of equity has not appeared. God never allows His just order to be destroyed by the sin of men without some of its outlines remaining unobscured. And finally, some kind of government, however deformed and corrupt it may be, is still better and more beneficial than anarchy." John Calvin, *The Epistle of Paul the Apostle to the Hebrews and the First and Second Epistles of St. Peter*, vol. 12 of *Calvin's Commentaries*, 271.
32 Calvin, *The Epistle to the Romans*, 281.
33 Richard Baxter, *A Holy Commonwealth* (Cambridge University Press, 1994), 70, 72.
34 Baxter, *Christian Directory*, IV.III, 744.
35 Baxter, *Christian Directory*, IV.III, 749.
36 Baxter, *Holy Commonwealth*, 178–210.
37 Baxter, *Christian Directory*, IV.III, 757.

38 Samuel Rutherford, *Lex, Rex* in *Puritanism and Liberty*, ed. A. S. P. Woodhouse (J.M. Dent & Sons, 1992), 204.
39 As Witte rightly points out, the concept of covenant became important among Calvinists in their justification of active resistance to tyranny. Based in God's biblical covenant with Israel, the concept of covenant underwrote Calvinists' understanding of political legitimacy. God relates to a Christian political society through a covenantal relationship, by which Calvinists meant that God promised to ensure the good of that society in exchange for the people's devotion to God's law. God's covenantal relationship with society is symbolized and enforced by its rulers, who act with God's authority and are responsible for defending God's law. But rulers are also bound in covenant to the people, a conviction from which the idea of popular consent grew. Both the idea of collective covenantal obligation and the grounding of political legitimacy in popular consent became hallmark axes of English and American Puritan political theology. For the role of covenant in Beza's political theology, for instance, see Witte, *Reformation of Rights*, 122–34.
40 Rutherford, *Lex, Rex*, 208.
41 Rutherford, *Lex, Rex*, 210.
42 Rutherford, *Lex, Rex*, 210–11.
43 Witherspoon, LMP, Lecture XII, *Works*, III:436.
44 Witherspoon, LMP, Lecture XII, *Works*, III:431.
45 Witherspoon, Letter from the Synod of New-York and Philadelphia, *Works*, III:13.
46 Witherspoon, *Druid #3*, *Works*, IV:438.
47 Witherspoon, *Druid #3*, *Works*, IV: 442.
48 Witherspoon, DPPM, *Works*, III:22.
49 Witherspoon, Letter from the Synod of New-York and Philadelphia, *Works*, III:14.
50 Witherspoon, *Druid #2*, *Works*, IV:433.
51 Witherspoon, LMP, Lecture X, *Works*, III:416.
52 Witherspoon, LMP, Lecture XIII, *Works*, III:440. Witherspoon also indicates the possibility that an analogous imperfect right of nations—that is, a right to mercy—might be a just cause in some circumstances. Finally, he suggests in this lecture that sometimes the anticipation of a violation is just cause for war, thus offering a foundation for justified preemptive warfare.
53 Witherspoon, DPPM, *Works*, III:36.
54 Oliver O'Donovan and Joan Lockwood O'Donovan, eds., *From Ireneus to Grotius: A Sourcebook in Christian Political Thought* (Eerdmans, 1999), 135.
55 For good introductions to the Western justified war tradition, especially its Christian roots, see Mark J. Allman, *Who Would Jesus Kill? War, Peace, and the Christian Tradition* (St. Mary's Press, 2008), 158–81; and Lisa Sowle Cahill, *Love*

Your Enemies: Discipleship, Pacifism, and Just War Theory (Fortress Press, 1994), chapters 4–6.
56 Calvin, *Institutes*, IV.20, 1499.
57 Calvin, *Institutes*, IV.20, 1501.
58 Calvin, *Institutes*, IV.20, 1500.
59 On the crusader motif, see Allman, *Who Would Jesus Kill?*, chapter 3.
60 James F. Childress, *Moral Responsibility in Conflicts: Essays on Nonviolence, War, and Conscience* (Louisiana State University Press, 1982), 69–71.
61 Israel Evans, as quoted in Kidd, *The God of Liberty*, 126–7.
62 Abraham Keteltas, "God Arising and Pleading His People's Cause" (1777), in *Political Sermons of the Founding Era, 1730–1805*, vol. 1, ed. Ellis Sandoz (Liberty Fund, 1998), 579–605.
63 Jacob Cushing, "Divine Judgments Upon Tyrants" (1778), in *Political Sermons of the Founding Era, 1730–1805*, vol. 1, ed. Ellis Sandoz, 607–26.
64 Kidd, *The God of Liberty*, 128.
65 Kidd, *The God of Liberty*, 130.
66 Witherspoon, Letter from the Synod of New-York and Philadelphia, *Works*, III:14.
67 Witherspoon, Letter from the Synod of New-York and Philadelphia, *Works*, III:12.
68 Witherspoon, *Memorial and Manifesto*, *Works*, IV:443.
69 Witherspoon, *Druid #2*, *Works*, IV:434.
70 Witherspoon, *Druid #2*, *Works*, IV:435.
71 Witherspoon, *Memorial and Manifesto*, *Works*, IV:370.
72 Witherspoon, Sermon 45, *Works*, III:77–78. Jeffry Morrison identifies the minister as John Rosborough, killed in Trenton because Hessian mercenaries thought he was Witherspoon. See Morrison, *John Witherspoon and the Founding of the American Republic*, 13.
73 To my knowledge, Witherspoon never acknowledged in print the war atrocities committed by Americans during the war, including the destruction of Native American communities and the torture techniques like tar-and-feathering, to which British soldiers and politicians were subjected.
74 Witherspoon, LMP, Lecture XIII, *Works*, III:440.
75 Witherspoon, LMP, Lecture XIII, *Works*, III:442.
76 Witherspoon, LMP, Lecture XIII, *Works*, III:444.

6

The Failure of Character

John Witherspoon was one of the most important leaders in the American fight for independence from Britain. He contributed to the effort as a politician, participating in state and continental congresses and serving on too many committees to count. He also served as one of the Revolution's chief apologists, what these days we call a "thought leader," providing the moral rationale for the Revolution and helping to garner support in the colonies and abroad. As we have seen, his moral justification for independence was rooted in his broader understanding of the importance of political character—the cultivation of virtuous dispositions toward general benevolence, concern for the common good, and respect for natural rights—among citizens and leaders. Defense of the rights and common good of the colonists was the reason independence from Britain was righteous and necessary, and to Witherspoon's mind, a commitment to benevolent and rights-respecting character was the guarantor of success in the struggle.

While he was voicing this moral opposition to what he saw as British tyranny, however, Witherspoon was participating in another social system of oppression, the industry of racial chattel slavery. The historical evidence suggests that Witherspoon owned slaves during his time in New Jersey, and that at least one of his sons may have as well. History also testifies that Witherspoon failed on numerous occasions to use his platform as a political leader and respected orator to publicly speak out against the enslavement of Black people. How should we understand the disconnect between this silence on slavery (and his own complicity) and his ardent defense of natural rights and human good in the struggle with Britain?

Slavery and Early American Christianity

While racial slavery did not dominate the political and economic landscapes in Scotland as it did in the American colonies, Witherspoon would have been aware of it, insofar as his home country remained part of a larger British slave-trading society. In fact, we know that Witherspoon had a close relationship with at least one enslaved Black person.[1] In the colonies, though, he was surrounded by the implications of chattel slavery. By the time of Witherspoon's death, there were nearly seven hundred thousand enslaved Black persons in the United States, representing almost one fifth of the total population.[2] Slavery existed in every colony, even allegedly abolitionist Vermont. Of course, slavery was most concentrated in the South, and its importance as a regional economic generator in that region made slavery a contentious topic between North and South, during the war and afterward. Regional rivalries constantly threatened the alliance between the colonies in their fight against Britain, and northern calls for the end of slavery were widely seen as an attack on the economic health of the southern colonies. A persistent effort to end slavery during the Revolution would have shattered the alliance between the thirteen colonies and substantially altered (or threatened) the independence movement.

The conflict between the northern and southern states around slavery was replicated within Witherspoon's New Jersey, for the colony itself was stratified by the issue. West Jersey reflected a strong abolitionist presence (led by the Quakers) in that region. By contrast, the economy of East Jersey was quite dependent on slavery, particularly around its ports. The College of New Jersey literally sat at the intersection of these two distinct cultures. Citizens and leaders of the colony would debate abolition vigorously during Witherspoon's time there, and as a local leader of prominence, he was involved in those debates. The conflict around slavery in New Jersey eventually culminated in the Gradual Abolition of Slavery law, passed in 1804. Unfortunately, this legal nod to abolition accomplished nothing of the sort, permitting only that Black people born after July 4, 1804, be emancipated when they reached their 20s and offering nothing to those enslaved in the state before that date. Ironically, the Gradual Abolition of Slavery law allowed for such gradual redress that New Jersey became the *last* northern state to abolish slavery, nearly a year after the Civil War's end.[3]

In New Jersey and throughout the colonies (North and South), Christian thinkers were among those who publicly defended slavery as a moral institution compatible with America's dominant religion. Many of slavery's apologists argued its consistency with the Bible; Dutch Reformed pastor Samuel B. How, for instance, pointed to passages in Genesis, Exodus, Philemon, and 1 Timothy to show that the Bible offers plenty of uncritical references to slaveholding, nowhere outlaws it, and is generally more concerned with humane relationships between masters and slaves than with questioning the appropriateness of the practice.[4] Presbyterian pastor Frederick Ross argued that "the relation of master and slave is sanctioned by the Bible," for it is an order of relation in "the same category as those of husband and wife," meant to govern "fallen and degraded man" and provide order to a state of human depravity.[5] Some southern Christians, including spokespersons for the Southern Baptist Convention, insisted that the morality of slavery was at worst a matter of private conscience about which individual Christians should have the right to disagree.[6] The argument for slavery's compatibility with biblical principle was a common one, highly persuasive in a culture in which a literal reading of the Bible was regarded as the highest moral authority for individuals and the nation.

Slavery's defenders normally took for granted that Black people were not the intellectual or moral equals of Europeans, sometimes appealing to curious theories of biblical history to validate that assumption. Some apologists traced Africans' lineage back to Cain, arguing that subjection to slavery was a manifestation of the curse God appropriately placed on that son of Adam as a consequence for introducing violence into the human community (Gen. 4). Other biblical defenders of slavery traced Africans back to Ham, Noah's son who was cursed for gazing upon his father's naked body (Gen. 9). Both of these textual arguments roughly fit with a trendy anthropological interpretation that emerged in the seventeenth century called polygenesis, or the belief that there is more than one human race.[7] Although strictly speaking, polygenesis contested the traditional Christian belief that all human beings descended from Adam and Eve, the idea did allow white Europeans to draw strong distinctions between themselves and the other races and cultures they discovered through colonization and conquest. To suggest biblically or anthropologically that there are distinct species differences between white and Black people made it possible for Christian Europeans to suspend any concern for the human rights of those they enslaved. They were not human, after all, at least not in the same way that Europeans thought about themselves. Worse yet, they deserved whatever hardship they experienced, as the extension of the biblical curse put on their ancestors long ago.

Because they assumed Black people were inferior, defenders of slavery sometimes argued that the institution was actually a benevolent system, for enslavement provided for the basic needs of a people who could not effectively care for themselves. Slavery was an extension of Christian charity, a form of paternalistic care for inferior beings, who in exchange for their labor were given reliable access to food and shelter. Characterized in this way, as a benevolent good, slavery was not only consistent with biblical principles, but it could actually be interpreted as a fulfillment of Christianity's commendation of benevolent other regard. Thus, the directions given to slaves and masters in the New Testament "household codes" could be seen as governing norms for a fundamentally charitable domestic relationship:

> Slaves, obey your earthly masters with respect and trembling, in singleness of heart, as you obey Christ, not with a slavery performed merely for looks, to please people, but as slaves of Christ, doing the will of God from the soul. Render service with enthusiasm, as for the Lord and not for humans, knowing that whatever good we do, we will receive the same again from the Lord, whether we are enslaved or free. And, masters, do the same to them. Stop threatening them, for you know that both of you have the same Lord in heaven, and with him there is no partiality.[8]

Rather than judging slavery as a categorical evil, the Bible suggests that there are good ways for masters to treat their slaves and good ways for slaves to live in obedience to their masters, and if the parties infuse their relationship with Christian sentiment, then ownership of other human beings can satisfy the moral expectations of Christian faith.

An even more creative defense of slavery offered in the eighteenth and early nineteenth centuries depicted it as a voluntary association. Catholic bishop John England defended slavery in South Carolina by insisting that "the natural law then does not prohibit a man from bartering his liberty and his services to save his life, to provide for his sustenance, to secure other enjoyments which he prefers to that freedom and to that right to his own labour, which he gives in exchange for life and protection."[9] England represented slavery as simply another kind of voluntary market exchange, labor for care, morally indistinguishable from other market exchanges. In fact, England went so far as to invoke the Christian idea of natural law, arguing that slavery is the exercise of a basic human right to control one's goods, in this case, the possession of one's body. Apparently missing the irony in his argument, England argued that opposition to slavery was an affront to the natural rights of both slaveholder and slave.

Of course, biblical and natural law arguments depicting a humane version of enslavement that could satisfy God's moral expectations required substantial gaslighting regarding the actual treatment of slaves in the colonies. Enslaved Black persons were subjected to levels of terror and torture that ran afoul of even a conservative biblical argument for the right treatment of slaves. In a culture that allowed most white Americans to ignore—or remain safely oblivious to— the severity of enslaved Black persons' experiences, it was enough for many to say that the Bible prohibits only the mistreatment of slaves, not slavery itself. This was a powerful argument in the eighteenth century, a time when the Bible's authority was accepted as unquestioned by most Americans. If the Bible did not prohibit slavery, and in fact included examples of holy figures participating in the practice, that was all many Americans needed to accept its moral validity.

Christian opponents of slavery in Witherspoon's time challenged the religious and moral justifications for the practice, as well as the convenient oblivion of many Americans (particularly in the North) to its violence and cruelty. One important voice of opposition was Witherspoon's good friend Benjamin Rush. Rush was zealously opposed to slavery. He wrote about its incompatibility with Christian morality and a reasonable society, and he advocated for its swift end. His investment in abolition is particularly insightful for our understanding of Witherspoon's position on the issue, given the close association the two men enjoyed in their shared work for education and the independence movement.

In *An Address to the Inhabitants of the British Settlements, on the Slavery of the Negroes in America*, published in 1773, Rush argued for an immediate end to the slave trade and a careful but reasonably paced emancipation of enslaved people in the colonies. In calling for abolition, he took on all of the common arguments used to justify the practice. Against the claim of its economic indispensability, he disputed the argument that Black people were better suited for the hard conditions of southern and Caribbean labor than white people, and he suggested that the industries now dependent on slave labor would adjust. He also insinuated that if there was an economic cost to abolition, that would not necessarily be a bad thing, as it could serve as a curb on the vices that unfettered economic gain encourages in the financially powerful.[10] Citing the biblical arguments in defense of slavery, he rejected the references to Cain's curse (and by extension, Ham's) as "a vulgar notion," dismissed the relevance of Old Testament instances of slavery as rooted in a different set of historical circumstances, and insisted that the institution contradicted all the values latent in Jesus' words and ministries.[11] He considered the idea that slavery was a useful tool for evangelizing Africans to be abhorrent, and he pointed out (in vivid detail) the obscene contradictions between the brutalizing behavior of slaveholders and traders and the gospel used to underwrite the industry.[12] "Let such, therefore, who vindicate the traffic of buying and selling Souls," wrote Rush, "seek some modern System of Religion to support it, and not to presume to sanctify their crimes by attempting to reconcile it to the sublime and perfect Religion of the Great Author of Christianity."[13]

An important part of Rush's Christian opposition to slavery was his rejection of one of its core premises, that Black people are not truly human in the same way white people are and thus do not deserve the same treatment as white Europeans. From the opening pages of his diatribe, Rush insisted on the full humanity of Black people:

> I need hardly say any thing in favour of the Intellects of the Negroes, or of their capacities for virtue and happiness, although these have been supposed, by some, to be inferior to those of the inhabitants of Europe. The accounts which travellers give us of their ingenuity, humanity, and strong attachment to their parents, relations, friends and country, show us that they are equal to the Europeans, when we allow for the diversity of temper and genius which is occasioned by climate. We have many well-attested anecdotes of as sublime and disinterested virtue among them as ever adorned a Roman or a Christian character.[14]

Rush insisted that Black people were the intellectual and moral equals of Europeans, attributing the character liabilities that whites exaggerated and attributed to Black people as "the genuine offspring of slavery," products of their dehumanizing experiences and another sign that people are not meant to be deprived of liberty. Asserting the full moral worth of Black Africans and Americans, Rush then declared them entitled to all of the natural rights European Americans assumed to be theirs. Throughout the treatise, he applied the obligations of the "rights of mankind" and "human nature" to America's responsibility to its enslaved population, appealing to his fellow Americans' "sense and virtue" to commit to "the cause of Humanity and general Liberty."

Rush imagined three parts to an American commitment to abolition. First, he called for the immediate outlawing of slave importation. Second, he called for a public campaign of shame directed at anyone implicated in the institution of slavery, until it became socially untenable to participate in it. Finally, he turned his attention to the question of emancipation, where he distinguished between older and younger generations of enslaved persons. For those who had been enslaved for so long that it resulted in physical, intellectual, or behavioral liabilities that would make independent living problematic, he argued that they should remain in the care of those who considered them "property." Here Rush does not make clear whether he is simply resigned to a reality of gradual emancipation, where enslavement is the "lesser evil" to ensure the care of older victims, or if he is making a justice argument that those who created the conditions of their infirmities should bear the burden of caring for them. What is clear is that Rush believed emancipation might come too late for an older generation of Black people. For the younger generation, however, Rush prescribed education, including moral and religious education, to prepare them for freedom. He demanded that they be "instructed in some business, whereby they may be able to maintain themselves," and then he argued that the law should dictate a timetable by which they would be emancipated and enjoy "all the privileges of free-born British subjects." In this way, America would "bear a testimony against a vice which degrades human nature, and dissolves that universal tie of benevolence which should connect all the children of men together in one great Family."[15]

Doctor Witherspoon and Slavery

Like his friend Benjamin Rush, John Witherspoon thought slavery was an immoral practice and institution, and that abolition was necessary for the new nation to get on the right side of benevolence and a respect for human rights. Or at least, that is the conclusion we might draw from his record as a teacher at the College of New Jersey. As we shall see, however, Witherspoon was not the vocal public opponent of slavery that Rush was, and in fact, Witherspoon's acquiescence to the presence of slavery in his home state—and in his home—paints a muddier picture of his position on this issue. Consequently, it also raises questions about the consistency of his commitment to a public character based in respect for the good and humanity of other human beings.

In the tenth of his *Lectures on Moral Philosophy*, immediately after an overview of natural rights—including the right to liberty—that all human beings possess as remainder from the state of nature, Witherspoon directly took up the issue of slavery.[16] He acknowledged that no society can exist with perfect equality between members, for "in every state there must be some superior and others inferior" in the maintenance of political order. He also acknowledged that how much inequality and "degree of subjection" a healthy society can host is a difficult question, perhaps one that requires the virtues of discernment and prudence to consider in specific contexts. Within a society that hosts inequality, he was willing to imagine voluntary slavery existing, by which he likely meant a kind of extended indentured servitude, where a person barters their liberty for some kind of provision or opportunity. He also allowed for the use of slavery as punishment for a crime, and in fact indicated his preference for forced labor over death as a legal punishment.

In this lecture, however, Witherspoon made clear his moral opposition to involuntary slavery of the kind practiced in the colonies. He argued that it was "certainly unlawful to make inroads upon others, unprovoked, and take away their liberty by no better right than superior power." This remark seems to be a clear and unequivocal objection to the African slave trade industry, and its placement in a lecture on natural rights and liberties suggests that Witherspoon thought involuntary servitude, when not a punishment for violating the social compact, was a transgression of human rights. Implicit in the linkage he provides here is an affirmation of the moral equality of Black persons, that he would assert the relevance of his concern for natural rights to them. Witherspoon knew that some defenders of slavery argued that the practice was actually benevolent, in that it introduced members of "barbarous nations" into better circumstances, "more of the comforts of life," a more refined culture, and "a more eligible state" than they would have in Africa. Witherspoon made clear, however, that even if this benevolent yield exists, "it does not justify the practice." For, he pointed out, "it cannot be called a more eligible state" if those taken against their will consider it "less agreeable to themselves." He even anticipated the proslavery argument that the Bible does not prohibit slavery by suggesting that slavery in the Bible is only of the punishment variety, for domestic offenses or as a consequence of war.[17] He also suggested that the "law of Moses" is more concerned with laying down requirements for the proper treatment of slaves than it is justifying the practice in the abstract. He ultimately declared that "it is very doubtful whether any original cause of servitude can be defended, but legal punishment for the commission of crimes."

In the following lecture, Witherspoon analyzed various domestic relationships, including the "relation of master to servant."[18] Notably, here he used the term "servant" rather than "slave," a deliberate word choice that allowed him to distinguish between voluntary and involuntary servitude and reject the latter as morally unjustifiable. He acknowledged that some members of society may "make it their choice, finding they cannot live otherwise better, to let out their labor to others for hire." He made clear, however, that in those arrangements a master can only presume a right over the "labor and ingenuity" of his servant for the agreed-upon time period. For Witherspoon, an indentured servant "retains all his other natural rights," and since life and liberty are inalienable rights, Witherspoon insisted that a master "can have no right either to take away life, or to make it insupportable by excessive labor." Implicit in this lecture, too, is an indictment of involuntary slavery as practiced in the colonies.

These philosophy lectures represent Witherspoon's most direct critique of the institution of slavery, marshalling his teachings on natural rights to label the practice inhumane.[19] In what otherwise reads like a rejection of slavery as practiced in the colonies, however, he included this aside: "I do not think there lies any necessity on those who found men in a state of slavery, to make them free to their own ruin."[20] At best, Witherspoon seemed to be saying that as bad as the institution is, no single slaveowner is obligated to sacrifice his own good to extract himself from the practice. At worst, Witherspoon was drawing a distinction between the acquisition of slaves from the African continent and the trading of slaves who were already in the colonies. Because the vast majority of slaves in the American South in Witherspoon's time were second- and third-generation slaves born in the Americas, this latter interpretation would amount to a moral pass for most Americans implicated in slavery.

Witherspoon's objection to slavery in his *Lectures on Moral Philosophy* was consistent with the teachings on natural rights in which they were embedded. He suggested that slavery was wrong because all human beings—including Black victims of slavery—have a basic right to life and liberty and control over the voluntary use of their property and labor. To argue this way was not just a critical commentary on the institution of slavery but an attack on the moral and anthropological assumptions on which that institution depended for its justification. In his invocation of natural rights to argue against slavery, he implied that Black Americans were the intellectual, moral, and species equivalent of white Americans. Importantly, there is no evidence to suggest that Witherspoon subscribed to polygenesis. Instead, his apparent regard for the humanity of Black persons resembles Rush's convictions, including his insistence that Black Americans have the same right to the protection of their natural rights as Europeans, as fellow descendants of Adam and as reflections of the *imago Dei*.

Witherspoon's actions in at least two cases affirmed this philosophical and theological commitment to the humanity of Black people. As president, we know that he welcomed at least three Black students to the College of New Jersey. Before the war, Bristol Yamma and John Quamine, two African free men, studied with Witherspoon at the behest of Samuel Hopkins and Ezra Stiles. In the last year of his life, Witherspoon also welcomed a man named John Chavis from Virginia to study with him. Given Witherspoon's convictions regarding education and its purpose as intellectual and moral preparation for the character of public citizenship, the fact that he would welcome Black students to study with him was a powerful testament to their equality in his eyes.

Another indicator of Witherspoon's respect for the humanity of Black people took place earlier in his career. As pastor of the Beith congregation in Scotland, Witherspoon took under his wing a young Black man named Jamie, instructed him in the faith, and agreed to baptize him. He gave Jamie (or allowed Jamie to choose) the surname Montgomery, the maiden name of Elizabeth Witherspoon. What makes Witherspoon's relationship with Jamie Montgomery noteworthy is that when Witherspoon befriended him, Jamie was caught up in a legal battle over his freedom. Jamie had been a slave in Virginia, purchased and shipped to Scotland to be educated with the intent of reselling him and netting a profit for his owner. Jamie claimed, however, that he was a freeman by virtue of being baptized, and the authority he invoked for that claim was none other than the minister who baptized him, John Witherspoon. The man who claimed ownership over Jamie argued that baptism did not make a slave free, that spiritual equality in Christ was not the same thing as political equality, and that Rev. Witherspoon had assured him that when he baptized Jamie, he made clear to the young man that this would have no impact on his slave status. Both sides invoked Witherspoon as an expert, but Witherspoon left no direct evidence for us to judge which invocation was accurate. It is not far-fetched, though, to believe that Jamie got the idea that his baptism was an emancipatory act from his minister, given what we know about Witherspoon's moral judgment on slavery, his conviction that it was a violation of natural right, and the close association in his moral theology between spiritual, moral, and political equality. In fact, it is plausible that Witherspoon baptized Jamie with at least partial intention that he might sabotage the alleged owner's claim on him.

If Witherspoon gave evidence of his respect for the full intellectual and moral capability of Black persons, we should pause to acknowledge that his description of Native Americans is less flattering. Although Witherspoon invited at least one Native student to the college, he peddled in negative stereotypes of indigenous Americans. In his "Description of the State of New Jersey," he reported that, according to what he had observed and read, Native Americans were good hunters and ferocious warriors, but they were also lazy, misogynistic, sometimes cowardly, and resistant to European standards of civilization. Efforts to enculturate them on reservation plots within the colony had largely failed, and the Natives either retreated back to the woods or died out. Witherspoon admitted that his experience with the Native peoples was shallower than others', given the fact that he had arrived in New Jersey recently, but he did not seem to hold high hopes for their assimilation into English culture. "There have been some of them educated at this college, as well as in New-England; but seldom or never did they prove either good or useful." Given his anthropological assumption that all human beings belong to the same species, originating from Adam and Eve and reflecting the *imago Dei*, Witherspoon was likely not making a judgment here on Native Americans' inherent ability to intellectually or morally "improve." Instead, what we have here is probably a commentary on Native *culture*, no less offensive to modern ears, but not a denial of the humanity of the Native Americans he judged so resistant to European "refinement."[21]

Witherspoon's belief in the fundamental intellectual and moral equality of Native and Black persons can be traced back to those same two intellectual traditions that shaped his broader moral foundations: Calvinism and Scottish moral philosophy. Among his theological and philosophical influences, he would have encountered some thinkers who were comfortable with racial slavery and others who judged it a moral abomination. As we have seen, Christian thinkers in the eighteenth century regularly offered biblical justifications for American slavery, rooted in assumptions about racial differences and reflecting Christianity's historical comfort with slavery as a social institution. Calvinists in Europe and America were among those who believed that slavery could be an acceptable tool of social order and political warfare. Before the eighteenth century, few English-American Calvinists were explicitly antislavery, because Calvinists placed a high priority on social order as a reflection of God's ordering and political power as derivative of God's sovereignty.[22] Whether motivated by a paternalistic concern for human beings considered intellectually or morally deficient, or used as a consequence of justified warfare, slavery was for many

Calvinists simply an institutional given that contributed to the stability of an appropriately hierarchical social order. Within this priority on order, Calvinists like William Ames placed a great deal of emphasis on "contentment," or the acceptance of one's social lot in life. Many Calvinists tended to be social conservatives, allergic to threats to social peace, so for them the moral responsibility of those who were enslaved was to live righteously within that lot, not to challenge the differentials of power.

Calvinists were also biblicists, and to most of them (certainly before the eighteenth century), the acceptance of slavery as a tool of state power was embedded in the Bible itself. The Bible occasionally offered moral parameters for the relationship between slaves and masters, but it never offered an explicit rejection of the practice itself. Its uncontested status in scripture led many Calvinists to assume God's comfort with the institution. As Gordon Mikoski argues, "to condemn slavery outright was . . . tantamount to undermining the authority of Scripture."[23] In fact, Mikoski interprets the Jamie Montgomery case as Witherspoon's attempt to have it both ways, to signal a "theoretical repugnance about the practice of the institution" without challenging scripture directly on the issue. Deference to the Bible helped other English-American Calvinists of the eighteenth century, like Jonathan Edwards and George Whitefield, justify their possession of slaves as well as the broader social practice.

While many Calvinists of the early modern era condoned slavery, there were minority voices to the contrary. The radical Calvinist Samuel Rutherford railed against slavery as part of his insistence on natural rights: "Every man by nature is a free man born, that is, by nature no man cometh out of the womb under any civil subjection to king, prince, or judge, to master, captain, conqueror, teacher, etc., because freedom is natural to all."[24] Roger Williams was invested enough in the equality of human beings that he objected to slavery, though later in life he supported the use of slavery as a consequence of war.[25] Of particular interest is Richard Baxter's opposition to slavery. Witherspoon was evidently fond of Baxter's work, and in his mammoth *Christian Directory* Baxter took up the responsibilities between masters and servants as part of his treatment of "Christian Economics," or domestic duties. In the first part of his discussion, Baxter dealt with servants as a broad category that included people engaged in a limited period of service and those in perpetual servitude. Immediately, he declared that masters have a fundamental responsibility to the laborers in their charge, to provide for their human needs (food, shelter, rest) and their spiritual good. He reminded masters that "in Christ [your servants] are your brethren and fellow-servants; and therefore rule them not tyrannically, but in tenderness and love; and command them nothing that is against the laws of God, or the good of their souls."[26] Baxter claimed a fundamental equality between masters and servants, one that imposes duties on the relationship despite the power differential. As if to reinforce the basic value of servants and slaves in the eyes of God, he insisted that the Golden Rule should govern the relationship, reminding masters to "do as you would be done by, if you were servants yourselves."[27]

Baxter then launched directly into a commentary on "those Masters in foreign Plantations who have Negroes and other Slaves." To slaveholders in the Americas, Baxter demanded that they respect the "difference between men and brutes. Remember that they are of as good a kind as you; that is, they are reasonable creatures as well as you, and born as much natural liberty."[28] At the very least, for Baxter this meant that the natural and spiritual needs of enslaved people must be respected and provided for. He insisted that slaveowners satisfy the physical needs of their slaves as members of their own households, and he suggested that failure to provide them Christian education is "rebellion against God, and contempt of Christ the Redeemer of souls."[29] Fundamentally, he instructed his slaveholding readers to treat their slaves as the human beings that they are. Directing a pointed accusation to English slaveholders in the Caribbean and American South, he wrote, "How cursed a crime is it to equal men and beasts! Is not this your practice? Do you not buy them and use them merely to the same end, as you do your horses? To labor for your commodity, as if they were baser than you, and made to serve you? Do you not see how you reproach and condemn yourselves, while you vilify them as savages and barbarous wretches?"[30]

The longer Baxter's discussion of African slavery goes on, the clearer it becomes that he intended an indictment of the slave trade itself, including both the brutal practices and the denial of Africans' humanity that underwrote the institution. Like many of his contemporaries, Baxter did not condemn slavery categorically; he allowed that voluntary perpetual servitude may be an appropriate remedy for extreme poverty, and involuntary slavery may serve as a proper recourse for criminal behavior or the consequence of war. But to Baxter, the African slave trade was something entirely different:

> To go as pirates and catch up poor negroes or people of another land, that never forfeited life or liberty, and to make them slaves, and sell them, is one of the

worst kinds of thievery in the world; and such persons are to be taken for the common enemies of mankind; and they that buy them and use them as beasts, for their mere commodity, and betray, or destroy, or neglect their souls, are fitter to be called incarnate devils than Christians, though they be no Christians whom they so abuse.[31]

Baxter called the African slave trade what it was, evil, and he was no more inclined to excuse second-hand slaveowners than he was those doing the acquisition off the African coast. Anticipating the question of whether buying a Black person already enslaved was as bad as kidnapping them in the first place, Baxter says unequivocally, "It is [your] heinous sin to buy them, unless it be in charity to deliver them." In fact, once a man has purchased another, he has an obligation to set him free. Baxter's hypothetical interlocuter then asks, "But may I not sell him again, and make my money of him, seeing I leave him but as I found him?" Baxter's response is direct: "No; because you have taken possession of him, and a pretended propriety, then the injury that is done him is by you."[32] It is your sin now, says Baxter, and your responsibility to remedy that sin by setting the enslaved person free.

Baxter's bold opposition to racial slavery in the seventeenth century anticipated (and in some ways outdid) the abolitionist perspectives of men like Samuel Hopkins, Ezra Stiles, Jonathan Edwards, Jr., and other Calvinists in Witherspoon's time. Given Witherspoon's fondness for Baxter's work, he likely would have been familiar with his objection to slavery as well. In addition to this theological influence, Witherspoon's position on slavery likely was shaped by his study of Scottish philosophy. British philosopher John Locke, who influenced many in the Scottish Enlightenment as a resource and foil, justified slavery and was a principal author of the Carolina constitution that allowed slavery in those colonies. Thomas Jefferson, of course, followed in Locke's footsteps in his participation in slavery in Virginia. David Hume was convinced that Black people were naturally inferior to white people and, it recently has been discovered, supported a friend's bid to purchase an American slave plantation, despite his critique of slavery in ancient Rome.[33] But for other thinkers among the Scots, common themes like natural rights and benevolence led them to view slavery as immoral. Francis Hutcheson, for instance, rejected the idea of involuntary slavery as antithetical to the "natural equality" that he believed all human beings possess. Natural equality bestows on all people natural rights, including the right to life and liberty, a conviction that prompted Hutcheson to reject Aristotle's argument that some people are naturally born for slavery.[34] Hutcheson's beliefs about natural equality led him to reject all uses of slavery, including as punishment or a consequence of war, and he (along with contemporaries like Adam Smith) influenced many in the abolitionist movement of the eighteenth century.[35] As we have seen, Witherspoon was deeply familiar with Hutcheson's work as well.

It is impossible to know for sure what precise combination of these influences led Witherspoon to the antislavery perspective reflected in his philosophical writings, but interestingly, in the few places Witherspoon comments on slavery, he does so primarily through philosophical argument, not religious claims. Witherspoon's clearest rejection of slavery appears in his *Lectures on Moral Philosophy*; there is no reference to slavery in his *Lectures on Divinity*, and no sermon text that includes negative commentary on the institution exists in his corpus, even though public preaching against slavery was a common tactic for abolitionist ministers. It may be fair to conclude that Witherspoon found the philosophical argument against slavery more compelling than the attempt to biblically oppose it.

It is also important to note that Witherspoon's critique of the morality of slavery did not make him an explicit abolitionist, certainly not one who called for immediate emancipation. While he apparently considered slavery wrong, his public writings also make clear that he did not think the solution to that wrong was the immediate elimination of the institution. Like the vast majority of abolitionists in his time, he may have believed Black Americans were generally unready for sudden freedom, so that a process of gradual emancipation would have seemed more responsible. Witherspoon also made it clear that he thought the institution was on its way out politically anyway, and as naïve as that optimism seems on this side of the Civil War, it also did not set him apart from many abolitionists. Finally, Witherspoon was painfully aware of the threat to the Revolution posed by an inter-colonial debate over slavery, given the South's investment in it, so his priority on American independence may have influenced his preference for a gradual address of the issue. Judging by his writings, Witherspoon may have believed slavery to be immoral, but that did not lead him to push for a radical and quick solution to this social problem.

Witherspoon the Slaveholder

In fact, it apparently did not even push him to disassociate himself from the practice. Despite evidence in Witherspoon's writings that he considered involuntary servitude a violation of natural rights, the historical record suggests that he himself owned slaves. After Witherspoon's death in 1794, an appraisal of his property included two slaves among the listings. Neither the origin of the slaves nor what happened to them after his death is known. For instance, the slaves could have been part of the absorption of property that came with his second marriage, to Ann Dill, but we cannot know for sure. There is no evidence to suggest that Witherspoon purchased them himself; neither is there evidence to eliminate that possibility. We also do not know the nature of his relationship with these two people. In fact, it is even possible that the two persons mentioned in the appraisal were not slaves but servants, given that white colonists often failed to differentiate between the two arrangements when it came to Black domestic workers.[36] But if we assume, as most scholars do, that the appraisal at Witherspoon's death indicates complicity in racialized slavery, how do we make sense of this fact, given his understanding of moral character?

Some scholars point to his ownership of slaves as clear evidence of moral hypocrisy. Despite all of Witherspoon's emphasis on natural rights and liberties when he was advocating for independence from Britain, when it came to the plight of enslaved Black Americans, he signaled his relative lack of concern by participating in the perpetuation of the institution. In fact, his critics say, he transgressed not only his broader investment in natural rights, part of the foundation of his theory of political character, but his more specific pronouncements on slavery itself, which he judged immoral based on that commitment to rights-based character. For critics looking for additional evidence that hypocrisy is the most straightforward explanation of Witherspoon's record on this issue, we might return to his discussion of slavery in the *Lectures on Moral Philosophy*, where he declared it "doubtful whether any original cause of servitude can be defended," but then provided himself and other slaveholders an out when he said, "I do not think there lies any necessity on those who found men in a state of slavery, to make them free to their own ruin." Was Witherspoon referring to his own financial circumstances, which were precarious throughout his tenure at Princeton, when he excused slaveholders from the responsibility to remove themselves from the practice?

While the evidence for contradiction exists, there is a lot we do not know about the circumstances of Witherspoon's alleged status as a slaveowner, and thus there is a real limit to the reliable conclusions we can draw about his experience and its consistency with or betrayal of his moral teachings. Did he actively acquire the slaves or passively inherit them with his second wife's property? Did they get added to his household when he was a middle-aged, active leader in revolutionary politics or when he was a sickly blind man on his deathbed whose affairs were largely governed by others? Did Witherspoon end up with slaves as part of his integration into the comforts of Princeton society, a local class that included slaveowners like the Stockton family? Do any of these details of acquisition matter in our assessment?

Perhaps Witherspoon acquired the individuals in order to prepare them for eventual emancipation, following the lead of his friend Benjamin Rush, an ardent abolitionist who at least once purchased slaves as a way to free them. To be a slaveholding abolitionist would not have made Witherspoon unusual in his time, and if this were his motive, it would ultimately be consistent with his moral rejection of slavery. But even then it would not absolve Witherspoon of all critique. Some may argue that a moral end does not justify immoral means. Others might argue that the utilization of slave practices to participate in the betterment of Black Americans smacks of paternalism, with white abolitionists deciding that a period of additional involuntary servitude was an acceptable cost for the chance to prepare them appropriately for social integration. As Lesa Redmond remarks, the abolitionist strategy of preparing slaves for introduction into free society "entails a recognition of Black liberty that is predicated upon white men determining when those in bondage are 'ready' for freedom and further determining how best to utilize that 'freedom' once it has been seemingly earned."[37]

With the uncertainty around his motives, Witherspoon's apparent complicity in slavery looks suspect in combination with his apparent reluctance to publicly advocate for emancipation, gradual or immediate. With the prominence of Witherspoon's bully pulpit, he could have been a powerful voice for freedom for Black Americans, but he wrote or did little on the subject outside of his classroom lectures, a fact that distinguishes him in history from more vocal abolitionists like Hopkins, Rush, or Jonathan Edwards, Jr. When he did have an opportunity to publicly stake ground for emancipation in New Jersey, he came up small. From at least as far back as 1774, activists (primarily led by Quakers) had engaged New Jersey assemblies with petitions calling for abolition. Tensions within the state and the interruption of the war resulted in little progress for the abolitionists when in 1790, they again petitioned the state legislature to outlaw slavery. Witherspoon, writing on behalf of a three-person committee charged with considering the issue, declined the invitation. On behalf of the committee, Witherspoon pointed to recent legal developments in New Jersey that outlawed both the importing and exporting of slaves, as well as the mistreatment of slaves, as progress toward the end of emancipation. He also hypothetically floated the idea of a law (similar to Pennsylvania's) that would award freedom to all enslaved persons by the age of twenty-eight, though he naively imagined that in that time slavery would peter out as an institution on its own. Given the progress already made, their belief that slavery was in its death throes, and their concern that "precipitation in the matter may do more harm than good," the three-person committee rendered the judgment that "it is not necessary nor expedient at this time, to make any new law upon the subject."[38] On the one hand, the committee's judgment clearly conveyed sympathy for the abolitionist cause and supported the idea of gradual emancipation. On the other hand, it did nothing to further the cause.

As the work of a committee, it is difficult to know how much this report reflected Witherspoon's own views. The general sentiment toward gradual emancipation fit with what he shared in his lectures and writings, and the fact that the committee recommended no action could reflect the reality that moderate Witherspoon was flanked on the committee by an abolitionist and a slavery apologist. Similarly, Witherspoon participated in a public statement on slavery issued by the Presbyterian Church, but how much the statement reflected his own views is obscured by the involvement of a committee. In 1787, the Presbyterian Church's Synod of New York and Philadelphia was presented with an overture that called upon every Presbyterian congregation and family "to do everything in their power consistent with the rights of civil society to promote the abolition of slavery." The overture based this plea on the unity of human beings as creations of God, the Christian responsibility to general benevolence, and a respect for "the rights of human nature."[39] After tabling discussion for a couple of days, the synod took up the overture and eventually settled on a recommendation for gradual emancipation. The statement, which Witherspoon likely helped craft (the minutes confirm he was in attendance), avoided the direct condemnation of slavery in the original overture, but it recommended that slaveholders create reasonable timetables for the emancipation of their slaves and prepare them for freedom by providing them with education and property. Again, a committee which Witherspoon helped lead took a moderate public approach to the contentious issue of slavery, endorsing the wish that the institution would disappear, but cautious in calling for radical change.

To the extent that these cases reflect Witherspoon's own stance (or at least a stance with which he was comfortable associating), they suggest a conservative approach that, when combined with his own personal involvement in slavery, understandably looks self-serving. Other parts of Witherspoon's record are similarly unflattering. For as much as Witherspoon dominated the mission and culture of Princeton during his tenure as president, he apparently never challenged the presence of slavery at the college. The college's first nine presidents owned slaves, as did trustees, faculty, and even students.[40] Slaves contributed significantly to life at the college from its earliest years, including during Witherspoon's time.[41] There is no evidence that Witherspoon ever spoke out against the infiltration of slavery into college life, and in fact, abolitionism had no significant presence at the college at all during his time as president. Furthermore, while Witherspoon privately taught several Black men, he did not push for his students of color to matriculate as formal students at the college; indeed, no Black undergraduates were enrolled at Princeton until the middle of the twentieth century.[42]

If Witherspoon believed that the epitome of public character was benevolent regard for human beings' natural rights, and if he believed that slavery violated the natural rights of Black people, why did he fail to publicly speak out against the institution, especially when it manifested on his own doorstep? If Witherspoon believed that higher education prepared people for effective public citizenship, and if he believed Black people capable of the kind of civic contribution that higher education empowered (a belief that seems implicit in his willingness to tutor several Black students), why did he not use his power at Princeton to welcome Black students into the full intellectual life of the college? To do so certainly would have made Witherspoon ahead of his time on the matter of rights for Black Americans, but given his aggressive commitment to rights on other political fronts, these are legitimate questions to ask. What made Witherspoon relatively radical when it came to political independence and nation-building but not when it came to racial justice?

One possible explanation for the apparent inconsistency between his philosophical opposition to slavery and his actions (or inactions) may be that his ideological commitments were neutralized to a certain degree by his own sense of personal need and convenience. As caretaker of a 500-acre estate like

Tusculum, Witherspoon may simply have failed to embrace the self-sacrifice it would have required to live without the help of the slaves he evidently owned. Likewise, perhaps a failure of imagination prevented Witherspoon from seeing how the college could continue its work without its dependence on slaves. If Witherspoon's hypocrisy was self-serving, he would hardly be the first person of privilege in history to fail to "walk the walk" of their theoretical commitments to justice, but of course that is no excuse for his failures. The easiest explanation for Witherspoon's private or public inaction on the issue of slavery is that he applied his assurance that "I do not think there lies any necessity on those who found men in a state of slavery, to make them free to their own ruin" to his own circumstances.

If this is the case, it may help us make sense of another moment in Witherspoon's intersection with slavery. At some point after his arrival in America, Witherspoon purchased land in what is now northeastern Vermont, around present-day Ryegate. By 1773, he was selling off some of that land, and a year later he gave some parcels to his oldest son, James. James traveled to Vermont to develop the land until war called and he left to join Washington's army. (James was killed in battle in 1776.) One account of local history suggests that James Witherspoon developed about twenty-five acres of land, complete with a house and outbuildings, with help from a team of laborers, "some of whom are said to have been colored slaves."[43] Now it is possible that this report is incorrect, that James's work team included Black laborers that the locals *assumed* were slaves; Vermont officially abolished slavery in 1777, but slaveholding persisted (albeit quite rarely) in the region before and after that date.[44] It may be that the anecdotal account of James's slaveholding reflects nothing more than "local interpretations of Black labor and caste in northeastern Vermont" at the time.[45]

If some of James's laborers were enslaved, the circumstances of his acquisition of them, as well as their lives after 1777, have been lost to history. But the possibility that James possessed Black slaves raises indirect questions about his father. If John was so opposed to slavery, how would his son come to participate in chattel slavery? Does this simply mark a moment of ideological opposition between John and James? Or does the possibility that James had slaves make it likelier that John willingly did as well? Perhaps James was raised in a household that, despite his father's classroom opposition to the institution, included enslaved persons (as the appraisal of his estate suggests), which would make it easier for James to justify the practice when his own needs required them. Too much missing information prevents us from knowing with certainty the facts surrounding

James's laborers, just as we lack adequate information to know for sure that his father unapologetically owned slaves. But the worst-case interpretation of this spotty historical record suggests a significant moral disconnect between Dr. Witherspoon's moral evaluation of slavery and his family's behavior.[46]

As we have already noted, however, there is at least one other way to interpret Witherspoon's actions, if we assume that the members of his household counted as such at his death were, in fact, slaves. Witherspoon could have been practicing the gradualist abolitionism to which he otherwise subscribed. Most abolitionists at the time were gradualists, believing that for a variety of reasons it was wise to wean America slowly from its dependence on slavery. Perhaps this is the explanation for the apparent presence of slaves in Witherspoon's household. If so, he not only was conforming with the majority view among abolitionists, he also was consistent with his own broader moral worldview, for moderation was a hallmark of Scottish philosophy and Calvinist theology. One implication of a realist anthropology that took seriously human beings' sin and commitment to self-interest was that moral reform would have to move slowly to achieve its ends without risking dangerous social upheaval. The respect for social institutions and deference to political authority evident in conventional Calvinism may have made Witherspoon reluctant to instigate too radical a social change (though he managed to get over any Calvinist conservatism when it came to political rebellion).[47] Theologically and philosophically, then, he may have been more comfortable with gradual social change around slavery than the more disruptive change being demanded by those who preferred the immediate emancipation of all slaves, and this gradualism may have informed his personal actions as well as his tepid public advocacy of abolition.

Oddly enough, Witherspoon's moral commitment to benevolence may have been partially to blame for his lack of leadership in the abolitionist project. One form that benevolent regard for others can take is paternalism, a condescending confidence that one knows better what is in the best interest of other people than those people know themselves. If benevolent paternalism animated Witherspoon's preference for gradual emancipation because it allowed for the preparation of Black people for social integration, then this would be a motive that Witherspoon shared with many abolitionist activists. We may even acknowledge the righteousness of Witherspoon's intent, but the disempowerment that resulted from a paternalistic regard for Black people is still open to significant critique. Whether Witherspoon's commitment to gradual emancipation reflected social conservatism or benevolent paternalism, it was compatible with his assumption that slavery's days in America were numbered anyway. Witherspoon thought the momentum of liberty from the independence movement would bleed into the social commitment to slavery, and that the institution would die out within a generation or so of his life. As we know from this side of history, that assumption proved ineffective and naïve.

Besides a philosophical commitment to slow reform, the most compelling explanation for Witherspoon's limited contribution to antislavery efforts may be that he judged radical commitment to emancipation politically unwise. Witherspoon may have been employing a pragmatic political strategy on a number of different levels. At home at the College of New Jersey, Witherspoon's fundraising and student recruitment depended on drawing from southern colonies. In comparison to the more parochial Harvard, Yale, and College of William and Mary, Princeton under Witherspoon's leadership was uniquely successful in attracting students and benefactors from well beyond its immediate region. This reach resulted in the long list of prominent families from Virginia and the Carolinas who sent their sons to study with him and contributed to the College of New Jersey becoming the first truly national college. But it also meant that Witherspoon had to be careful not to alienate constituencies from these slaveholding states. In fact, the local politics of New Jersey also required him to step carefully around the issue of slavery, as the institution was popular and important to the economy of East Jersey. For the good of his college's standing, locally and among the thirteen colonies, Witherspoon may have been reluctant to align himself publicly with abolitionist agendas.

This would have been a concern for Witherspoon beyond the health of his school. The unity of the colonies was always at high risk during the Revolution, and one of the aggravating issues to that unity was slavery. The northern and southern colonies were aware that they hosted distinct cultures and economies, and while they struggled to free themselves from Britain, a great deal of distrust existed between the regions too. Each thought that the other would prioritize their own economic needs over the other's, to the point that many involved in the independence movement feared that colonial cooperation would collapse into regional claims of independence and superiority before freedom from Britain had been achieved. Witherspoon clearly was very worried about disunity among the colonies, if the number of pleas to stick together in his public speeches and sermons is any indication. He was adamant that a strong central government was necessary to the success of independence, in part to compel the colonies into a relationship of mutual support and dependence. For Witherspoon, *the*

United States always promised a more secure future than *these* United States. Given this concern about unity, it is quite likely that Witherspoon sacrificed a robust public commitment to emancipation to what he considered the higher moral and political priority: political independence from Britain and a healthy start to the new republic. Perhaps Witherspoon's shortcomings on the issue of slavery reflected his unwillingness to touch the third rail of early American politics.

If Witherspoon made political calculations that discouraged him from speaking out forcefully against slavery, this could be read as consistent with his moral worldview in some ways—at least his moral anthropology, which always balanced the hope for collective virtue against a Calvinist acknowledgment of the reality of self-serving sin. Even so, his failure to combat slavery was inconsistent with the priority he placed on natural rights, the foundation of his vision of good political character. To explain Witherspoon's inactivity on emancipation as political calculus is not to excuse or condone it. However he made sense of it, from our perspective, we may judge Witherspoon's record on slavery as a failure of character as he himself defined it.

Notes

1 The account of Witherspoon's relationship with the enslaved Jamie Montgomery will be important later.
2 "Black and slave population of the United States from 1790 to 1880," *Statistica*, https://www.statista.com/statistics/1010169/black-and-slave-population-us-1790-1880.
3 Noelle Lorraine Williams, "New Jersey: The Last Northern State to End Slavery," The New Jersey Historical Commission, https://nj.gov/state/historical/his-2021-juneteenth.shtml.
4 Edwin S. Gaustad, ed., *A Documentary History of Religion in America to the Civil War*, 2nd ed. (Eerdmans, 1993), 489–91.
5 Gaustad, *Documentary History*, 501–2. See also Mark A. Noll, *The Civil War as Theological Crisis* (The University of North Carolina Press, 2006), 33–5. Noll argues that the apparent biblical equivocation on the morality of slavery is why the Civil War was as much a religious as a political crisis.
6 Gaustad, *Documentary History*, 496–7.
7 Sean McGever, *Ownership: The Evangelical Legacy of Slavery in Edwards, Wesley, and Whitefield* (InterVarsity Press, 2024), 58.

8 Eph. 6:5-9, NRSVUE.
9 Gaustad, *Documentary History*, 487.
10 Benjamin Rush, *An Address to the Inhabitants of the British Settlements, on the Slavery of the Negroes in America* (Philadelphia, PA: John Dunlap, 1773), http://name.umdl.umich.edu/N10229.0001.001, 7.
11 Rush, *Address*, 3, 12.
12 Rush, *Address*, 15-16, 21-4.
13 Rush, *Address*, 13.
14 Rush, *Address*, 1-2.
15 Rush, *Address*, 26.
16 Unless indicated otherwise, all references in this and the following paragraph are to Lecture X, *Works*, III:419-20.
17 Witherspoon, LMP, Lecture XI, *Works*, III:428. Witherspoon rejected the enslavement of POWs in modern war. He declared "the practice of ancient nations, of making their prisoners of war slaves" to have been "unjust and barbarous." He implies that doing so violated the human rights of those who may have fought in a war but were not responsible for the decision to go to war. He also warned that the practice invites one's enemies to utilize it as well, and his comment here has clear allusions to the conflict with Britain. Finally, he argued that POWs do not make very cooperative servants, so the practice of enslaving them does not serve much practical purpose.
18 All references in this paragraph are to Lecture XI, *Works*, III:428.
19 Other evidence of Witherspoon's views on slavery includes a mention of it in "A Description of the State of New Jersey," a piece he evidently wrote at the urging of Mr. Marbois's questions about the colony/state. Among his observations is the "great humanity" with which the Low Dutch people who dominate the state regard "their slaves and other servants," including that they do not hesitate to eat together in multiracial meals. See *Works*, IV:407. Witherspoon offered this observation without any moral commentary on the institution of slavery itself.
20 Witherspoon, LMP, LectureX, *Works*, III:419.
21 Witherspoon, "New Jersey," *Works*, IV:411.
22 See Jonathan Edwards as an example of a Calvinist thinker who emphasized the importance of social order as a reflection of God's ordering, in a way that led him to not only excuse but participate in slavery. McGever, *Ownership*, 103.
23 Gordon S. Mikoski, "Partial Iconoclasm: John Witherspoon's Presbyterian (Political) Theology and Slavery," *Theology Today* 80:4 (2024), 409.
24 Rutherford, *Lex, Rex*, as quoted in A. S. P. Woodhouse, *Puritanism and Liberty*, 206.

25 For more on Williams's mixed legacy on slavery, see John M. Barry, *Roger Williams and the Creation of the American Soul: Church, State, and the Birth of Liberty* (Viking Press, 2012), 158, 240–1, 356.
26 Baxter, *Christian Directory*, 460a.
27 Baxter, *Christian Directory*, 460b.
28 Baxter, *Christian Directory*, 461a.
29 Baxter, *Christian Directory*, 461b.
30 Baxter, *Christian Directory*, 461b.
31 Baxter, *Christian Directory*, 462b.
32 Baxter, *Christian Directory*, 462b.
33 Felix Waldmann, "David Hume Was a Brilliant Philosopher but also a Racist Involved in Slavery," *The Scotsman*, July 17, 2020, https://www.scotsman.com/news/opinion/columnists/david-hume-was-a-brilliant-philosopher-but-also-a-racist-involved-in-slavery-dr-felix-waldmann-2915908.
34 Hutcheson, *System of Moral Philosophy* (1755), I: 299–301.
35 Peter Wirzbicki, "John Witherspoon, the Scottish Common Sense School, and American Political Philosophy," *Theology Today* 80:4 (2024), 395–405.
36 Richard M. Balzano, "Informants and Artifacts: Local Histories' Representations of Bondage and the Precarious States of Freedom in Northeastern Vermont," *Vermont History* 90:1 (2022), 8. For a discussion of the mystery around the enslaved persons in Witherspoon's household—who they were, where they came from, and what happened to them—see Kevin DeYoung, "John Witherspoon and Slavery," *Theology Today* 80:4 (2024), 355–68.
37 Lesa Redmond, "John Witherspoon and Slavery: Ideology versus Praxis," *Theology Today* 80:4 (2024), 391.
38 For a copy of the record from the relevant New Jersey Assembly proceedings, see Sean Wilentz, "John Witherspoon and the Abolitionist Travail," *Theology Today* 80:4 (2024), 334–54, especially Appendix IV, 354. Wilentz argues (347) that the committee's judgment should be read as progress in historical perspective, since its report embraces the idea of eventual emancipation in a state where proposals for gradual abolition had been repeatedly rejected by the assembly over two decades.
39 Synod of New York and Philadelphia, *Minutes* [manuscript], May 26 and May 28, 1787. PHS Call number: VF BX 8951 .A3 1758–1788. See also Sean Wilentz, "John Witherspoon and the Abolitionist Travail."
40 For an extensive narrative account of the presence of slavery at Princeton, see the Princeton & Slavery Project at https://slavery.princeton.edu.
41 Lolita Buckner Inniss tells the story of two such slaves as a run-up to her study of James Collins Johnson and the experience of slaves at Princeton in the nineteenth

century. See *The Princeton Fugitive Slave: The Trials of James Collins Johnson* (Fordham Press, 2019), xiii–xiv.

42 Inniss, *The Princeton Fugitive Slave*, xx.

43 Edward Miller and Frederic P. Wells, *History of Ryegate, Vermont, from Its Settlement by the Scotch-American Company of Farmers to Present Time* (St. Johnsbury, VT: Caledonian Company, 1913), 557. As quoted in Balzano, "Informants and Artifacts," 7.

44 Balzano, "Informants and Artifacts," 4–5.

45 Balzano, "Informants and Artifacts," 8.

46 For more connections between slavery and Witherspoon's extended family, see the Princeton & Slavery Project at https://slavery.princeton.edu/stories/slavery-in-the-witherspoon-family. Most of these stories connect the Witherspoon clan to slaveholding through marriage into other families.

47 As we have seen throughout this study of Witherspoon, Calvinism hosts quite a bit of diversity, and that is true on this issue of social conservatism versus radicalism too. Witherspoon may have been influenced by his Calvinist worldview to take the social debate over slavery slowly, but other Calvinists interpreted the same tradition to require immediate emancipation. The Scottish Covenanters, who participated in abolitionist efforts in Vermont and the American South, combined an ultra-literal reading of the Bible with theocratic aspirations for human government to call for the immediate end to slavery as an affront to God's will. See Joseph S. Moore, "Covenanters and Antislavery in the Atlantic World," *Slavery & Abolition* 34:4 (2013), 539–61; Randolph A. Roth, "The First Radical Abolitionists: The Reverend James Milligan and the Reformed Presbyterians of Vermont," *The New England Quarterly* 55:4 (1982), 540–63.

7

Witherspoon and American Political Character

To this point, this book has been concerned with understanding John Witherspoon's vision of good political character—what he thought it looked like, how it was best cultivated, and how optimistic he was that good character could drive the effort toward American independence and the formation of a new republic. In this final chapter, I want to consider the implications of Witherspoon's vision in our time. Of course, the United States in the twenty-first century is a very different society than the one Witherspoon's peers were trying to create. The United States is more religiously diverse, more geographically expansive, and more politically centralized than it was during the Revolution, the Articles of Confederation, and the early days of the Constitution. The issues that tax us sometimes look very different than they did in the eighteenth century. And of course, we live on the other side of slavery than Witherspoon did, though we continue to grapple with the legacy of that atrocity. All of this is to say that a consideration of Witherspoon's relevance to our moment requires more than a simple cut-and-paste of his philosophical vision onto our context. At the same time, I suggest that Witherspoon's preoccupation with political character is an enduring concern in our time, and critical reference to his vision—both the virtue in it and the hypocrisy—may help us navigate important crises in the American character of the twenty-first century.

In many ways, Witherspoon personified the ideological basis for American independence. As a prominent representative of that historical moment, he gives us a sense of the intellectual, moral, and political grounds for the Revolution and the ethos in which the new republic was forged. Indeed, because of his moral bilingualism, he is one of the few figures from the period who captures both major ideological drivers of the Revolution. His political thought represented the Enlightenment-based ideals of many of the Founders, with his cautiously optimistic moral anthropology, his commitment to natural rights, and his respect for pluralism. With his typically Scottish concern for the social nature of human beings, he balanced the celebration of individual worth and liberty with a recognition that civil society is not just protection against encroachment on individual rights but an environment in which individuals can exercise their natural rights, defend the rights of others, and collectively engage in projects of true human flourishing. In this way, Witherspoon could speak much more naturally about the interconnectedness of individual rights and the collective good than a Hobbesian or even Lockean social project might.

Witherspoon also reminds us that the birth of the United States was not forged by the Enlightenment alone. Open to modern philosophical learning, Witherspoon was still an orthodox Calvinist, respected by many religious leaders of his day for his commitment to traditional doctrines and enthusiasm for both the intellectual and affective dimensions of the Christian religion that endeared him to revivalists and rationalists alike. He helped to make the case for the Revolution in theological terms, especially in his emphasis on religious liberty as the fundamental right at stake in the war. Along with Congregationalist, Presbyterian, Baptist, and Quaker leaders, he encouraged pious Americans to be patriotic, arguing for the compatibility between piety and patriotism while avoiding the crusading impulses of many of his preacher contemporaries. Early American historians increasingly recognize the indispensability of religious leaders to the independence movement, as they were often more effective in stoking local support than high-minded intellectuals like Jefferson. Witherspoon reminds us that the story of the American Revolution cannot be adequately told without highlighting the role that clergy like him played in its success.[1]

As a public intellectual, Witherspoon made the case for independence and articulated his vision for the new republic in the Continental Congress, in newspapers on both sides of the Atlantic, from pulpits in Princeton and elsewhere, and in the classrooms of the College of New Jersey. Witherspoon's impact goes well beyond serving as the personification of the Revolution's rhetorical underpinnings, however. Among his many important students was James Madison, and Witherspoon's impact on this particular founder cannot be exaggerated. Madison's own religious views are difficult to reconstruct, given that he was not as forthright as Jefferson in his correspondence with friends. Undoubtedly, though, his study with Witherspoon reinforced a basic respect for religion that he harbored and that drove his investment in "separation of church and state" as much as his concern about the effect of sectarian discord on public health. As Ralph L. Ketcham observed, "Madison's tolerant, sympathetic, and interested attitude toward religious questions and institutions was recurrent and consistent," a respect for religious adherents that was encouraged by his study with the Presbyterian Witherspoon.[2] Furthermore, "one of the most striking features of Madison's life was the warm feelings of mutual respect which generally existed between him and a wide variety of religious groups," relationships that Ketcham attributes to Madison's sympathy for religious concerns.[3] These "warm feelings" allowed Madison to forge alliances with religious constituencies in his fight for religious liberty in Virginia and on the national stage, the most consequential of which was his friendship with Baptist preacher John Leland. As William Lee Miller emphasized, "Madison had the best formal education of any of the major founding fathers, and he made good use of it. Much of it was in the context of an antiestablishment Protestantism. It gave him a knowledge of the tradition of dissent that Jefferson did not have and that few of the other major figures in the nation's founding would have."[4]

The ideological nature of Madison's commitment to religious freedom also was at least partially formed in Witherspoon's classrooms.[5] Like his teacher, Madison rejected the Lockean idea of toleration in favor of full-blown religious liberty, arguing that toleration "implied that there was some institution or belief in a superior position from which to do the tolerating."[6] By contrast, Madison availed himself of the dissertations on freedom of conscience and the importance of inalienable natural rights that he heard from Witherspoon to argue beyond an ethos of toleration for a civic commitment to complete religious liberty and the institutional separation of church and state. Witherspoon's tutelage paid dividends in Madison's defense of the Virginia Bill Establishing Religious Freedom in 1786, his work on the Bill of Rights soon thereafter, and his behavior toward religion while president. None of this was born from a hostility toward religion but instead reflected a respect for religion and conscientious conviction as human experiences beyond the purview of government to control.

Through his studies with "the old doctor," Madison also acquired a moral anthropology that made him encouraged about the potential for democratic governance while also sanguine about the temptations that naturally accompany the accumulation of power. Like Witherspoon, Madison subscribed enough to a general Enlightenment optimism in human rationality and virtue to advocate for a politics of self-rule. At the same time, "his tough assessment of the frailty of man's nature, the finiteness of human understanding, and the occasional inclination of the world to be simply 'out of joint,' would have warmed the heart of Presbyterian John Witherspoon."[7] From this understanding of the human condition, Madison developed principles of political realism that emphasized the importance of that quintessential American system of checks and balances to the defense and exercise of rights. We can imagine Madison internalizing from Witherspoon a version of that adage theologian Reinhold Niebuhr would articulate 150 years later: "Man's capacity for justice makes democracy possible; but man's inclination to injustice makes democracy necessary."[8]

Witherspoon the teacher shaped the opening moments of the United States most notably through his influence on Madison, but he also taught many other students who went on to serve the cause of independence, as the oft-repeated list of political actors who studied with him testifies. More broadly, Witherspoon helped to shape the distinctive character of early American higher education by teaching students who themselves would go on to establish or lead colleges in the new nation. At least three of Witherspoon's students founded colleges of their own. Former Witherspoon pupils would lead Union College in New York, Jefferson College in Pennsylvania, Washington and Hampden-Sydney in Virginia, Mount Zion in South Carolina, three colleges in North Carolina, two colleges in Georgia, and five institutions in Tennessee, in addition to the two disciples who followed him as president of the College of New Jersey.[9] Furthermore, Witherspoon influenced Benjamin Rush's philosophy for educational reform that he put into service in the form of three colonial colleges he helped establish.[10] In fact, Rush claimed (perhaps somewhat hyperbolically) that Witherspoon "gave a new turn to education and spread taste and correctness throughout the United States."[11]

From Witherspoon, these college leaders inherited a publicly oriented mission that has been the philosophy of American higher education through most of its history. For Witherspoon, like the Puritans and Gershom Carmichael before him, like Rush and Ben Franklin in his own time, and like generations of college leaders to follow, American higher education had a civic purpose: to train citizens and leaders to contribute to the public good. Under Witherspoon, Princeton would move beyond a primary concern for training ministers to include innovative tracks of study that would serve future teachers, lawyers, politicians, and public intellectuals. To cater to this vocational range, Witherspoon would complement the study of classical languages and medieval modes of learning with more practical elements, like modern languages, natural philosophy (science), moral philosophy, and politics. In doing so, he not only reshaped the curriculum at the College of New Jersey but significantly influenced the template for higher education in the United States until at least the advent of the modern research university.

Similarly, Witherspoon was a force of nature in the evolution of the Presbyterian Church in the United States into a distinctively American denomination. He furthered the cease-fire between revivalism and rationalism among Presbyterians, helped organize the first General Assembly on this side of the Atlantic, and trained many of the clergy in the next generation of American Presbyterians.[12] He helped to marshal Presbyterian support for the Revolution through his own preaching and the public letters of the Synod of New York and Philadelphia. He joined the ranks of dissenting American Protestants who protested the imposition of an Anglican bishop in the colonies, out of concern for religious freedom.[13] Discomfort with religious establishment also led the Presbyterians, with Witherspoon's leadership, to change language in the Westminster Confession, that historic creed of British Calvinism, to weed out its endorsement of civil interference in the realm of religion. These changes made the Presbyterians' confession more suitable for use in a pluralistic democracy that features "separation of church and state," and it helped to institutionalize a commitment to religious liberty among American Protestants.

For his political, pedagogical, and ecclesial impact, Witherspoon deserves to be part of the telling of early American history much more than he is. Overshadowed by the likes of Jefferson, Franklin, Adams, and Madison, Witherspoon was just as important as these thinkers, for the substance of his impact in the Revolution and as a symbol of a distinct stream of influence on the early republic. Witherspoon reminds us that the ideological formation of the United States is the product of more than Enlightenment philosophical reasoning. Religious thinkers, activists, and communities contributed to the independence movement, the early experiment with representative democracy, and the moral and political values on which the United States was founded. Moreover, his importance is more than historical. His commitment to the importance of a politics of character, based in respect for rights and a commitment to the common good, is a part of the American moral tradition that begs to be revisited in our moment. Witherspoon's views on character, including his own failures of character, offer historical wisdom to the political and cultural challenges facing the United States in the twenty-first century.

Our Crisis of Political Character

Witherspoon reminds us that a concern for public character is in America's DNA, as is a myopic appreciation for its moral application. We need to deal with whether those moral blinders render his ideals irrelevant, but for now we can acknowledge that Witherspoon was hardly alone in his conviction that the new American nation's health depended on the cultivation of character among citizens and leaders. Founders like George Washington, John Adams, Benjamin Rush, and Benjamin Franklin were concerned that upstanding moral character among citizens and leaders was necessary to ensure civic peace and order. Encouraging what Franklin called "Publick Religion" would instill in Americans "a creed of honesty, diligence, devotion, public spiritedness, patriotism, and obedience," and, as Franklin's term implies, they assumed that support of religious devotion (in a nonsectarian manner and consistent with the principle of religious freedom) would aid commitment to those virtues.[14] Patrick Henry echoed this concern for public character and religion's role in maintaining it when he sponsored a bill to support religious teachers in Virginia. The bill began with the assumption that "WHEREAS the general diffusion of Christian knowledge hath a natural tendency to correct the morals of men, restrain their vices, and preserve the peace of society," thus signaling both his concern for public character and his conviction that religion was key to nurturing it.[15] Many eighteenth-century political thinkers believed that a flourishing and stable society required the encouragement of virtue among the population.

This tradition of associating good public character with civic health and counting the encouragement of virtue among the responsibilities of a healthy society continues in our day. A priority on character sometimes is associated exclusively with political or religious conservatism, but concern for character need not be conservative. More moderate thinkers like David Brooks, Michael Sandel, Jim Wallis, and the late President Carter—in very different ways—have advocated for the civic importance of moral character that does more than simply reinforce conservative positions on social issues.[16]

In fact, if social conservatives served as the public voice for public virtue at the turn of this century, since 2016 they have been conspicuously quiet. Concern about character in American public life is now widespread among social moderates and liberals, prompted by the convention-busting audacity of Donald J. Trump. One by one, Trump has obliterated traditional expectations of those who aspire to the presidency. Certainly Trump did not invent the challenge to character in modern politics. Being constantly surrounded by corruption, Trump's presidencies remind us of the Nixon era. With his long-standing record of abusing or debasing women, Trump recalls our willingness to ignore or tolerate similar behavior from JFK and Bill Clinton. But beyond the precedent of modern presidents, Trump has made little attempt to hide his contempt for conventions of character. Instead of playing the part, he proudly belittles opponents, boasts of transgressions, dismisses military and political heroes as "losers," directs ridicule toward people with disabilities, incessantly undermines trust in the media, stokes racial hostilities, and threatens those he does not like or who do not "treat him well" with incarceration or deportation. He also lies as a matter of course. The *Washington Post* counted 30,573 specific instances of Trump uttering intentional falsehoods in his first term alone.[17]

Many Christian evangelicals who were a reliable source for calls to character at the turn of the century counted themselves among the most ardent supporters of this politician who enthusiastically attacked character norms. In the late 1990s, evangelical leaders and their allies insisted that moral character was an important criterion by which we should select leaders and hold them accountable. They attacked President Bill Clinton as unsuitable for the presidency because of his reputation as a philanderer; the entire Monica Lewinsky scandal was an attempt to use legal processes to force a moral referendum on Clinton's lack of character. By the early 2000s, this concern for public character yielded a political agenda with definable policy priorities. Evangelicals and their allies successfully pushed George W. Bush into the presidency with their insistence that his "compassionate conservatism" would protect American "moral values" better than the Clinton-dominated Democratic Party.[18]

By 2016, though, these same evangelicals were backing Donald Trump, claiming that his moral indiscretions were irrelevant to his suitability for leadership, relying instead on his friendliness to religion and his promise to overhaul the Supreme Court to ensure the end of *Roe v. Wade*. Trump's norm-busting behavior did not alienate his evangelical base; it actually emboldened his supporters, even religious ones, and Trump won over 70 percent of the evangelical vote each time he ran for office. In the meantime, Trump's political opponents tried in vain to get traction by appealing to character, with Michelle Obama famously declaring during the 2020 campaign that "when they go low, we go high," and Vice President Kamala Harris incessantly calling into question Trump's moral fitness for office in the 2024 election cycle. Trump's opponents inevitably found that the charges against Trump's character did not stick, and they usually abandoned the effort soon after, because benevolent character was apparently no longer a priority for conservative and evangelical voters. Over the decade that Trump has been president or a presidential candidate, his behavior has been so normalized in our political culture that he now has frequent imitators, and it is unclear whether the seemingly antiquated conventions of political decorum are even binding anymore.

At the risk of a bit of historical simplicity, we might imagine Witherspoon looking upon the state of American politics in our day as a tragic confirmation of his concern for character. Witherspoon argued that the health of the American republic depended upon a collective commitment to the common good, propelled by a virtuous priority on benevolence for others, exercised by leaders and citizens. That benevolence, he thought, shows itself in a respect for equal protection under the law, a sense of mutual duty, and a concern for the protection of rights. For Witherspoon, the good of the individuals and the common welfare of society are inextricably tied together. The current political environment in the United States would suggest that he was right. Without a shared respect for fellow citizens, it is difficult to encourage an investment in the common good. When mutual concern is replaced by suspicion and animosity, we lean into our differences and disagreements rather than the ties that bind us. The common good, then, cedes ground in our concerns to a competition between special interests in what is presumed to be a zero-sum game, where my good and others' goods are seen as mutually exclusive rather than fundamentally tied together. This, of course, is precisely the circumstance Witherspoon so feared, that in his time individual states or regions would abandon their united effort for independence to pursue their own interests at the expense of other states. Substitute political parties, identity groups, and ideological echo chambers for regional rivalries, and Witherspoon's deepest fear becomes our American reality. Without a basic sense of trust, other-regard, and what Danielle Allen calls "political friendship" between fellow citizens, we lose sight of what makes us the *United* States.[19] The law becomes a tool to wield against one's enemies, and rights become the bounty of those in power.

We might argue that one limitation to transplanting Witherspoon's call for political character to our moment is that the United States is a much different nation than it was two hundred odd years ago. We now live in a pluralistic society in which there is no shared consensus on moral norms and values, so that to appeal to a specific vision of healthy character is to reference norms that do not enjoy universal support, more reflective of a time when Christianity dominated the American ethos than our own moment, when religion's public influence significantly wanes. Witherspoon's claim, however, was that the mutual commitments that define good political character are deeply *human* norms and values, not simply a reflection of Christian particularism. He defined character as a commitment to legitimate concern for the well-being of one's neighbor and the collective good, reverence for the peaceful order that comes from the rule of law, and a deep investment in the protection and promotion of human rights. He rooted these values in his particular Christian worldview, but he also believed that they were rationally justifiable and obviously necessary for a healthy and flourishing civil society. The simultaneous erosion of benevolent character, national solidarity, and investment in the common good in our time seems to be empirical evidence that he was onto something. In particular, he emphasized the need for character in those we invest with leadership responsibilities, so that their discernment, wisdom, and benevolent concern can lead our collective disagreement and decision-making. When we entrust the public good to leaders of questionable character, who lack benevolence and a commitment to rights and duty, we shall, as Witherspoon predicted, "soon pay dear for [our] folly."

What a society committed to law, rights, and the common good requires in particular circumstances is a matter of interpretation and discernment. Different citizens holding the same commitments to these fundamental goods may nonetheless interpret their manifestation in public policy and practice in different ways. Witherspoon knew that, but he also believed that a common commitment to virtue, rights, duty, and the common good would shape how Americans debate and decide among the different options before them. In other words, Witherspoon thought public character would not clearly resolve all conflict, but it would shape the character of our conflict in constructive ways, including the character of our dissent. It is common enough these days for activists and public intellectuals alike to object to the imposition of moral parameters on social protest, when bigotry, injustice, and hate operate—and succeed—by throwing off moral restraints. Witherspoon, however, worried about a strategy of political dissent that called for fighting fire with fire. He objected to the maltreatment of POWs, even though he knew that American soldiers were abused by the British. He insisted on directing respectful language to the enemy, even though he himself was ridiculed and even burned in effigy by royalists. He rejected the demonizing rhetoric that came with viewing the Revolution as a crusade, a divine cause against infidels.

Obviously Witherspoon did not object to social protest, dissent, or civil disobedience—he was, in fact, a leader in a war of rebellion! But Witherspoon insisted that good character had a place even in violent resistance, let alone nonviolent social protest. In fact, he argued that the character of the just society for which we struggle ought to color the nature of our dissent. In this way, he thought about the relationship between character and social protest in a way similar to Martin Luther King's advocacy for nonviolent resistance. King believed that the means and attitudes of social resistance should match the vision of the just society that we seek, and that if we employ tactics of injustice in our fight, "the new order we seek will be little more than a duplicate of the old order."[20] The character of our dissent matters; it witnesses to the moral order we struggle to make reality.

Religion and Public Good

Also like King, Witherspoon was confident that religion could be a potent source of public character. Their confidence in religion, specifically Christianity, looks more complicated, however, from our historical vantage point. Some of the most important ideals of American democracy undoubtedly stemmed not just from Enlightenment thought but also from an evolution in Christian political theology. Early modern Protestant political theology taught that defense of personal liberty was a theological extension of the Christian commitment to human dignity, and an investment in the common good was a reasonable interpretation of the Christian doctrine of neighbor-love. Modern Catholicism often leans into the same themes. Witherspoon was a part of the early translation of Christian ideals into democratic aspiration, but as we know well, Christianity has not always been on the right side of the political good. Christian thinkers ardently defended slavery in the American South through the Civil War, and Christian groups continued to speak for—and sometimes violently enforce—white dominance over people of color even after abolition. The Christian religion has been invoked to stymie women's rights, to object to rights and freedoms for LGBTQ+ persons, and to baptize the excesses of capitalism that continue to oppress people in poverty. Much of American history and contemporary politics challenges Witherspoon's confidence in the Christian religion to promote benevolent political character, especially in a United States that is much more diverse than the one he lived in.

The concern for Christianity's more dubious political potential is especially heightened in our era due to the bravado of Christian nationalism. Christian nationalism is a political movement that perpetuates the myth that the founders intended the United States to be an explicitly Christian nation. Claiming that Witherspoon and his revolutionary peers established this nation on biblical principles and intentionally integrated Christian values into the political order, Christian nationalists have marshaled their considerable political and cultural infrastructure to undermine an American commitment to religious disestablishment. They argue that the United States was ordained by God to protect and propagate a very specific understanding of Christianity, so they celebrate the confusion of Christian identity and patriotism, refuting generations of interpretation of the First Amendment. They push for the display of the Ten Commandments in public schools and on government grounds, argue that prayer in school is essential for national health, and take the commitment to "one nation, under God" in the Pledge of Allegiance as symbolic affirmation that real Americans are Christian and real Christians are patriotic.[21]

What makes Christian nationalism distinct from simply a misunderstanding of history is that it weaponizes its interpretation of the nation's past in service to what are ultimately racist and antidemocratic aspirations. Because they purport to believe that the "original intent" of the founders was a Christian nation, Christian nationalists treat secularism and pluralism as national threats. Often collapsing ethnic, racial, and religious identities, they support strict immigration laws to limit the non-Christian population, and they campaign for leaders who will govern according to their Christian priorities—traditional male-dominated families, hostility toward gay, lesbian, and transgender people, and restrictions on the sexual and reproductive freedoms of women. Christian nationalism is ultimately not about religious orthodoxy. Instead, it is the use of religious myth to energize the hold on power of what Robert Jones and others call "White Christian America."[22] White Christian America is the legacy of two religious demographics: white mainline Protestants and white evangelicals/fundamentalists. Together they represent a constituency that has been accustomed to holding power in national life, but their power is waning, and they know it. Trends suggest that in a matter of decades, white Americans will be a minority population in the United States, so behind all of these efforts to undermine democratic institutions and resist the deepening of American pluralism is a desperate grasp for power by well-funded political leaders and a shrinking demographic. For this reason, the movement is often appropriately referred to as *white* Christian nationalism, because a vision of racial purity is at least as important to the cause as any religious ideals.

Students of Christian nationalism rightly point out that it is a political movement, not a variety of Christian religion. Christian nationalism is ultimately not about orthodoxy but power. Christian nationalism is not a synonym for evangelicalism; lots of evangelicals identify or sympathize with the nationalists' agenda, but others oppose its baptism of political power as blasphemy. Furthermore, Christian nationalism counts among its adherents non-evangelical Protestants, non-Christians, and secularists who find its power grab for white America appealing, even if they do not all subscribe to the religious orthodoxy the movement uses for cover. The "Christian" part of the movement is essential to its success, however. Christian nationalism co-opts the language and traditions of Christianity in order to baptize its antidemocratic efforts. It claims that an orthodox rendering of Christian values is on its side, so that all Americans should want the same things for public life that they do. And because Christian nationalists speak the language of traditional Protestant faith so effectively, many American evangelicals have come to believe that this vision of America is right and worthy of pursuit. Christian nationalists were instrumental in funneling the American evangelical vote toward President Trump in the 2016, 2020, and 2024 elections.

Besides an appeal to a selective interpretation of Christianity, of course, Christian nationalists also peddle a popular misinterpretation of American history. They insist that most, if not all of the important founders were practicing, orthodox, evangelical Christians. Sometimes they offer severely contorted renderings of founders that real historians know were unorthodox in their thinking, men like Thomas Jefferson, Thomas Paine, John Adams, and George Washington. The reality is that unorthodox thinkers were just as instrumental in the founding of the United States as traditional Christians, and most of them had no interest in the official establishment of one religious sect over others. Admitting the difficulty in making someone like Jefferson look like an establishment evangelical, Christian nationalists will more often emphasize the contributions of men who likely did hold traditional religious convictions, like Samuel Adams and John Jay. Some proponents of Christian nationalism include Witherspoon as one of their own, pointing to his Calvinist orthodoxy and public calls for revival in national piety as evidence that he desired the establishment of Christianity as the official religion of the new republic.[23]

As we have seen, however, this read of Witherspoon misstates his convictions regarding the proper relationship between "church and state." Yes, Witherspoon believed that religion could positively contribute to the character of the nation. But he believed that such a constructive contribution took the form of moral influence and alliances, not enforced doctrinal conformity, for he believed that piety could make Americans more virtuous only if they were first free to identify with religion on their own. In other words, religious *liberty* was the key to his confidence in religion's constructive social potential. Religious liberty in service to benevolent mutual regard was his primary political concern, and as a result, he never endorsed the kind of establishment Protestantism—with its penchant for violent enforcement—that Christian nationalists now claim for him.

In fact, Witherspoon gives us historical inspiration for rejecting the power grab of Christian nationalism while still embracing the potential of religion to positively shape public character in the United States. Like virtue theorists before and after him, Witherspoon believed that character is best cultivated in communities of mutual learning and accountability, with traditions of moral education and opportunities to practice and habituate other-regarding dispositions. These days, social observers increasingly attribute the deterioration of social connections and investment in a common good to the evaporation of formative sub-communities to which Americans can belong.[24] In response, Witherspoon stands as a voice from the past to suggest that religion often can serve as one locus for communal moral formation, encouraging virtues that, when exported, may contribute to an ethos of mutual respect and concern in the public arena. Many contemporary thinkers echo Witherspoon's suggestion that the substance of religions, including Christianity, can encourage a society that values democracy, defends human rights, and encourages commitment to the common good.[25]

Schools of Character

Religious communities were not the only place Witherspoon looked for moral formation and leadership in the new nation. As we have seen, he also believed that the family played an important role in cultivating public character in children. He assigned the encouragement of civic character as one of the responsibilities of government. And he believed that what we now call liberal education was about preparing young people for their duties in a democratic society. But each of these arenas is a contestable priority in contemporary American public life.

The importance of family to moral formation is perhaps the least controversial of Witherspoon's claims, but for decades American religious and political conservatives have pushed a particular interpretation of "family values" that makes echoing Witherspoon's emphasis difficult in our context. One of the most prominent sources for family values in American evangelicalism, for instance, has been Focus on the Family, an organization founded by psychologist and evangelical leader James Dobson. Through multimedia outreach to parents and pastors, Focus on the Family promotes heterosexual marriage, male family leadership, and parenting that is deeply informed by what it calls "biblical principles." It stridently opposes divorce, gay marriage, non-traditional family forms, and abortion.[26] Driven largely by Dobson's prominence as a spokesperson for the Christian Right, Focus on the Family and evangelical organizations like it have so dominated the public perception of "family values" that the term itself is now seen by Americans along the political spectrum as code for conservative views on sex, marriage, and family.

In this context, it is difficult to consider Witherspoon's priority on the family as a resource for moral formation without reinforcing the view that there is only one way to imagine a character-compatible family. Without a doubt, when Witherspoon talked about the family, he was assuming a household with two heterosexual parents. Even with this traditional assumption, though, Witherspoon's normative vision for the healthy family was progressive for his time and deviated significantly from how modern evangelicals talk about domestic life. Witherspoon was notably less hierarchical than what conservative evangelicals typically propose for a good family, apparently because his beliefs about healthy family life were based on his own experiences. He did not insist, as today's evangelicals do, that male authority in the household is a biblical template; instead, he recognized that parenting and domestic organization require skills and capacities that are not gender-specific. He acknowledged that wives were sometimes better equipped for family leadership than their husbands, and in these cases, he counseled husbands to defer to their partners. Witherspoon's portrait of the ideal family also featured parents who modeled good behavior with firmness, but without physical punishment and authoritarian control of their children. What we get from Witherspoon is a highly disciplined but decidedly nonhierarchical norm for the family, one that served as a laboratory for healthy relationships beyond the domestic arena.

Granted, the close association of "family values" with conservative views of sex, gender identity, and reproductive decision-making makes it hard to point to the family as a tool of character formation in a pluralistic society without invoking a particular set of cultural and political values. Witherspoon reminds us, though, of the risk of abandoning "family values" as a component of political character. Moral formation is most successful when it begins early, and the raising and schooling of young children present an opportunity to instill in them the value of benevolent mutual regard for civic life. It invites us to habituate in our children an investment in the collective good. Sociological and psychological research confirms that extended families, LGBTQ+ couples, and other forms also serve as successful family structures in which children can develop morally as well as intellectually and physically. Given what we know about the power of hate and competitiveness when modeled for young children, we do well to follow Witherspoon's prescription that a focus on the family is indispensable to the encouragement of a society of other-regarding character, even if many of us would expand our sense of what counts as a healthy formative family environment beyond the traditional nuclear form.

The association of government with character formation is also highly contestable in our day, and not just because of the erosion of standards of moral behavior and the dearth of other-regarding, rights-respecting character among political leaders. From the New Deal era through the Carter presidency, government was widely seen as a vehicle for discharging our collective commitment to the common good. Social welfare programs, anti-poverty initiatives, benefit entitlements, civil rights enforcement, and nondiscrimination regulations were all manifestations of the principle that the mechanisms of government can be utilized to discharge society's duty to the well-being of its members and the common good. In other words, government can be a means to maximize general benevolence. In the 1980s, however, Ronald Reagan taught Americans that "government is not the solution to our problem; government is the problem."[27] Thus began a drift into deregulation, *laissez-faire* economics, and minimalist government that became so pervasive that even the opposition party internalized it to win elections and maintain power. Bill Clinton's 1996 attack on "welfare as we know it" is the most blatant example of the universal adoption of hostility to government.

Given this entrenched suspicion of government in contemporary American politics, Witherspoon's insistence that government should both model and cultivate civic character is a hard sell. A civil society of good character, according to Witherspoon, maximized the general good of its citizens and, above all, protected and promoted natural rights. The erosion of programs that keep citizens out of poverty, the capitulation to corporations that exacerbate the wealth gap and dominate public assets like health care, and the deterioration of legal protections around civil rights (like voting) and natural rights (like bodily autonomy) all betray a society that is no longer collectively invested in the common good. Beyond its provision for basic human needs, government can help normalize a commitment to what the Constitution calls the "general Welfare," a necessary reaffirmation in a moment in which individual freedom ("Don't tread on me") is emphasized beyond—and often at the expense of—any duty to the common good. Combined with the failures of public leaders to model other-regarding character, government's structural retreat from its responsibility to safeguard basic rights and dignities is, from the perspective of "the old doctor," a discouraging sign of a morally disordered society.

The corrective for this disorder may be the inspiration of a new generation of other-regarding and rights-respecting civic leaders, and Witherspoon believed this was an important function of what we now call higher education. His confidence in higher education reflected the broader American tradition of liberal education as an institution with a civic purpose, the training of publicly minded citizens and leaders. But colleges and universities enjoy almost as little public confidence as government in our time. Some of that suspicion reflects a problem that goes the whole way down in the history of American higher education. Higher education is a privilege of the elite; only about 40 percent of Americans have a four-year college education, and liberal arts education remains an especially inaccessible luxury.[28] Students from the bottom fifth of wealth distribution in the United States make up only 5 percent of students in elite institutions.[29] In part because so many Americans are not exposed to it, higher education has become less valued in the United States than it was in the last century when the GI Bill, Pell Grants, and other government programs enacted the assumption that access to college was a public good. Now higher education is broadly seen as unavailable to many, socially irrelevant, and ideologically suspect. Conservative commentators in particular accuse colleges and universities of serving as breeding grounds for radical leftist agendas, a charge that has some grounding in truth if the low number of conservative faculty members on college campuses is any indication.

Any reliance on higher education for the cultivation of political character and democratic health in our day must wrestle with the reality of socioeconomic privilege and ideological imbalance on our college and university campuses. But the proper response is not to abandon education as unimportant but to reclaim the historic mission of college, especially the liberal arts. As Amy Gutmann suggests, the "institutional mission of colleges and universities at all levels is to increase opportunity, to cultivate creative understanding, and . . . to contribute to society. At their best, universities recruit hardworking, talented, and diverse student bodies and help them develop the understandings—including the roles and responsibilities of the professions in society—that are needed to address complex social challenges in the twenty-first century."[30] Colleges and universities serve this public mission when they train students for civically minded vocations while also offering a laboratory for citizenship in a pluralistic society, an educational space in which they can engage and learn from real cultural, religious, intellectual, and ideological difference. Constructive engagement with difference is the refiner's fire of public character, but it is hard to host when campuses are effectively segregated along racial lines, or when intolerant ideological orthodoxies govern, whether they are of the conservative or liberal variety. It is also difficult to do when higher education, especially liberal education, is a commodity easily attainable only by the wealthy. Colleges and universities, public and private, embrace their civic responsibility to cultivate public character when they explore new ways to make college affordable and accessible to a greater proportion of the population. This public mission requires a corresponding public investment in educational institutions, especially public universities, at a moment in which state allocations to their universities are constantly shrinking.

Witherspoon and America's Original Sin

John Witherspoon reminds us that a shared commitment to natural rights, mutual benevolence, and the common good is the recipe for a healthy democracy, and these moral commitments require communities and institutions to habituate them in citizens and leaders and to keep us in relationships of accountability to one another. But what if all this reflection on Witherspoon's political ethic of character, including its relevance to our time, is fundamentally misguided given his hypocrisy in the matter of character, his apparent complicity in the great moral crime of American history, the enslavement of Black human beings?

Witherspoon's connection with slavery is not something we can or should dismiss superficially. The disconnect between his moral teachings and the institution of slavery is part of his legacy too. In a way, this is another front on which Witherspoon helps our national reflection, for he personified the moral hypocrisy that is baked into our collective DNA. Naïve hagiography of someone like Witherspoon does as much a disservice to this truth as declarations that slavery or racism is something we have left in the past. As we consider whether Witherspoon can serve us as a historical resource in a promotion of character for our moment, we must take seriously the question: does his considerable moral failure on this front disqualify him as a useful voice worth learning from?

Of course, this question is too infrequently asked of other so-called founding fathers of the United States. The interrogation of Jefferson's relationship with Sally Hemmings has received more national attention in recent decades, but it is still subjected to whitewashing denials of a sexual relationship or claims that the relationship was mutual and romantic. Too often underappreciated is the power differential that makes Jefferson's relationship with Hemmings problematic regardless of the details, or the contextual reality that Hemmings was just one of hundreds of Black people Jefferson owned. Beyond the obvious examples of slaveholding founders, we know that many of the white members of abolitionist movements in the eighteenth and nineteenth centuries protested slavery while harboring racist assumptions about Black Americans' intellectual abilities and cultural compatibility with a predominantly white population. Critical understanding of the views on race held by white people on both sides of the slavery debate should chasten our celebration of these figures, a caution that extends to Lincoln as well, whose views on race were not always or entirely enlightened.[31] And if we take seriously the racism that is part of the biographical record of our national leaders, must we also call into question the authority of the foundational texts they penned, texts that themselves reflect the racism of their authors?[32]

Do we have any other options, besides the whitewashing of history that conveniently ignores the more sinister failures of figures like Witherspoon or the complete dismissal of such figures as constructive historical resources for our consideration of a healthy public life? Karen V. Guth, in a remarkable volume on what she calls the ethical treatment of "tainted legacies," identifies five common responses to a troubled and traumatic historical legacy like Witherspoon's.[33] "Deniers" simply ignore the problematic aspects of that historical record—by arguing that the problems do not exist, by peddling in moral equivalence (e.g., "everyone has flaws"), or by attributing the problems to historical context. In the case of Witherspoon, some apologists have attempted to challenge the assumptions that he indeed was a slaveholder. We have seen that the evidence against Witherspoon is telling but inconclusive, and some of Witherspoon's defenders lean into the spotty evidence to defend him against the charge of slaveholding. More often, defenders of Witherspoon point to his historical moment, arguing that racism was prevalent, that slavery was a contested but widespread part of colonial culture, and that virtually no one was arguing for its immediate abolition. The implication is that we should not hold Witherspoon's involvement in slavery against him, because as a product of his era, he hardly could be expected to know better. To grant Witherspoon such an easy out is to misrepresent his historical context, in which he was surrounded by thinkers and activists who were quite critical of slavery as a moral abomination. It also dangerously minimizes the harm of slavery, to the detriment of our responsible address of its enduring impact on US society.

What Guth calls "separationists" might defend Witherspoon's positive legacy by employing a slightly different tactic. Separationists acknowledge both the appealing part of his historical impact and the more problematic parts of his biography but then assert that they have very little to do with one another. In other words, separationists argue that it is possible for us to benefit from Witherspoon's teachings on political character while conveniently leaving his slaveholding in the past. But as we have seen, if Witherspoon was a slaveholder, that was an important part of who he was as a moral and political leader, as important as his teachings on political character. His teachings on political character and his willingness to live with slavery as a reality were inextricably intertwined. The foundation of his concept of character was benevolent regard for other human beings and a deep commitment to human rights, two moral ideals violated by the institution of slavery. The separationist, then, asks us to compartmentalize in a way that is impossible for historical memory or ethical consistency.

Guth contrasts these two common attempts to defend historical legacies from their tainted dimensions to another one, which she calls the "abolitionist" response. The abolitionist refuses to separate the admirable parts of a historical legacy from their problematic aspects. They are one and the same person, tradition, or history, and the unethical part of that legacy negates the usefulness or virtue of the allegedly good part. In fact, some abolitionists may argue that the immoral part of the legacy reflects the "true self" of a figure like Witherspoon better than his moral platitudes. As Guth writes, "the risk of reinforcing the negative ideology, burdening victims, or corrupting the entire legacy is too great for abolitionists to risk engaging with the tainting legacy," so they reject the authority of such legacies and ban them from any canon of cultural authority.[34] As Guth rightly points out, however, the abolitionist's rejection of someone like Witherspoon's moral failings comes with a corresponding risk. That risk is that the abolitionist fails to take seriously enough the enduring power of a tainted legacy. Witherspoon's part of American history continues to have an entrenched and formative influence on subsequent generations, including our own.[35] Abolitionism may signal righteous indignation regarding morally compromised aspects of our past, but it actually undermines its own project by inviting the misguided view that systemic injustices are only a product of a past that we can easily jettison.

Two other common responses to tainted legacies that Guth identifies are what she calls "revisionists" and "redeemers." The revisionist assessment of history takes seriously the good parts and the problematic remainders and refuses to ignore one part of that history in service to the other. What revisionists argue is that a holistic approach to that history prompts reassessment. In the case of Witherspoon, that reassessment might require us to update his legacy as a prophet of political liberty and a pioneer in American higher education to include his identity as a slaveholder. Witherspoon revisionists might argue, for example, that statues of the man on the campus of Princeton University should remain in place, but with a plaque that tells the whole story of his life and moral record. Slightly different in their intent, redeemers, says Guth, "aim to salvage good from the ashes," not by ignoring the problematic parts of the legacy but by "putting tainted goods in the service of life-saving causes."[36] A redemptive redirection of Witherspoon's legacy might similarly include symbolic markers to prompt public consideration of the role of Black people in the early maturation of Princeton. Guth appreciates much of the constructive work that revisionist and redemptive approaches to these kinds of tainted legacies undertake, but she still worries that they risk reinforcing the authority of the legacy and absolving it of judgment too quickly.

The approach that Guth recommends is a significant variation on the revisionist and redemptive approaches that also captures some of the righteous moral indignation of the abolitionists. She calls hers a "reformer" approach, and she distinguishes it from the others in several ways. The reformer approach insists on decentering the specific legacy in question—in our case, Witherspoon himself—to interrogate the historical and social systems of oppression in which they were embedded, by which they were formed, and for which they stand as representatives. In our case, Guth might suggest that the questions around what to do with Witherspoon's tainted legacy should prompt a larger discussion about the history of oppression he represents and its impact on subsequent iterations of American society. Her approach also invites us to look beyond Witherspoon himself to consider the moral authority of victims of the oppression he participated in and symbolizes. In other words, Guth argues that Witherspoon's tainted legacy should draw our attention past Witherspoon to uncover and preserve the moral testament of enslaved Black Americans and the powerful defense of their own humanity in the face of a dehumanizing institution.

Finally, Guth argues that a reformer approach ought to prompt us "to reform the larger social, cultural, political, and economic structures whose unjust power arrangements, policies and practices, and *de facto* and *de jure* modes of operation have enabled, facilitated, and excused the various violations of tainted legacies."[37] Ultimately, the point of consideration motivated by these legacies should not be the "great men" or their traditions, but the ongoing project of rejecting destructive and dehumanizing systems and creating a more equitable and just society.

Guth's reformist approach to tainted legacies represents the good that I think can come from a legitimately critical appreciation for Witherspoon's story. Witherspoon personified the moral disconnect that goes all the way back to the origins of American society. In his participation in—or at the very least, permissiveness to—racial oppression, Witherspoon embodied the United States' original sin. To struggle with Witherspoon's record is to struggle with the soul of our nation, but it is a wrestling match well worth the effort and woefully overdue. Much of the pushback on contemporary efforts aimed at racial justice ignores the fact that we are collectively starting from a deficit. Racism is not an unfortunate detail of America's past. It is a historical commitment to inequality that is baked into our systems and structures and persists to this day. To take Witherspoon as a complicated figure is to take seriously our complicated past, to wrestle with our highest ideals and our deepest inhumanities, and to ponder the question of how one nation can be so committed to the aims of liberty while it actively and aggressively maintains institutions of unfairness and oppression. To take that kind of collective soul-searching seriously positions us to reform and restructure our society in a way that inches closer to justice.

This project of moral reform is also where Witherspoon may help us, perhaps despite himself, for if he personified those demons of the American tradition, he also elegantly articulated its highest ideals, ideals that will serve our efforts at a more just society—concern for the common good, respect for the basic humanity of other persons, and a robust commitment to human rights. What Guth says about historical, cultural, political, and religious legacies in general, we certainly can say about the legacy of political moral ideals that Witherspoon represented:

> They create the moral environment in which we exist, they are the air our psyches breathe, and they shape our ways of seeing, thinking, and valuing. They structure our behavior, our ways of life, and our modes of organization. We are indebted to them in ways we can easily identify and in ways we cannot fully acknowledge. Legacies do not merely produce heirloom objects that we can receive or reject, but entire frameworks from which we cannot escape and which we still need.[38]

The moral legacy of political character is one we abandon to our own peril, for it contains the very ingredients we need to construct the antidote for the injustice and oppression Witherspoon also represents, and which is embedded in our political, economic, and cultural systems.

Holding on to the good and the bad in a legacy like Witherspoon's is to engage in what I call "chastened history." It reminds us that a mixed moral record is who we are as a country; great moral aspiration and tragic moral failure are simultaneously present in our national bloodstream. Figures like Witherspoon, Jefferson, Washington, and others personify the imperfections and hypocrisies that pervade our national character. There is educational good to be had by continuing to focus on these figures, but to begin telling fuller stories of their roles in American politics and culture. When we ignore them because of their moral failings, we miss out on the opportunity to learn more critically from our past. Of course, study and veneration are not the same thing. To the degree that statues, for instance, encourage uncritical celebration of figures from a racist past as part of a narrative of "the good ol' days," there is a compelling argument that such memorials compromise rather than contribute to a critical understanding of our past. Removal of markers that encourage such uncritical veneration may have a constructive purpose, but "tainted" public markers could serve the project of public education, and in these cases, the most constructive recourse may not be to remove them. Often *more* history is better history, and augmenting public markers of historical figures to include the more problematic parts of their backgrounds can contribute to a more chastened examination of our nation's past.

To acknowledge this history accurately is to invite us to confess our own complicity and to take seriously the entrenched nature of our national problems and failures. The United States has not "solved" the problem of racism, and its persistence in systems and structures makes more sense when we admit the way that racism has been a consistent force in history, represented by some of the most beloved figures in that history. Similarly, true accountability for the genocide committed against Native Americans starts with acknowledgments of land seizures, like those recited at select university events. Real justice for persons with differences requires that we wrestle with the fact that definitions of "disability" historically are social constructions, reflecting the abilities of the privileged "normal," while ableist norms have been used to animate attempts to "fix" those who are different. Interventions like the eugenics movement a century ago, or the more recent development of pharmaceutical "cures" for mental health issues, the clinical approach to neurodiversity, or the cultural fascination with bioengineered enhancement technologies all reflect the ways our social norms discount those who do not match the characteristics and priorities of a dominant majority. A chastened familiarity with this history equips us to see how malevolent attitudes in American culture have begotten oppressive systems and structures, and vice versa.

In the process, a chastened approach to history serves us better than a categorical rejection of history because it allows us to retain the better angels of our political traditions and utilize them as raw ingredients for an antidote to the injustices that plague us. If we ignore Witherspoon and Jefferson as relics of an immoral age, if we disown the Declaration and the Constitution as racist documents, then we deprive ourselves of the very ideals on which we can build a collective future that is more just than they were able to see. Jefferson was a slaveholder, but he also gifted our foundational documents with aspirations of natural rights on which we can craft new expectations of American public life, in spite of his failings. Witherspoon was complicit in slavery, and yet he also provided us with a vision of political character rooted in the protection of human dignity and obligation to the common good, ideas that can be used to critique Witherspoon's moral myopia but also imagine a society better than the one for which he labored. The Declaration and the Constitution were written by slaveholders with the deprivation of Black humanity built into their texts, but they also bequeathed to us ideals of life, liberty, and the pursuit of happiness, a commitment to the general welfare, the blessings of liberty, and the establishment of justice. These are the moral pillars on which a more just union might be imagined in our moment, to move beyond the failings of our past.

This chastened recollection of the ideals of American history is what Dr. King invited us to undertake in his "I Have a Dream" speech. Seamlessly weaving together invocations of biblical prophets, patriotic hymns, and appeals to the foundational documents of our nation, King pulled no punches when he indicted white America for giving Black Americans "a bad check; a check which has come back marked 'insufficient funds.'" Directing the ideals of America against itself, he laid bare the failures of a nation that talked a good game of life and liberty but failed to extend those goods to half of its population. But then, after rendering moral judgment, he utilized those same ideals and that same history to imagine a more hopeful future, when the content of character rather than skin color would guide our assessment of one another, and the "magnificent words of the Constitution and the Declaration of Independence" and their guarantee of "unalienable rights of life, liberty, and the pursuit of happiness" would represent "a promissory note to which every American was to fall heir."[39] Like many other white Americans of his time, Witherspoon failed to see this just society as clearly as King imagined it. But perhaps Witherspoon's vision of political character—as well as his failures to live up to that vision—can help direct us toward a more benevolent community in our time.

Notes

1 For more on the role of clergy in the Revolutionary effort, see Gary L. Steward, *Justifying Revolution: The American Clergy's Argument for Political Resistance, 1750–1776* (Oxford University Press, 2021) and Thomas S. Kidd, *God of Liberty: A Religious History of the American Revolution* (Basic Books, 2010).
2 Ralph L. Ketcham, "James Madison and Religion: A New Hypothesis," in *James Madison on Religious Liberty*, ed. Robert S. Alley (Prometheus Books, 1985), 185.
3 Ketcham, "James Madison," 184.
4 William Lee Miller, *The First Liberty: America's Foundation in Religious Freedom* (Georgetown University Press, 2003), 72.
5 For more on the way that his instruction at Princeton distinguished Madison's approach to religious freedom from the likes of Jefferson, see Miller, *First Liberty*,

76–7; also, Nicholas P. Miller, *The Religious Roots of the First Amendment: Dissenting Protestants and the Separation of Church and State* (Oxford University Press, 2012).
6. Miller, *First Liberty*, 5.
7. Ketcham, "James Madison," 192.
8. Reinhold Niebuhr, *The Children of Light and the Children of Darkness: A Vindication of Democracy and a Critique of Its Traditional Defense* (Charles Scribner's Sons: 1944), xxxii.
9. Collins, *President Witherspoon*, II: 223–4.
10. Michael Sullivan, "John Witherspoon: Religious Educator to the American Founding Generation," *Religious Education* 117:1 (2022), 84.
11. As quoted in Collins, *President Witherspoon*, II:209.
12. See James H. Smylie, *A Brief History of the Presbyterians* (Geneva Press, 1996), 62–5, for a brief discussion of the organization of the first General Assembly and Witherspoon's involvement in it. The sermon Witherspoon preached at the opening of that first Assembly, "The Success of the Gospel Entirely of God," can be found in *Works*, II:569–86.
13. Smylie, *Brief History*, 58.
14. John Witte, Jr., Joel A. Nichols, and Richard W. Garnett, *Religion and the American Constitutional Experiment*, 5th ed. (Oxford University Press, 2022), 54–5.
15. A Bill Establishing a Provision for Teachers of the Christian Religion (1784).
16. See David Brooks, *The Road to Character* (Random House, 2016); Michael J. Sandel, *What Money Can't Buy: The Moral Limits of Markets* (Farrar, Straus and Giroux, 2013); Jim Wallis, *On God's Side: What Religion Forgets and Politics Hasn't Learned about Serving the Common Good* (Brazos, 2013); Jimmy Carter, *Our Endangered Values: America's Moral Crisis* (Simon & Schuster, 2006).
17. Glenn Kessler, Salvador Rizzo, and Meg Kelley, "Trump's False or Misleading Claims Total 30,573 Over 4 Years," *Washington Post*, January 24, 2021, https://www.washingtonpost.com/politics/2021/01/24/trumps-false-or-misleading-claims-total-30573-over-four-years.
18. See my *In Defense of Civility: How Religion Can Help Unite America on Seven Moral Issues that Divide Us* (Westminster John Knox Press, 2010), chapter 1.
19. Danielle Allen, *Talking to Strangers: Anxieties of Citizenship since Brown v. Board of Education* (The University of Chicago Press, 2006).
20. Martin Luther King, Jr. *From Strength to Love* (Fortress Press, 1963), 55.
21. For several outstanding introductions to Christian nationalism and its threat to American democracy, see Andrew L. Whitehead and Samuel L. Perry, *Taking America Back for God: Christian Nationalism in the United States* (Oxford University Press, 2020); Philip S. Gorski and Samuel L. Perry, *The Flag and the Cross: White Christian Nationalism and the Threat to American Democracy* (Oxford University

Press, 2022); Katherine Stewart, *The Power Worshippers: Inside the Dangerous Rise of Religious Nationalism* (Bloomsbury, 2019).

22 Robert P. Jones, *The End of White Christian America* (Simon & Schuster, 2016).

23 David Barton, a pseudo-historian and a favorite of Christian nationalists, is the most prominent example of a Christian nationalist who reads Witherspoon as sympathetic to the "Christian America" cause. See John Fea, *Was America Founded as a Christian Nation?* (Westminster John Knox Press, 2011), 228.

24 See, for instance, Robert Putnam, *Bowling Alone: The Collapse and Revival of American Community*, revised and updated (Simon & Schuster, 2020).

25 For just a couple of examples, see David P. Gushee, *Defending Democracy from Its Christian Enemies* (Eerdmans, 2023), especially chapters 12–14; Jim Wallis, *On God's Side: What Religion Forgets and Politics Hasn't Learned about Serving the Common Good* (Brazos, 2013); James Calvin Davis, *Forbearance: A Theological Ethic for a Disagreeable Church* (Eerdmans, 2017), chapter 9; Davis, *In Defense of Civility* (Westminster John Knox Press, 2010); Abdulaziz Sachedina, *The Islamic Roots of Democratic Pluralism* (Oxford University Press, 2001).

26 Focus on the Family, https://www.focusonthefamily.com.

27 Ronald Reagan, Inaugural Address 1981, https://www.reaganlibrary.gov/archives/speech/inaugural-address-1981.

28 "10 Facts About Today's College Graduates," *Pew Research Center*, April 12, 2022, https://www.pewresearch.org/short-reads/2022/04/12/10-facts-about-todays-college-graduates.

29 Michael S. Roth, "How Higher Education Can Win Back America," *New York Times*, December 27, 2024, https://www.nytimes.com/2024/12/27/opinion/college-education-tuition-egalitarian.html.

30 Amy Gutmann, "What Makes a University Education Worthwhile?," in *The Aims of Higher Education: Problems of Morality and Justice*, ed. Harry Brighouse and Michael McPherson (The University of Chicago Press, 2015), 23.

31 "Examining Lincoln's Views on African Americans and Slavery," Lincoln Presidential Library and Museum, https://presidentlincoln.illinois.gov/education/educator-resources/teaching-guides/lincolns-views-african-american-slavery.

32 Inviting us to take these questions seriously is why the 1619 Project is such a powerful exercise in public scholarship. See *The 1619 Project: A New Origin Story*, ed. Nikole Hannah-Jones, Caitlin Roper, Ilena Silverman, and Jake Silverstein (The New York Times, 2021). For treatment of this question for the purposes of constitutional law, see Louis Michael Seidman, "America's Racial Stain: The Taint Argument and the Limitations of Constitutional Law and Rhetoric" (Georgetown University Law Center, 2022), https://scholarship.law.georgetown.edu/cgi/

viewcontent.cgi?params=/context/facpub/article/3467/&path_info=auto_convert.pdf.
33 Karen V. Guth, *The Ethics of Tainted Legacies: Human Flourishing after Traumatic Pasts* (Cambridge University Press, 2022).
34 Guth, *Tainted Legacies*, 63.
35 Guth, *Tainted Legacies*, 73–4.
36 Guth, *Tainted Legacies*, 79.
37 Guth, *Tainted Legacies*, 86.
38 Guth, *Tainted Legacies*, 15.
39 Martin Luther King, Jr. "I Have a Dream," in *A Testament of Hope: The Essential Writings and Speeches of Martin Luther King, Jr.* ed. James M. Washington (Harper Collins, 1986), 217–20.

Bibliography

Allen, Danielle. *Talking to Strangers: Anxieties of Citizenship since* Brown *v.* Board of Education. The University of Chicago, 2006.
Allman, Mark J. *Who Would Jesus Kill? War, Peace, and the Christian Tradition*. St. Mary's Press, 2008.
Ames, William. *The Marrow of Theology*. Translated by John Dykstra Eusden. Baker Books, 1968.
Augustine, *Basic Writings of Saint Augustine*, vol. 1. Edited by Whitney J. Oates. Baker Books, 1992.
Balzano, Richard M. "Informants and Artifacts: Local Histories' Representations of Bondage and the Precarious States of Freedom in Northeastern Vermont." *Vermont History* 90:1 (2022), 1–23.
Barry, John M. *Roger Williams and the Creation of the American Soul: Church, State, and the Birth of Liberty*. Viking Press, 2012.
Baxter, Richard. *A Christian Directory*, 1673, Reprint. Soli Deo Gloria Publications, 1990.
Baxter, Richard. *A Holy Commonwealth*. Cambridge University Press, 1994.
Berry, Christopher J. "Sociality and Socialisation." 234–47 in *The Cambridge Companion to the Scottish Enlightenment*, 2nd ed., edited by Alexander Broadie and Craig Smith. Cambridge University Press, 2019.
"Black and Slave Population of the United States from 1790 to 1880." *Statistica*. https://www.statista.com/statistics/1010169/black-and-slave-population-us-1790-1880.
Book of Confessions, The Constitution of the Presbyterian Church (USA), Part I. (2016).
Breen, Timothy H. *The Character of the Good Ruler: A Study of Puritan Political Ideas in New England, 1630–1730*. Yale University Press, 1970.
Brooks, David. *The Road to Character*. Random House, 2016.
Cahill, Lisa Sowle. *Love Your Enemies: Discipleship, Pacifism, and Just War Theory*. Fortress Press, 1994.
Calvin, John. *Institutes of the Christian Religion*. Edited by John T. McNeill. Westminster Press, 1960.
Calvin, John. *The Epistle of Paul the Apostle to the Hebrews and the First and Second Epistles of St. Peter*, vol 12 of *Calvin's New Testament Commentaries*. Edited by David W. Torrance and Thomas F. Torrance. Eerdmans, 1991.
Calvin, John. *The Epistles of Paul the Apostle to the Romans and to the Thessalonians*, vol. 8 of *Calvin's New Testament Commentaries*. Edited by David W. Torrance and Thomas F. Torrance. Eerdmans, 1991.

Carmichael, Gershom. *Observations upon Liberal Education*. Edited by Terrence O. Moore. Liberty Fund, 2003.

Carter, Jimmy. *Our Endangered Values: America's Moral Crisis*. Simon & Schuster, 2006.

Childress, James F. *Moral Responsibility in Conflicts: Essays on Nonviolence, War, and Conscience*. Louisiana State University Press, 1982.

Collins, Varnum Lansing. *President Witherspoon*, 2 vols. Arno Press & The New York Times, 1969.

The Constitution of the Presbyterian Church in the United States of America. Philadelphia, PA: Thomas Bradford, 1789, Internet Archive. http://archive.org/details/const00pres.

Cooper, Anthony Ashley. Earl of Shaftsbury. *An Inquiry Concerning Virtue in Two Discourses*. London: A. Bell, E. Castle, and S. Buckley, 1699.

Cuneo, Terence. "Reid's Moral Philosophy." 243–66 in *The Cambridge Companion to Thomas Reid*, edited by Terence Cuneo and Rene van Woudenberg. Cambridge University Press, 2004.

Cushing, Jacob. "Divine Judgments Upon Tyrants" (1778). 607–26 in *Political Sermons of the Founding Era, 1730–1805*, vol. 1, edited by Ellis Sandoz. Liberty Fund, 1998.

Davis, James Calvin. *In Defense of Civility: How Religion Can Help Unite America on Seven Moral Issues that Divide Us*. Westminster John Knox Press, 2010.

Davis, James Calvin. *Forbearance: A Theological Ethic for a Disagreeable Church*. Eerdmans, 2017.

Davis, James Calvin, ed. *On Religious Liberty: Selections from the Works of Roger Williams*. Harvard University Press, 2008.

"Declaration of Independence: A Transcription." America's Founding Documents, National Archives. https://www.archives.gov/founding-docs/declaration-transcript.

DeYoung, Kevin. "John Witherspoon and Slavery." *Theology Today* 80:4 (2024), 355–68.

DeYoung, Kevin. *The Religious Formation of John Witherspoon: Calvinism, Evangelicalism, and the Scottish Enlightenment*. Routledge, 2020.

Dorn, Charles. *For the Common Good: A New History of Higher Education in America*. Cornell University Press, 2017.

Edwards, Jonathan. *Ethical Writings*. Volume 8 of *The Works of Jonathan Edwards*. Edited by Paul Ramsey. Yale University Press, 1989.

Edwards, Jonathan. *Religious Affections*. Volume 2 of *The Works of Jonathan Edwards*. Edited by John E. Smith. Yale University Press, 1959.

Fea, John. *Was America Founded as a Christian Nation?* Westminster John Knox Press, 2011.

Finke, Roger, and Rodney Stark. *The Churching of America 1776–2005: Winners and Losers in our Religious Economy*. Rutgers University Press, 2005.

Foster, James. "Of the Civil Magistrate: John Witherspoon's Doubly Religious Toleration." *Global Intellectual History* 5:2 (2020), 264–78.

Gaustad, Edwin S., ed. *A Documentary History of Religion in America to the Civil War*, 2nd ed. Eerdmans, 1993.

"General Orders 15 May 1776." Founders Online, National Archives. https://founders.archives.gov/documents/Washington/03-04-02-0243.

Gorski, Philip S., and Samuel L. Perry. *The Flag and the Cross: White Christian Nationalism and the Threat to American Democracy*. Oxford University Press, 2022.

Geiger, Roger L. *The History of American Higher Education: Learning and Culture from the Founding to World War II*. Princeton University Press, 2015.

Gushee, David P. *Defending Democracy from Its Christian Enemies*. Eerdmans, 2023.

Guth, Karen V. *The Ethics of Tainted Legacies: Human Flourishing after Traumatic Pasts*. Cambridge University Press, 2022.

Gutmann, Amy. "What Makes a University Education Worthwhile?" 7–25 in *The Aims of Higher Education: Problems of Morality and Justice*, edited by Harry Brighouse and Michael McPherson. The University of Chicago, 2015.

Knud Haakonssen, "Natural Jurisprudence and the Theory of Justice." 195–212 in *The Cambridge Companion to the Scottish Enlightenment*, 2nd ed., edited by Alexander Broadie and Craig Smith. Cambridge University Press, 2019.

Haller, William. *Liberty and Reformation in the Puritan Revolution*. Columbia University Press, 1955.

Hanley, Ryan Patrick. "Magnanimity and Modernity: Greatness of Soul and Greatness of Mind in the Enlightenment." 176–96 in *The Measure of Greatness: Philosophers on Magnanimity*, edited by Sophia Vasalou. Oxford University Press, 2019.

Hobbes, Thomas. *Leviathan*. 1651. J.M. Dent and Sons, 1973.

Hutcheson, Francis. *Inquiry into the Original of Our Ideas of Beauty and Virtue*. Edited by Wolfgang Leidhold. Liberty Fund, 2004.

Inniss, Lolita Buckner. *The Princeton Fugitive Slave: The Trials of James Collins Johnson*. Fordham Press, 2019.

Jones, Robert P. *The End of White Christian America*. Simon & Schuster, 2016.

Kant, Immanuel. "An Answer to the Question: 'What Is Enlightenment?'" 54–60 in *Kant: Political Writings*, edited by Hans Reiss. Cambridge University Press, 1991.

Kessler, Glenn, Salvador Rizzo, and Meg Kelley. "Trump's False or Misleading Claims Total 30,573 Over 4 Years." *Washington Post*, January 24, 2021. https://www.washingtonpost.com/politics/2021/01/24/trumps-false-or-misleading-claims-total-30573-over-four-years.

Ketcham, Ralph L. "James Madison and Religion: A New Hypothesis." 173–96 in *James Madison on Religious Liberty*, edited by Robert S. Alley. Prometheus Books, 1985.

Keteltas, Abraham. "God Arising and Pleading His People's Cause" (1777). 579–605 in *Political Sermons of the Founding Era, 1730–1805*, vol. 1, edited by Ellis Sandoz. Liberty Fund, 1998.

Kidd, Thomas S. *God of Liberty: A Religious History of the American Revolution*. Basic Books, 2010.

King, Jr., Martin Luther. *From Strength to Love*. Fortress Press, 1963.

King, Jr., Martin Luther. "I Have a Dream." 217–20 in *A Testament of Hope: The Essential Writings and Speeches of Martin Luther King, Jr*, edited by James M. Washington. Harper Collins, 1986.

Lambert, Frank. *The Founding Fathers and the Place of Religion in America*. Princeton University Press, 2003.

Little, David. *Essays on Religion and Human Rights: Ground to Stand On*. Cambridge University Press, 2015.

Madison, James. "Memorial and Remonstrance against Religious Assessments, [ca. 20 June] 1785." *Founders Online*, National Archives. https://founders.archives.gov/documents/Madison/01-08-02-0163. [Original source: *The Papers of James Madison*, vol. 8, *10 March 1784–28 March 1786*, ed. Robert A. Rutland and William M. E. Rachal. The University of Chicago Press, 1973, 295–306.]

Mailer, Gideon. *John Witherspoon's American Revolution*. The University of North Carolina Press, 2017.

Marsden, George. *The Soul of the American University Revisited: From Protestant to Postsecular*. Oxford University Press, 2021.

McGever, Sean. *Ownership: The Evangelical Legacy of Slavery in Edwards, Wesley, and Whitefield*. InterVarsity Press, 2024.

Mikoski, Gordon S. "Partial Iconoclasm: John Witherspoon's Presbyterian (Political) Theology and Slavery." *Theology Today* 80:4 (2024), 406–13.

Miller, Nicholas P. *The Religious Roots of the First Amendment: Dissenting Protestants and the Separation of Church and State*. Oxford University Press, 2012.

Miller, Thomas P., ed. *The Selected Writings of John Witherspoon*. Southern Illinois University Press, 1990.

Miller, William Lee. *The First Liberty: America's Foundation in Religious Freedom, Expanded and Updated*. Georgetown University Press, 2003.

Moore, James, and Michael Silverthorne, eds. *Natural Rights on the Threshold of the Scottish Enlightenment: The Writings of Gershom Carmichael*. Liberty Fund, 2002.

Moore, Joseph S. "Covenanters and Antislavery in the Atlantic World." *Slavery & Abolition* 34:4 (2013), 539–61.

Morgan, Edmund S. *The Puritan Family: Religion and Domestic Relations in Seventeenth-Century New England*. Harper & Row, 1966.

Morrison, Jeffry H. *John Witherspoon and the Founding of the American Republic*. University of Notre Dame, 2005.

Niebuhr, Reinhold. *The Children of Light and the Children of Darkness: A Vindication of Democracy and a Critique of Its Traditional Defense*. Charles Scribner's Sons, 1944.

Noll, Mark A. *America's God: From Jonathan Edwards to Abraham Lincoln*. Oxford University Press, 2002.

Noll, Mark A. *The Civil War as Theological Crisis*. The University of North Carolina Press, 2006.

Noll, Mark A. *The Rise of Evangelicalism: The Age of Edwards, Whitefield, and the Wesleys*. InterVarsity Press, 2003.

O'Donovan, Oliver, and Joan Lockwood O'Donovan, eds. *From Ireneus to Grotius: A Sourcebook in Christian Political Thought*. Eerdmans, 1999.

Perkins, William. *The Whole Treatise of the Cases of Conscience* Cambridge: John Legat, 1606.

Polishook, Irwin H. *Roger Williams, John Cotton, and Religious Freedom: A Controversy in New and Old England*. Prentice-Hall, 1967.

Putnam, Robert. *Bowling Alone: The Collapse and Revival of American Community* (revised and updated). Simon & Schuster, 2020.

Redmond, Lesa. "John Witherspoon and Slavery: Ideology versus Praxis." *Theology Today* 80:4 (2024), 391.

Reid, Thomas. *Practical Ethics: Being Lectures and Papers on Natural Religion, Self-Government, Natural Jurisprudence, and the Law of Nations*. Edited by Knud Haakonssen. Princeton University Press, 1990.

Roth, Randolph A. "The First Radical Abolitionists: The Reverend James Milligan and the Reformed Presbyterians of Vermont." *The New England Quarterly* 55:4 (1982), 540–63.

Rush, Benjamin. *A Plan for the Establishment of Public Schools and the Diffusion of Knowledge in Pennsylvania; to Which Are Added, Thoughts upon the Mode of Education Proper in a Republic*. Philadelphia, PA: Thomas Dobson, 1786.

Rush, Benjamin. *An Address to the Inhabitants of the British Settlements, on the Slavery of the Negroes in America*. Philadelphia, PA: John Dunlap, 1773.

Rush, Benjamin. "Thoughts upon Female Education, Accommodated to the Present State of Society, Manners, and Government, in the United States of America. Addressed to the Visitors of the Young Ladies Academy in Philadelphia, 28th July 1787, at the Close of the Quarterly Examination, by Benjamin Rush, M.D." *The Universal Asylum and the Columbian Magazine*, April 1790 (Philadelphia), 209–13; May 1790, 288–92.

Sachedina, Abdulaziz. *The Islamic Roots of Democratic Pluralism*. Oxford University Press, 2001.

Sandel, Michael J. *What Money Can't Buy: The Moral Limits of Markets*. Farrar, Straus and Giroux, 2013.

Segrest, Scott Philip. *America and the Political Philosophy of Common Sense*. University of Missouri, 2010.

Smylie, James H. *A Brief History of the Presbyterians*. Geneva Press, 1996.

Steward, Gary L. *Justifying Revolution: The American Clergy's Argument for Political Resistance, 1750-1776*. Oxford University Press, 2021.

Stewart, Katherine. *The Power Worshippers: Inside the Dangerous Rise of Religious Nationalism*. Bloomsbury, 2019.

Stohlman, Martha Lou Lemmon. *John Witherspoon: Parson, Politician, Patriot.* Westminster Press, 1976.

Sullivan, Michael. "John Witherspoon: Religious Educator to the American Founding Generation." *Religious Education* 117:1 (2022), 74–87.

Synod of New York and Philadelphia, *Minutes* [manuscript], May 26 and May 28, 1787. Presbyterian Historical Society. Call number: VF BX 8951. A3 1758–1788.

"The Massachusetts Body of Liberties." 177–202 in *Puritan Political Ideas*, edited by Edmund S. Morgan. Bobbs-Merrill, 1965.

"The Westminster Confession of Faith (1646)." 192–230 in *Creeds of the Churches: A Reader in Christian Doctrine from the Bible to the Present*, 3rd ed., edited by John Leith. John Knox Press, 1982.

Townes, Emilie M. *Womanist Ethics and the Cultural Production of Evil.* Palgrave Macmillan, 2006.

Unger, Harlow Giles. *Dr. Benjamin Rush: The Founding Father Who Healed a Wounded Nation.* Da Capo Press, 2018.

VanDrunen, David. *Natural Law and the Two Kingdoms: A Study in the Development of Reformed Social Thought.* Eerdmans, 2010.

Waldmann, Felix. "David Hume Was a Brilliant Philosopher but also a Racist Involved in Slavery." *The Scotsman.* July 17, 2020.

Wallis, Jim. *On God's Side: What Religion Forgets and Politics Hasn't Learned about Serving the Common Good.* Brazos, 2013.

Wertenbaker, Thomas Jefferson. *Princeton: 1746–1896.* Princeton University Press, 1946.

Whitehead, Andrew L., and Samuel L. Perry. *Taking America Back for God: Christian Nationalism in the United States.* Oxford University Press, 2020.

Wilentz, Sean. "John Witherspoon and the Abolitionist Travail." *Theology Today* 80:4 (2024), 334–54.

Williams, Noelle Lorraine. "New Jersey: The Last Northern State to End Slavery." The New Jersey Historical Commission. https://nj.gov/state/historical/his-2021-juneteenth.shtml.

Wirzbicki, Peter "John Witherspoon, the Scottish Common Sense School, and American Political Philosophy." *Theology Today* 80:4 (2024), 395–405.

Witherspoon, John. *The Works of the Rev. John Witherspoon*, 2nd ed. 4 vols. Philadelphia, PA: William W. Woodward, 1802.

Witte, John. *The Reformation of Rights: Law, Religion, and Human Rights in Early Modern Calvinism.* Cambridge University Press, 2007.

Witte, John, and Joel A. Nichols. *Religion and the American Constitutional Experiment*, 4th ed. Oxford University Press, 2016.

Woodhouse, A. S. P., ed. *Puritanism and Liberty.* J.M. Dent & Sons, 1992.

Index

Note: Page numbers followed by 'n' denotes note numbers.

abolition   203–7. *See also* slavery
   Baxter on   199–200
   and the Covenanters   212 n.47
   in New Jersey   188, 203–4
   Rush and   191–3, 203
   Witherspoon and   201–5
Adams, John   5, 128, 130
Address to the Inhabitants of the British Settlements, on the Slavery of the Negroes in America (Rush)   191–3
Address to the Students of the Senior Class (Witherspoon)   76–7, 79
affections (philosophical term)   51–2, 55–62
   Edwards on   57, 82 n.27
   Witherspoon on   57–62
Ames, William   53–5, 198
   Conscience, and the Cases Thereof   102
   Marrow of Theology   73, 102
   on moral law   91–2
   on natural law   90
   on prudence   116–17
   on rights   102
   on virtue   73
Anabaptists   25–7
Aristotle   50, 76, 201
Articles of Confederation   163–4
Augustine, Saint: on human nature and sin   52–8
   on just war theory   173–4

Baxter, Richard   117–18, 168
   on slavery   198–200
benevolence   37, 57, 64–5, 72–8, 96–8, 105–6, 220. *See also* common good
   and paternalism   207–8
Black Americans, enslaved. *See* slavery
Body of Liberties   103–4

Calvin, John: on government   25–32, 127, 167–8
   on just war theory   174
   on natural law   92–4
   on natural virtue   63–4, 68–9, 72–3
   on providence   27–32
   on rights   100–1
   on sin   52–3, 55
Calvinism: in colonial America   23–5
   and the Enlightenment   23–4, 39–45
   on family   138
   human nature (sin and will)   41, 53–6
   influence on Witherspoon   23–5, 32–5, 42, 44–5, 57–62, 72–5, 91–5, 100–1
   moral law   89–91
   natural law   92–4
   political theology   25–35, 167–70
   rights   98–105
   in Scotland   13–18
   on slavery   197–200
Carmichael, Gershom   105–8, 113–14
children. *See* family
Childress, James F.   176
Christian Directory (Baxter)   117–18, 198–200
Christian Magnanimity (Witherspoon)   43–4
Christian nationalism   223–5
church and state relationship. *See* Calvinism: political theology; religious liberty
Church of England (Anglican Church)   13–14, 20, 166, 217
Clinton, William J.   219, 227
College of New Jersey (Princeton)   18–22, 33, 75–6
   An Address to the Students of the Senior Class   76–7, 79, 147

founding and early curriculum 143
graduation address *Christian Magnanimity* 43–4
slavery at 205, 211 n.40, 211 n.41
Witherspoon's presidency 18–19, 22, 147–51, 154 n.76, 196, 205, 208, 216–17
common good 7, 9, 23, 43–5, 49
　Calvin on 72–3
　Hutcheson on 73–5
　and rights 111–14
　Witherspoon on 74, 76–8, 97–8, 112–14, 220–1
conscience 40, 54–5, 83 n.44, 92, 94–5
Constitution, U.S. 10, 164–5, 228, 235–6
contemporary American moral values 218–29
　and Christian nationalism 223–5
　and evangelical Christians 219–20, 222, 226
　in higher education 228–9
　and religion 222
　and Trump 218–20
Continental Congress 1, 5, 21–2, 163
covenant 90–1, 112, 169, 184 n.39

Declaration of Independence 1, 4–6, 157, 166–7, 235–6
　and natural law 94
　and providence 32, 34
　and rights 99–100, 110
Dominion of Providence over the Passions of Men (Witherspoon) 1–5, 132–3, 171
　on moral character 42–43, 49
　and providence 32–3, 178
　reaction to 5–6
　on rights 99, 109
　on virtue 76, 79, 126–7
Druid (Witherspoon) 42, 67, 179
duty-based ethics 87–118
　Carmichael on 105–6
　Witherspoon on 89–91, 95–8

Ecclesiastical Characteristics (Witherspoon) 15, 17
ecclesiology 13–14, 16, 35
　Presbyterian 14, 35

education: in the family 137–42
　higher 9, 142–51, 228–9
　Turnbull on 144–6
　Witherspoon on 137–42, 146–51
　Witherspoon's legacy in 216–17
Edwards, Jonathan 57, 82 n.27, 198, 210 n.22
　on virtue 64–5
emancipation. *See* abolition
English Civil War 39, 101–2, 117, 168
Enlightenment, thinkers and concepts 23, 36–42, 44, 213–14. *See also* Scottish Enlightenment
Essay on the Connection between the Doctrine of Justification by the Imputed Righteousness of Christ, and Holiness of Life (*Essay on Justification and Holiness*) (Witherspoon) 15–16, 48 n.53, 58–60, 65

family: influence on moral character 137–42, 225–7
　Witherspoon on 138–42, 226
Franklin, Benjamin 129, 144, 218
freedom of conscience. *See* religious liberty
friendship 77, 97, 170

Golden Rule 88, 199
government, role in society 25–30, 227–8. *See also* leadership
　Calvin on 167–8
　Madison on 215–16
　philosophies of 158–65
　Rutherford on 168–70
　Witherspoon on 158–65
grace: and children 138
　and natural law 93
　and salvation 13, 16, 29
　and virtue 53–5, 58–9, 63–72
Great Awakening 19–20, 25, 46 n.13, 57. *See also* revivalism
Guth, Karen V. 230–4

Hobbes, Thomas 158–62
human nature. *See* moral anthropology; moral character; virtue

Hume, David   37–40, 44, 45, 100, 158, 200, 48 n.53
Hutcheson, Francis   17, 36–7, 40–1, 61
  on benevolence   73–5, 100
  "moral sense"   37, 40–1, 94
  on morality and affections   56–7, 66
  on rights   108
  on slavery   200–1

imago Dei   105, 196, 197
Independents (church)   13–14, 102
Institutes of the Christian Religion (Calvin)   27, 31, 63–4, 69. *See also* John Calvin

Jefferson, Thomas   34–5, 100, 126, 129, 165, 200, 224, 230, 235
just war theory   172–6
  and moral conduct in war   175–7, 179–81

Ketcham, Ralph L.   214–15
King, Martin Luther, Jr.   222, 236

leadership   29–32, 135–7, 142–3, 161–3, 218–21, 225–9
Lectures on Divinity (Witherspoon)   90, 147–8
  and Trinitarianism   34
Lectures on Eloquence (Witherspoon)   149–50
Lectures on Moral Philosophy (Witherspoon)   40, 61–2, 75, 94, 120 n.31, 130, 170
  concerning slavery   193–6
  and public virtue   50–1
legacies, historical: Witherspoon's   10–11, 230–6
  problematic   230–6
Lex, Rex (Rutherford)   168–9
Little, David   102, 46 n.18
Locke, John   39, 46 n.18, 100, 135, 158, 160
  on slavery   200

Madison, James   5, 129, 164–5
  on government   216
  on religion   214–15
  Witherspoon's influence   214–16
magnanimity   43–5
May 17, 1776   1, 4, 49
Memorial and Manifesto of the United States of North America (Witherspoon)   167, 178
Merritt, Eli   170–1
Montgomery, Jamie   196, 198
moral anthropology   23, 50–2, 165, 215
  Ames   53–5
  Augustine   52–3, 57
  Calvinist   53–6
  Edwards   57
  Hutcheson   56–7
  Shaftesbury   56
  Witherspoon   57–62
moral character   4, 7, 9, 23, 49–50. *See also* contemporary American moral values; religion
  Ames on   53–5, 73
  Calvinist   55–6, 63–4
  in contemporary American politics   218–29
  and duty   96–8
  Edwards on   64–5
  Enlightenment concepts about   36–42, 50–2, 56
  family influence on   137–42, 225–7
  and health of the new nation   7, 23, 43, 45, 49, 72, 79–80, 115–16, 125–51, 170–1, 180–1, 217–18, 225
  in higher education   142–51, 228–9
  in leaders   161–3, 218–19, 227
  in the Revolutionary War   178–81
  Williams on   70–1
  Witherspoon on   58–62, 65–71, 74–80, 125, 221
moral law   7–9, 40, 70
  and duty   96
  interpretation of   114–18
  revealed in scripture   90–4, 116
  Witherspoon on   89–95

Native Americans: oppression of   185 n.73, 235
  Witherspoon on   197
natural law   90, 92–5, 105–6
  Witherspoon on   94–5

natural virtue 63–71
  Calvin 63–4, 68–9
  Calvinist 69–71
  Edwards 64–5
  Witherspoon 65–8
New Jersey (colony/state) 21, 164, 166, 197
  slavery in 188, 203–4, 210 n.19

Observations upon Liberal Education (Turnbull) 144–6

Perkins, William 56, 70
political dissent: Calvin on 30–1. *See also* government
  role of religion 49, 101–2, 214–15
  Witherspoon on 32–3, 221–2
polygenesis 189, 192, 195–6
Practical Treatise on Regeneration (Witherspoon) 66
predestination 13, 35
Pre-Revolutionary America 1, 166–7, 172, 224
  conflict between colonies 170–1, 208–9, 220
Presbyterian Church in America 6, 19, 35, 134, 166. *See also* Synod of New York and Philadelphia
  Witherspoon's influence on 217
Presbyterian Church in Scotland 4, 13–17, 35, 131–2
  Moderate Party 15–17, 21, 132
  Popular Party 15–17, 132
Presbyterianism 14, 16, 35, 102
Princeton, NJ 1, 5, 7, 18
Princeton University. *See* College of New Jersey
providence (divine) 2–4, 16, 27–32, 135
  in the independence movement 3, 32–5, 135–6
prudence 116–18, 123 n.109
  Ames on 116–17, 123 n.111
  Baxter on 117–18
Puritans (American) 13, 94, 103–4, 128, 138

racism 11, 230–6
Reformation 25–6

Reid, Thomas 37, 39–40, 61–2, 100
religion: colonial American 19–25, 126, 217
  contribution to political character 8, 9, 125–37, 162, 217, 224–5
  and political duty 33–4
religious liberty 25, 39, 99–104, 217
  Madison and 165, 215
  Witherspoon on 108–9, 130–1, 134–5, 172, 214, 225
revivalism 19–20, 25, 47 n.21
  in the Presbyterian Church in America 20–1
Revolutionary War: American Christianity's influence on 214, 217, 224–5. *See also* just war theory
  and crusade rhetoric 176–7, 221
  Witherspoon's justification of 166–7, 169–75, 178
rights (human) 7–9, 98–115
  alienable and inalienable 99, 110–11
  Calvin on 100–1
  Carmichael on 105–7
  and common good 111–14
  Hutcheson on 108
  interpretation of 114–18
  perfect and imperfect 107–10
  Puritans on 103–5
  right of necessity 113–14
  and slavery 191–5
  Witherspoon on 107–18, 171–2, 193–5, 213–14ss
Rush, Benjamin 19, 46 n.11, 128
  and abolition 191–3, 203
  on higher education 146–7, 216
Rutherford, Samuel 168–70
  on slavery 198

salvation 13, 55, 60, 69, 72, 93, 138
Scotland 5, 6, 13, 131–2
  Beith church 15, 196
  Paisley church 15, 16, 18, 19, 140–2
Scottish Enlightenment 7–9, 16–18, 23, 37–8. *See also* Francis Hutcheson
  education 143–6
  human nature 40–1, 56–7, 61–2, 87, 94

influence on Witherspoon 38–45, 94, 200
rights 100
slavery 200–1
Turnbull 143–6Servetus, Michael 100, 101
Shaftesbury, Lord 17, 37, 61
on morality 56–7, 66
sin 41, 52–5
Witherspoon on 58, 94
slavery (Colonial American) 8, 10, 103, 106, 181
Baxter on 198–200
Christian opposition to 191–3, 198–200, 212 n.47
and Christianity 188–93
moral arguments in favor of 189–91, 197–8
in New Jersey 203–4
Rush on 191–3
in Vermont 206
Witherspoon and 8–10, 193–6, 201–9, 229–34
Smith, Adam 37, 44, 45, 201
Synod of New York and Philadelphia: letter 127, 133, 135, 170, 178. *See also* Presbyterian Church in America
overture supporting abolition 204–5

Ten Commandments 69, 73, 88, 90–2, 101, 104, 223
Ames on 91–2, 102
Treatise Concerning Religious Affections (Edwards) 57
Trump, Donald J. 218–20, 222
truth 78–9, 85 n.90
Turnbull, George 143–6

University of Edinburgh 14, 18, 143–4
Hugh Blair 37

Vermont 188, 206, 212 n.47
virtue (general) 49–50, 54, 64–5, 70, 75, 96
friendship as a virtue 77
instilling in children 137–42
and moral law 89–95
truth as a virtue 78–9
virtue (public) 4, 7, 9, 23, 43–5, 49–50
Calvin on 72–3
Hutcheson on 73–4
Williams on 71
Witherspoon on 50, 72, 74–80
vocation 29–30, 148–9

Washington, George 5–7, 136, 176, 224
letter from Witherspoon 33–4, 43
Westminster Confession 17, 34–5, 90, 133–4, 217
Williams, Roger 39, 121 n.67, 122–3 n.102, 128, 135
Bloody Tenent 128
and Quakers 121 n.73
on rights 104–5
on slavery 198
on virtue 70–1
wisdom 114–18
Witherspoon, Elizabeth (wife) 15, 18, 19
Witherspoon, James (son) 206–7
Witherspoon, John: and Calvinism 23–35
and the Enlightenment 36–45
in New Jersey 18–22
as a Revolutionary leader 22–6, 32–5
in Scotland 13–18
"wrath of man" sermon. *See Dominion of Providence over the Passions of Men*

About the Author

James Calvin Davis is the George Adams Ellis Professor of Liberal Arts at Middlebury College, where he has taught ethics and religion for twenty-five years. An expert in Anglo-American Calvinism and religion in American public life, he is the author or editor of five previous volumes, including *On Religious Liberty: Selections from the Works of Roger Williams* (2008).